# Magical Dogs 3

# Magical Dogs 3

## On the Road

Patti Kerr

*Kim ~*
*Happy 60th !*
*Prayers your magical dog*
*comes home soon.*
*♡ Patti Kerr*

**Along the Way Press**
Flemington, New Jersey

MAGICAL DOGS 3: On the Road

Cover Design: James Lebbad (Lebbad Designs)
Editor: Joy Stocke (Tree of Life Books)
Text Design: Susie Kenyon (Sans Serif Book Designs)
Front Cover Photo: Joseph Frazz Photography
Back Cover Headshot: Dave Norton

ISBN: 978-0-9845989-3-9

Disclaimer:
This book and any associated products (including websites, blogs, e-books, promotional products, and other products) are provided for entertainment and informational purposes. The author is not a veterinarian or dog care professional and does not advocate any particular product, item, technique, or position contained herein. Nothing herein should be interested as a substitute for the advice and care of a professional. The publisher and author cannot be held responsible for any inconvenience or damage caused by any subsequent changes or the use (or misuse) of information contained or implied herein.

*This book is dedicated to my very own magical dogs,*
*Brooke, Ava, and Kimber;*
*and every dog who has come (or will come) into my life.*
*You change and bless me—in all the best ways.*
*I am forever grateful.*

# Contents

# Prologue:
# The Magic Is Back

THE IDEA FOR THIS BOOK CAME ABOUT MANY YEARS AGO IN Sagadahoc Bay, Maine. After spending a year writing the draft of my first *Magical Dogs* book and finally sending it off to my editor, I was mentally exhausted.

"Ava," I said. Ears perked, head tilted, she looked up at me with her big brown puppy eyes. "I think we need a break. It's time for a road trip!"

Immediately, Ava, our lovable Polish lowland sheepdog, began barking and running around in circles, clearly excited. Ava lived for road trips and adventures with my partner Robb and me. So, the following week, Robb, Ava, and I hopped into our 1992 Toyota motorhome and hit the road.

Our destination was the Gulf of Maine, specifically Georgetown Island where, nestled on the southern tip, was Sagadahoc Bay Campground. We'd never been to that part of Maine and it looked to provide us with the peace and quiet we wanted and needed. The campground also had a waterfront location and was pet-friendly. Perfect.

Pat, one of the owners, was waiting to welcome us. Standing alongside her were two apricot-colored standard poodles, their tails wagging. "Meet Monty and Dylan, my helpers and the official campground greeters," she said, handing us a map of the campground. "If you'd like, I can arrange to have a fresh Maine lobster meal delivered to you while you're here. Either way, come back and visit. We're always in the office and Monty and Dylan love the company."

Pulling into our site, the sound of dogs barking emerged from the motorhome next to us. We parked, got out, and took a short walk around the campground to shake off some of our road weariness. It was cozy, well-maintained, and picturesque. We wanted to explore it some more but decided to first head back and get settled.

While setting up, the sounds of barking emerged again from the motorhome next to us. After several minutes, the door to the motorhome opened, a woman poked her head out, and sighed. "Sorry for all the noise."

We laughed, pointing down at Ava who was now barking along in unison.

As the woman proceeded down her steps, two dogs followed close behind. She walked toward us, pointing to the slightly-larger dog. "This is Jeb. He's a six-year-old terrier mix. And this," she said, pointing to the smaller dog, "is Benny. He's a fourteen-year-old Jack Russell and is almost-blind and mostly-deaf."

Benny, oblivious that we were talking about him, made a beeline for Ava. It was clearly a case of love at first sight or, in Benny's case, love at almost-sight. For the rest of our time at Sagadahoc, when given the opportunity, Benny never left Ava's side.

"I haven't seen Benny like this with another dog," the woman said a few days later, shaking her head in amusement. "He's actually not too keen on other dogs, but then Benny is always full of surprises and constantly keeps us entertained."

"We recently had a wedding at our house and afterwards Benny was nowhere to be found. We were frantic, and kept searching and calling everyone who had been at the wedding, without any luck. Several hours later, we got a call from the Port-O-John company. Apparently, shortly after the party ended and amidst all the chaos of cleaning up, Benny climbed into one of the Port-O-Johns. The company came, picked up the Port-O-Johns, and Benny never made a sound. After returning to their facility, they opened the door, and there sat Benny, looking up at them with his big goofy dog grin. That's our Benny. Always ready for fun or an adventure."

"Like your dog, both of our dogs love to travel. This is our first month of retirement so we're heading out on a year-long trip around the country. Our plan is to drive down the East Coast and slowly work our way across the South. That will allow us to stay ahead of any cold weather and snow. Sagadahoc is our first stop and it's been the perfect place to start our trip. We love it here—and so do the dogs."

It didn't take us long to understand why they loved Sagadahoc. It was peaceful and quiet and, just like the tides, our days at Sagadahoc rolled by with ease. Twice a day the tide changed. As it did, life and the view at the campground changed, too. At ebb tide, with the land that was previously underwater now exposed, locals showed up, buckets in hand, to go clamming. Robb, Ava, and I took advantage of the low tide to go for long walks across the bay. Later, after the tide rolled back in, Robb and I relaxed on a rustic wooden swing at the water's edge watching Ava run along the beach, barking, and chasing the seagulls and loons circling overhead. Later, Ava curled up next to us, as we watched the sun go down. Once back in our motorhome, I pulled back the curtains and stared out the window at the Seguin Island lighthouse off in the distance. As Maine's second oldest lighthouse, it has guided mariners through fog, storms, and out of harm's way since 1857. Its quiet presence, night after night, was both calming and reassuring. And the fact that it sat on what was called "Sixty-Four Acres of Magic" made it even more perfect.

On our last full day at Sagadahoc, Pat arranged to have Leom Kelly, a local lobsterman, and his wife Cathy, prepare and deliver what turned out to be a scrumptious Maine lobster meal.  It was the perfect ending to our time in Maine.

Afterwards, I walked to the office to thank Pat for her hospitality. Monty and Dylan were there to greet me, tails wagging. Pat and I sat down and talked about our lives and dogs.

"My husband, Eric, grew up on this land," she explained, gazing at the campground outside their sliding glass door. "It's been in his family since 1722 and five generations of his family have lived here. It used to be a mini-farm with pigs, turkey, cows, and a big orchard out back. With so much vacant land, Eric's parents always talked about starting a campground but they never acted on it. After Eric and I got married, we wanted to share the beauty of what we have with others so we decided to open the campground."

Monty came over and peacefully sat down next to me. As I began to pet him, I told Pat about the book I'd just written.

"Really," she mused. "That's great. Dogs have always been a part of our life, this land, and the campground. Since I'm allergic to cats and dogs, I always used an inhaler or took a pill because I wanted a way to still have them in my life. Then one day I met our first apricot-colored poodle, a ten-week-old puppy named Kampa. For the first time ever, I didn't wheeze or break out. I was amazed and grateful.

"We adopted Kampa and he became the campground greeter, welcoming everybody the moment they arrived. He waited patiently in the office until they were settled at their site before walking over and waiting outside their motorhome to see if they would open their door and invite him in. Most of our guests did and Kampa walked in and sat down. People always talked to Kampa because they knew, on some level, he understood what they were telling him. Then, before wearing out his welcome, he walked back to the door to be let out so he could return to the office ready to greet our next guests."

Pat smiled wistfully. "Kampa quickly became the love of my life. He loved everyone—and everyone loved him. A guest once said that Kampa was a person in a poodle suit and it was true. He was great, but Monty and Dylan are great dogs, too. The truth is every dog is a great dog. I'm proud that we are a pet-friendly campground because we've never had a problem with the dogs. Like the sign in our office says: Dogs Welcome, People Tolerated. If your dog can vouch for you, you're welcome at our campground.

Laughing, I thanked her once more and walked back to our motorhome.

The next morning, we packed up and walked down to the beach one last time. As we sat on the swing watching Ava run, I turned to Robb and half-jokingly, said, "How cool would it be to travel around, meet extraordinary dogs and their owners, and write a book with their stories?"

Always my champion, Robb shook his head in agreement. "It would be very cool. Do it."

I grinned. "Maybe I will."

We returned home and I finished writing *Magical Dogs: Life and Lessons from Our Canine Companions* then went on to write *Magical Dogs 2: Connecting the Dots, Connecting the Dogs*. The idea for this book remained firmly entrenched in the back of my mind but, as the saying goes, "Timing is everything." It was certainly true for this book.

Three years after sitting on the swing with Robb in Sagadahoc Bay, I finally hit the road. My travels over the next few years were sporadic. While I could say it was due to good times, not-so-good times, or a worldwide pandemic, the truth is it was simply life. The result was this book took longer than I originally anticipated but it didn't matter because ultimately the stories came together at the perfect time in the perfect way and with the perfect cast of dogs.

At long last, it's time to bring the Magic back!

# Chapter I
# ✨ HOME SWEET ✨
# HOME

FOR ME, LIFE BEGINS AND ENDS AT HOME IN THE TOWN WHERE I, along with generations of my family before me, have lived.

Not only have I lived in the same town, I have also lived on the same street my entire life. For me, there is something about the continuity of living in one place that is both comforting and charming. I love that my neighbors are like extended members of my family and that, when I walk down the street, I know a lot of the people I meet. People whose children, grandchildren, and pets I know—and who, in turn, know me and my family.

By staying in one place, I never had to change schools and had the same friends growing up. The same was true for my sons who, until they moved out on their own, always lived in the same house on the same street in the same town.

I always told my sons our house wasn't just a house. It wasn't just four walls, a roof, and a collection of possessions. It was our home, our sanctuary, our one place in the world where they, and everyone who enters it, would feel safe and loved. An oasis from the outside world.

I spend the majority of my days at home. It's where I have made countless precious memories with family, friends, neighbors, and dogs. It's also where I dreamed of, and ultimately wrote, the *Magical Dogs* books so it is here, at home, where we shall begin our journey.

# Chapter 2

# BROOKE

*Cracking My Heart Open*

THOSE WHO HAVE READ MY FIRST TWO *MAGICAL DOGS* BOOKS are already familiar with Brooke and Ava so, for you, the following will be a quick review. For everyone else, while it isn't their entire story, it will bring you somewhat up to speed.

Growing up, it was tradition in our hometown that whenever the high school football team won a game, the band and cheerleaders marched up to the courthouse on Main Street to gather for a victory rally. Hundreds of excited kids took to the streets and followed to join in the celebration.

After one such victory, my brother and his friends were following the band as it made its way to Main Street. As the band turned onto Pennsylvania Avenue, the energy and excitement reached fever pitch for the crowd as well as for a Weimaraner who had just moved with its family onto the avenue. No longer able to contain his excitement, the dog darted out the front door of the house, ran across the street and, for whatever reason, picked my brother out of the crowd and bit him on the butt. Gratefully, his pants took the brunt of the bite, but Mom still brought him to the doctor.

The doctor gave my brother a precautionary rabies shot while the dog was quarantined. When the results of the dog's rabies test came back negative, that was the end of it for everyone—except me.

While I hadn't witnessed any of it happen it still instilled a belief in me that all dogs were mean, aggressive, and would randomly bite if given the opportunity. As a result, I grew up terrified of dogs.

My brother Joe's toy poodle, Pon, began to chip away at that fear when I was in high school. She was adorable but also incredibly patient, loving, and sweet and showed me another side to dogs.

In 1985, when I wrote My Life List (what many today call a Bucket List), number seven on the list was: Own a dog. As a single mom of twin sons, my life was busy enough at the time without adding a dog to the mix, so my goal remained on the list for "someday."

Fast forward to the spring of 2001. Robb and I had been married for several years and were talking about getting a dog. That year, for my birthday, someday arrived when Robb blessed me with a Polish Lowland sheepdog puppy. We named her Brooke.

Brooke looked like a miniature Old English sheepdog and was adorable, cuddly, funny, and smart. Robb, Brooke, and I spent almost every waking hour together and began traveling in our motorhome: to New England where Brooke ran full-speed into what looked like a grassy field but turned out to be a green colored swamp; to Long Beach Island where we walked and played on the beach; and to Disneyworld where she got to see my sons play in a professional paintball tournament. After buying a fixer-upper cabin in New York State, Robb, Brooke, and I started driving up there on weekends to clean it out and begin renovations. Brooke loved relaxing alongside us as we worked so, when it was done, we named it Brooke's Bungalow.

In our twelve years together, Robb, Brooke, and I had amazing adventures and incredible fun, but we also went through exceptionally difficult times: illness, death, and separation. Regardless of what we were going through, Brooke remained by our side, unfazed, uncomplaining, and always with an endless supply of unconditional love.

In 2008, one year after my mother passed from Alzheimer's, I began working on my first book. Brooke and I woke up, had breakfast together, then as I slipped in front of my computer to begin writing, she curled up next to me, her head resting on her purple-cheetah-print pillow, and slept. For almost two years, we kept the same routine. As a result, I stayed focused and finished *I Love You, Who Are You? Loving and Caring for a Parent with Alzheimer's.* That time spent with Brooke was transformative for me in many ways.

Looking back and writing about my family's experience with Alzheimer's (along with

Brooke

my experience as one of my mother's caregivers), allowed me to see our journey in a new, non-judgmental light. By adding the stories, advice, and tips of other caregivers, it allowed me to pay forward all my mother and grandmother had gone through with the disease in order to support others on a journey with a loved one living with Alzheimer's. The entire process was healing and made me appreciate the true power of writing.

In addition, having Brooke's quiet, loving presence by my side day-after-day was reassuring, calming, and showed me that sometimes the kindest thing we can do for another being is to sit quietly with them. From Brooke, I learned what it meant to be truly present for someone and how, without words, to provide comfort and support when it is most needed.

Brooke brought joy, fun, and laughter to our entire family. Because of her, we embraced our childlike qualities and enjoyed the simple pleasures of going for walks, taking time to play, and being together. Having her fuzzy little presence waiting at the door, ecstatic to see us (whether we'd been gone for five minutes or five hours), reminded all of us that the most important thing in life is to share and show love.

Brooke knew how to share and show love better than anyone I had ever met. She was born on February 13 so we nicknamed her our fuzzy little Valentine. Having never had a dog, I was unaware what true unconditional love—the kind of love Brooke, and every dog, gives so freely and easily—felt like or how it would change me. I also didn't realize the full impact of her love or the extent of how much she changed me until she passed shortly after her twelfth birthday.

Because of Brooke, I was no longer the same person I had been. She filled gaps and healed wounds—some I had been aware of; others I hadn't even realized were there. One of the most remarkable transformations she brought about was that I was longer terrified of dogs. The fear had completely vanished and I now craved their companionship.

I had also never before grieved a pet. I was unbelievably heartbroken and unprepared for the inconsolable sadness that completely engulfed me. Even though Brooke let us know in a variety of ways, starting on the day she passed, that she was fine, I still felt hollow and lost. So, eventually, I turned to the one thing that had helped me heal in the past: writing.

Writing the first *Magical Dogs* book gave me the opportunity to share Brooke's story. In looking back at the totality of our journey together, it helped me heal, but I also realized that my life with Brooke didn't occur by happenstance or simply because of a Life List I had written years before. Rather, it had unfolded with intention and purpose.

Brooke came into my life to crack my heart open, show me the beauty, love, kindness, and purity of a dog, and push me out of my comfort zone so I could grow into the next phase of my life.

While writing about Brooke and our journey together was very healing, by sharing stories of so many other incredible dogs, I experienced another level of healing, understanding, and purpose that ultimately changed the entire trajectory of my life.

For me, all the extraordinary, amazing, life-altering things that unfolded during my time with Brooke (and beyond) can be summed up in one word: magical.

After she left this world, Brooke sent us yet another blessing: our next magical dog, Ava.

# Chapter 3
## AVA

*Cracking Our Hearts Open*

ROBB AND I WERE SHATTERED AFTER BROOKE PASSED. THE HOUSE was too quiet and every space within it held memories of her so we packed up and headed to Mexico.

While there, we laughed, cried, and talked about Brooke and how to move forward. One afternoon, as we sat staring at the ever-changing azure waters of the Bay of Banderas, Robb told me that, before we came to Mexico, he had emailed several places to see if anyone had a female Polish Lowland sheepdog.

"I explained that I'm not ready," he said, and paused, watching the waves lap the shore, "but that I might be in the future."

"The truth is I can't even think about another dog right now," he said solemnly, staring down at the ground. "I honestly don't know if I'll ever be ready." Pausing again, he shifted his gaze from the water and looked at me. "All I know is that if we ever get another dog, it has to be a Polish Lowland sheepdog, female, and the runt of the litter."

Ava

In other words, it had to be a dog just like Brooke.

Robb stayed in Mexico while I returned home to spend Easter with my family. It helped to be with all of them but, being home in New Jersey without Robb or Brooke, was depressing. I felt incredibly alone and visited my father incessantly. Unable to sleep at night, I spent hours online looking at dogs available for adoption. Like Robb, I wasn't serious; it was just something to pass the time. Thinking back on what Robb had told me, I sent out a few emails as well telling people if, at some point down the road, they got a female Polish Lowland sheepdog to please let me know. I never said a word about Robb's requirement that it be the "runt of the litter."

I decided to return to Mexico—and Robb. While packing, my phone rang and a woman introduced herself as an AKC breeder of Polish Lowland sheepdogs in North Carolina. "I have a puppy I want to tell you about."

I began our conversation with an apology. "I appreciate the call but honestly, you're probably wasting your time. We aren't ready for another dog and I'm not sure when or if we'll ever get another dog."

"That's fine," she said. "I understand. I just wanted to talk to you."

And so we talked—about Brooke. I told her everything about her, our life together, and how brokenhearted we were now.

"The truth is, I was only looking at dogs online to pass the time. Robb definitely isn't ready for another dog and I'm not sure if I am." Then, not wanting to appear rude, added, "But tell me about the puppy anyway."

"She's almost six weeks old, and absolutely adorable, but she's tiny. She was only four ounces when she was born . . . the runt of the litter."

Hearing those five words—"the runt of the litter"—made my hair stand up on end. This puppy fulfilled all three things on Robb's checklist for our next dog: a Polish Lowland sheepdog, a female, and the runt of the litter.

I tried to remain calm. "She sounds wonderful. I appreciate the call but, again, we aren't ready. In fact, I'm getting ready to head back down to Mexico and won't be home for a few weeks."

"That's fine. There's no pressure. Is it alright to send you some photos of the puppy?"

I agreed. What harm could a few pictures do, I thought.

That night, she emailed me pictures. The puppy was, without question, adorable. The next morning, I walked down to my dad's house, told him what happened, and showed him the pictures. He looked at them and, knowing how sad I was, immediately said, "Come on, Pat. Let's go get her."

"Pop," I said. "I cannot and will not make a decision like that without Robb being on board. Besides, we aren't going to buy a dog."

That afternoon, the woman called back. "There's something I forgot to tell you. The puppy is healthy, but her teeth don't properly align. Because of that, I can't breed her or list her with the AKC. She may need dental work after her adult teeth come in, so I'm not looking to sell her. I'm just looking for someone to love her. Think about it while you're away."

I gathered the pictures together, put them in my bag, and headed to the airport.

Robb was waiting for me at the airport in Puerto Vallarta and we immediately headed to our favorite little restaurant for lunch. I hadn't told him about the puppy or my conversations with the woman but, while relaxing over coffee, I pulled the photos out of my bag and placed them on the table in front of him. He looked at the top photo, then at me, confused.

"Something happened when I was home . . ." and I proceeded to tell him the story.

"I thought we talked about this," he said.

"We did. I just wanted to tell you what happened while we were apart. I honestly don't know what it means, if anything."

He looked through the pictures, slowly put them in a neat pile, and handed them back to me without saying a word. We spent our time together in Mexico relaxing, going for walks, and talking about Brooke. We didn't talk about the puppy until the day before we were going home. Taking hold of my hand, Robb looked at me, and gently said, "As for the puppy, I'm not sure what any of this means either but maybe together, we can figure it out. Let the lady know that, if the puppy is still available, when we get home we'll come meet her."

Three days later, Robb and I drove four hours to a hotel in Virginia to meet the woman and the puppy. One hour later, we got back in our car to drive back to New Jersey with our puppy, Ava.

The entire ride home, Ava sat in the back seat on the dog bed the woman gave us and stared at me. Once home, she ran, hopped, played, and explored my backyard. Robb stood off to the side, watching. I took her in the house and she began sniffing her way around, completely at ease—almost as if she'd been here before. I went outside to tell Robb, but he and his car were gone.

Robb and I have been in a committed relationship for over twenty-five years but maintain separate residences because it works for us. So, on that day, he chose to leave my house and drive to his house. All of my calls to him went straight to voicemail and texts went unanswered.

A few days later, Ava had her first appointment with our veterinarian, Dr. Elena Braz, and, much to my delight, Robb showed up to drive us. On the way, he told me Ava had triggered very strong emotions in him about Brooke and, rather than subjecting the puppy and me to that, he had decided to leave. He also said that after today's appointment, he was going to drive to the cabin—alone. OK, I thought, Ava and I will give you the space you need.

From her first day with me, Ava did so many things like Brooke, from laying on the floor and pushing a tennis ball back and forth between us with her nose to unwrapping boxes and presents with ease and without assistance. There were so many things that made me think of Brooke and I couldn't help but wonder if Ava was, in fact, a gift from Brooke.

Knowing it was important for the three of us to begin making memories at the cabin, she and I drove to the cabin and surprised Robb. When we arrived, he was happy, but hesitant, to see us. We gave him his Father's Day gifts, and Ava immediately started unwrapping them—just like Brooke had always done. He looked at me, then continued to watch her, never saying a word. At the end of the day, the three of us were sitting on the back deck when Ava walked over, sat down in front of Robb, and looked up at him. Hesitating momentarily, he reached down, picked her up, and held her as they stared into one another's eyes. When he brought her closer, she instantly laid her head on his chest, looking perfectly content. Robb's face began to soften. You could almost hear his heart starting to crack open once again. I smiled, confident at last that the three of us were going to be a family.

We spent the rest of the spring, summer, and early fall between New Jersey and the cabin in New York State. On Halloween morning, Ava and I dropped Robb at Newark Airport. He was heading back to Mexico for six weeks and I decided to make the most of that time by working with, and training, Ava.

Since Robb had taken charge of Brooke's training, I was uncertain and lacked the confidence in my ability to train Ava so I brought a steady stream of trainers in to help us. Each one had their own (and very different) approach to training and each one only lasted one session. None of them felt like the right fit and, with every one who came and went, it only added to my anxiety and lack of confidence which was now trickling down to Ava. She, too, was becoming anxious.

I finally signed us up for a puppy class and, at our first class, Karen, the trainer, gave us basic tasks to work on. I left the class with a newfound confidence. As we continued training with Karen, my confidence grew. Eventually, Ava and I worked together and she got her Canine Good Citizen certification. With every new step and challenge we faced together, along with a sprinkling of her signature spunk and sass, she showed me how to stay present in the moment and face life with confidence and courage.

The start of our journey with Ava definitely wasn't smooth sailing due to Robb's initial hesitancy and my lack of confidence. However, I believe that, too, was part of Ava's journey and purpose in coming to us. She never once wavered in her affection or devotion to either of us but stayed the course and kept loving us. Her antics and playful spirit continued to bring endless moments of love, joy, and laughter back into our life, family, and home.

Ava now has visual problems. Our veterinary ophthalmologist says she is blind in one eye but, if you were here with us, you would never know. She runs and plays like she always has and is still filled with the same spunk and sass. The only change is that, as her vision decreases, she has softened a bit. Never much of a cuddler, she now comes over more frequently throughout the day to seek more physical connection. She looks up at me, and just like when she was a puppy, I still feel the same intense connection we had in those early days. Only now, with years of history, moments, and memories together, the connection is much more intense.

While we don't know how her visual problems (or anything) will ultimately play out, we will let Ava continue to be our guide and handle the future like only she can: with courage, confidence, spunk, a little bit of sass, a whole lot of love, and a sprinkling of magic. And, most important, we will handle it together.

# Chapter 4

 # KIMBER

*Kindness Brings New Life,*
*New Hope, and a New Dog*

KINDNESS SOMETIMES HAS A SIMPLE, SOLITARY IMPACT ON A person or the world. Other times it creates unexpected, far-reaching ripples whose impact can be felt for an extended period—or forever—which is precisely the type of kindness that started our journey with Kimber.

In April 2018, I saw on Facebook that Animal Alliance of New Jersey, a local rescue, was having an adoption event at the landscape center where my daughter-in-law, Melanie, worked part-time. It was a gorgeous spring day and, while I needed more wildflowers for my garden, the dogs were the main draw for me.

Unbeknownst to me, Melanie had visited with the dogs several hours earlier before starting her work day. That night she sent me a text: "Did you see the little tiny shepherd mix puppy today?"

I responded that I wasn't sure which one she meant since there were so many puppies at the event.

She replied: "I think he was mostly tan, small in stature, and had a black patch halfway down his tail. He was very sweet and, when he approached me, began nibbling my arm and bracelet. I was just curious if you knew anything about him."

I pulled out the business card for Animal Alliance of New Jersey I had grabbed off their table and sent them a message inquiring about the puppy. Several hours later, I got a response: "Sounds like one of the "C" puppies. There were four "C" puppies. Cooper, Carson, and Chace were at the event. The fourth "C" puppy was adopted a few days ago. His name was Cameron."

My heart stopped: Cameron. Six months prior, in October 2017, my beautiful, blue-eyed grandson Cameron was born. Six days later he passed. Our family was stunned, shocked, and distraught.

Melanie and my son, Sean, asked others to do an act of kindness in honor and memory of their son, Cameron. It was a profound and heart-felt request but, for me, it held additional significance. As a mother and grandmother, I believed one of my purposes in life was to protect my family yet I had been unable to protect Cameron, Sean, or Melanie. I had been helpless to change the outcome of Cameron's all-too-short journey on this earth but now, this—an act of kindness—was something tangible I *could* do.

For months, I had considered volunteering for an animal rescue and had visited several but none felt like the right fit. Now, thanks to a puppy and my grandson, I felt connected to Animal Alliance of New Jersey and attended their Volunteer Orientation. The orientation affirmed what I already suspected: I had found my place, my tribe, as well as another way for me to channel kindness into the world.

I began going to Animal Alliance during the week to walk dogs and, on weekends, helped at adoption events. Being with the dogs and watching them find their person and forever home was healing in ways I never anticipated. I began to get more involved until, in May 2019 (one year after attending the Volunteer Orientation), my father unexpectedly passed.

In July, I sent Katie, the volunteer coordinator for Animal Alliance, a message: "I'm sorry I haven't been around to help. When things settle down, I promise to get involved again. I may also be interested in fostering at some point but would like some guidance before I commit or make a decision."

I wasn't convinced fostering was a good fit for me, or Robb's and my life, but trusted that, once I got additional guidance and information, I could make an educated decision. There was no rush. In the meantime, I would continue to follow my heart, intuition, and Cameron's Acts of Kindness. Together they were helping heal my heart while also leading me in unexpected and beautiful directions.

Now, whenever a friend's dog passed over the Rainbow Bridge, I did an act of kindness in honor and memory of the person and their dog. I never knew in advance what act of kindness I was going to do. Instead,

I sat, waited, and prayed for the perfect opportunity to come along—and it always did.

On August 27, 2019, my friend John posted on Facebook that his dog, Abby Lee Grace With the Beautiful Face, had crossed the Rainbow Bridge. From the multitude of photos and posts of him, his wife Jaci, and their dog Abby, I knew the incredible love and connection that existed between the three of them and that they were now, understandably, heartbroken. I sat, waited, and prayed for the appropriate act of kindness to bubble to the surface and, just a few days later, Katie sent out an urgent email to all Animal Alliance volunteers.

Animal Alliance had pulled a mama dog and her four pups from a shelter in Georgia. After transporting them to New Jersey and getting them settled at the rescue, the washing machine broke and water had overflowed straight into the room housing the mama dog and her pups. Katie had one simple request: Was there anyone who could foster the mama dog and her puppies until they got their room dried out?

It was Labor Day weekend. Ava was at the cabin with Robb and I had no plans, which meant I was available to do it. The bigger question was *could* I do it? I had never done anything like this before but, after reading through Katie's email several more times, it finally hit me: *This* was the act of kindness I was meant to do in honor of John and Jaci, and in memory of Abby Lee Grace With the Beautiful Face.

Pushing doubt aside, I emailed Katie back, told her I would do it, and prepared my house for the mama dog and her puppies. I blocked off my kitchen from the rest of the house, set out food and water dishes and a dog bed, covered my kitchen floor with sheets and towels, then headed to Animal Alliance.

Annie, the Executive Director, met me, gave me more sheets, towels, puppy pads, food, and a crate then helped me get Mama Kimber and her pups settled in my car. Waving to Annie, I drove off, excited and nervous.

My neighbor Tara was waiting at my house when we arrived. After carrying the food and supplies into the house together, Tara proceeded to bring the puppies in while I turned my attention to Kimber. As I grabbed hold of her leash, she looked at me and, without any hesitation, hopped out of my car and calmly walked alongside me into the house.

Once inside, she looked around, laid down, and exhaled. It felt like she had given me, and my home, the stamp of approval and that she knew she and her pups were safe.

My flawless attempt at puppy-proofing my kitchen, quickly unraveled as the puppies, King, Kai, Khloe, and Katlyn, immediately began chewing the legs on my kitchen table and chairs. I got another gate and blocked off the dining nook but, next, they found tiny nooks and crannies to crawl into. I tried to stay on top of things but the puppies were non-stop energy and mischief—and there were four of them! What in the world had I gotten myself into?

Kimber Grace with the Pretty, Pretty Face and the Wiggly Waggly Tail

That night, I decided to sleep on the floor in the kitchen with them. Having never been in this situation, I wasn't sure if it was the right thing to do, but I did it anyway—and didn't sleep a wink the entire night.

The pups were still nursing and therefore very demanding of Kimber. She was a sweet, caring mama but also clearly exhausted. Starting the next morning, I corralled the puppies into the crate every few hours so I could take Kimber into my fenced-in backyard and give her time alone to relax, decompress, and enjoy some peace and quiet.

The second time we went outside together, Kimber began to calmly explore my yard as I sat down in the grass. Suddenly, she stopped, turned her head, looked at me, walked back, and rested her head on my shoulder. I began to pet her and she stood motionless for several minutes. Finally, she raised her head, backed up, looked into my eyes, turned, and continued to walk around my yard.

I was stunned. The moment she looked into my eyes, something inside me shifted. An overwhelming calm and peace washed over me like I had never before experienced. As we headed back into the house, I tried to put it out of my mind but every time I looked at Kimber, she was staring back at me. I wondered if she had felt it, too.

That night, exhausted, I decided to sleep on the couch so I would be nearby to hear if they needed me while also giving myself some space and distance to hopefully get some sleep.

After getting comfortable, I began to doze off when I heard whimpering coming from the kitchen. I ignored it, thinking it would stop, but instead it got progressively louder. Now fully awake, I crawled across the room in the dark to see what was happening. As I got close to the gate, I was shocked. All four puppies were curled up together in the dog bed, sound asleep. It was Kimber. She was laying on the other side of the gate crying.

I grabbed my pillow and blanket from the couch and settled down on the floor on the opposite side of the gate thinking it would appease her. The crying and whimpering continued and then she began to paw at the gate. Not wanting the puppies to wake up, I tried quietly talking to her but her whimpering continued until, finally, she leapt over the gate, licked my face, laid down next to me, and we both went to sleep.

The next afternoon, I brought Kimber and her pups back to Animal Alliance. I was looking forward to getting home and taking a nap but, after dropping them off, my heart ached for Kimber. What had begun as an act of kindness in honor and memory of John, Jaci, and Abby Lee Grace With the Beautiful Face had evolved into so much more. That moment in my backyard when Kimber put her head on my shoulder was the start of a very intense, and very real, connection between her and me.

I continued walking dogs at Animal Alliance, always making sure I walked Kimber, too. At adoption events, I asked to be teamed up with her and, since it was increasingly difficult for me to see her going from the event straight back to the rescue, I started bringing her to my house the day before and after adoption events.

One by one, all of Kimber's puppies were adopted but there was still no interest in Kimber. My heart broke for her so I decided to bring her to my house while we waited for her forever home and family to surface. Without realizing it, I was doing what I had briefly mentioned to Katie a few months earlier: I was fostering a dog. Even though I wanted guidance before attempting to foster, I didn't need it because everything with Kimber happened organically, naturally, and perfectly.

At adoption events, Kimber stayed huddled up next to me. People walked past her as if she were invisible. I tried introducing her to people, telling them what an amazing dog she was, but no one was interested, so I began posting about her on my Facebook page. Every day, I posted new messages and photos of Kimber telling people about her and upcoming adoption events.

One day, my friend, Kathryn, told me she was going to come to the next adoption event to meet Kimber. I was excited thinking that perhaps this was Kimber's chance at a forever home. Kathryn came to the event but left without saying a word. The following weekend, she came to another adoption event but this time, before leaving, told me with absolute conviction, "I love her, Patti, but Kimber is very clearly your dog. She's already chosen you."

"Trust me, Kathryn," I assured her. "She's not my dog. What you're seeing is just who she is. She's sweet and amazing and a great dog. I'm just helping her find her forever home. Maybe it's with you. Please think about it."

Another friend, Jane, echoed Kathyrn's words, "She's already chosen *you*, Patti." As more and more people agreed, I politely reminded all of them that I was simply her foster and that we weren't looking for, or ready, to adopt another dog.

While waiting patiently for her forever family, Kimber and I went for walks. We hung out in my gazebo with our neighbor, Linda, who constantly told me what a good dog Kimber was. It was true. She laid next to me, her head in my lap, and never barked or gave me any cause for concern. And, just like that morning in my backyard, every time she looked at me with her soft brown eyes, it felt like she was peering into my soul. She was special and I knew someone was going to be incredibly lucky to have her in their life and home—we just needed to find them.

Robb, Ava, and I had plans to go away for a long weekend, and after getting permission from Annie to bring Kimber with us, we hopped in our motorhome and headed to a campground an hour away in Sussex County. For three days, we hiked, ate, relaxed, played, and had a wonderful time. On our way home, Ava fell asleep in the passenger seat next to Robb while Kimber slept peacefully next to me on the couch in the motorhome. A half hour from home, I got a text from Katie: "We have an application for Kimber. We need you to bring her back so the people can meet her."

I read the text to Robb then, looking over at Kimber peacefully sleeping next to me, started to cry. "Honey, this is what you've been working so hard for," Robb reminded me. "This is what we wanted for her." I knew he was right but I couldn't help myself. Every time I looked at her, I cried.

Friday afternoon, the people came to my house to meet Kimber. I had met them before and liked them so I was hopeful. It went great so, the next day, they brought their dog to meet Kimber and that went well, too. Early Sunday morning, I brought Kimber to their home and, once again, all went well. They decided to adopt Kimber and arrangements were made for them to pick her up from my home at noon on Wednesday. At long last, Kimber had found her family.

Tuesday night, Kimber and I went for a walk then curled up in my bed to go to sleep. In the dark, I listened to her breath. She was peaceful, calm, happy. The next morning, I was a mishmash of emotions. We went for a walk and sat in my backyard together until, as scheduled, the man arrived at noon to pick her up. I helped Kimber get settled in his car. She looked at me with her beautiful, soulful eyes and, as soon as they pulled out of my driveway, I broke down.

Four hours later, Christina, a Facebook friend who had been following my posts about Kimber, sent me a message: "Isn't this your foster dog?" Under the message was a picture of Kimber.

"Yes. Where is she?"

"She's running loose in our apartment complex outside Milford."

"Please keep your eyes on her, Christina. I'm on my way."

I sent Robb a quick text then, heart pounding, got in my car. Thirty minutes later, I pulled up to see Christina standing, waving her hands to get my attention. Grabbing a leash and harness, I ran over to her. "Where is she?"

"She ran up behind the apartments," Christina answered, pointing up the hill. "I tried to follow her but she's fast and I lost sight of her."

I took off running up the hill calling Kimber's name the entire way.

The hill got steeper the higher I got and then, at the top I looked out at acres and acres of open fields. Unsure which direction to head, I ran first in one direction, and then the other.

"Kimber . . ." I called. "Kimber . . . !"

I saw and heard nothing. I continued running and calling for her but the enormity of what I was facing was overwhelming. Unfamiliar with this area and, knowing Kimber was as well, I realized I needed help so headed back down to grab my cell phone out of my car and call Hound Hunters of New Jersey to ask for their help or guidance.

Nearing my car, I saw the man who had adopted Kimber standing across the street from his house, motioning me to come closer. With his other hand, he placed a finger to his lips indicating I should be quiet, then pointed toward his house. Sitting in his front yard was Kimber.

I quietly sat down in the grass and said, "Is that my Kimber Grace?"

Her ears perked, her head turned in my direction and, as soon as she saw me, she ran toward me. Reaching me, she looked at me, her tail wagging furiously, a huge smile on her face. I hugged her, buried my face in her fur, and slipped my harness over her head.

The man apologized profusely and explained. "I was taking our dog out. She's older and moves slowly so I checked on Kimber. She was laying under our dining room table and I thought she would stay there but the second I opened the front door, she bolted past me like a rocket."

Together, we walked Kimber back into his house. "Right now," I explained, "all she knows is me and the rescue. She needs time to decompress and get to know you, your family, and your routine. It's important to keep at least one, and preferably two, harnesses and leashes on her until she settles in." He agreed, and apologized once again. After taking my harness and leash off Kimber, I gave her a hug and walked out to my car.

Backing out of their driveway, I stopped to check for oncoming traffic. I didn't see any cars but, from the corner of my eye, saw a strangely familiar black dog sitting on the man's front lawn watching me: Kimber. I opened the passenger door of my car and she ran over, jumped in, sat down, and looked at me as if to say, "Can we just stop this now and go home?"

But the people had adopted her. She was their dog. So, once again, I put my harness and leash on her and brought her back into their house.

After another warning about keeping a harness and leash on her, I told him, "I'm planning on going to Delaware on Friday to visit my son and his family. Do you think you'll be alright with Kimber?" He assured me they would be fine.

"I'm going to reach out to you every day," I said, "but if you have any questions or concerns, please reach out to me or the rescue. We're here to help."

On Thursday, I checked in with them and they texted me a picture of Kimber. She was still huddled under their dining room table but they assured me everything was fine. Friday morning, I checked in with them and, once again, everything was fine so, confident they were settling in together, I drove to Delaware.

Saturday morning, everything still seemed to be going fine but that afternoon I got a text from them saying it wasn't working out and they were going to return Kimber to the rescue. I was shocked and immediately sent a text to Annie. She confirmed that they had been in touch with her as well and would be bringing Kimber back the next day.

I called Robb to tell him the latest development and, without hesitation, he said, "She's been through too much. Go get her. She's ours."

The next morning, I left Delaware, drove back to New Jersey and straight to Animal Alliance, picked up Kimber, and brought our girl home.

While I will never know exactly how old Kimber is or all she went through before coming into our lives, I do know that she and her puppies had been strays living under someone's shed in Georgia. Every time the people tried to get them out, Kimber, in an attempt to keep her family safe, barked at them. They finally called Animal Control who got them out from under the shed and brought them to a local shelter. At that point, Animal Alliance of New Jersey stepped in and brought them to New Jersey.

Even though Kimber had been staying with us and was already somewhat familiar with us and many of our routines, we still had a long way to go. She still cowered at times if I went to pet her, wasn't completely comfortable with Robb, and was reactive if people came into our house or yard. We remained patient and continued to work with her and slowly things started to change.

I pulled up the initial post Animal Alliance had made about her and read: "She's a sweet and affectionate young girl with the most beautiful, shiny black coat, gorgeous face, and clear deep eyes. Kimber likes to play and enjoys going for walks, as well as anything that involves the company of her human companions. She's at her happiest when she's being shown love and affection. She's very good-natured and well-behaved and would make a spectacular addition to any family."

All of that was true, especially the parts about enjoying the company of her human companions and being at her happiest when she was being shown love and affection. She constantly laid next to me and put her paw on me or rested her head in my lap. She always wanted to touch me. At night, if I was having difficulty falling asleep, she sensed it and belly crawled across the bed to me. After placing her paw on my shoulder and her head next to mine, she stayed like that until she was confident I was calm and relaxed.

I had her DNA tested because she had an extraordinary, almost uncanny, ability to launch herself, instantly and without effort, from a seated position to several feet in the air. I was convinced she was part kangaroo. The DNA results came back: 50% Australian cattle dog and 50% Karelian bear dog—no kangaroo.

As her personality continued to reveal itself , so too, did her name. We added Grace to her name in honor of Abby Grace, the dog who had started us on this journey with her. Then, in recognition of her astonishingly pretty face and stub of a tail that rarely stopped wagging, her name ultimately evolved into Kimber Grace with the Pretty, Pretty Face and the Wiggly Waggly Tail.

It was obvious that, at her core, Kimber was an incredibly happy dog. Every morning we followed the same routine: breakfast, a walk, followed by a mid-morning nap yet every morning, she acted like it was the first time we were having breakfast or going on a walk. Every morning, the second her eyes opened, her head popped up, followed by her body, and she began jumping around on the bed, excited to greet another day. As we made our way to the kitchen, she followed alongside me, hopping, skipping, and jumping for joy the entire way. Everything in the world—

from eating breakfast to going for walks to just being together—brought her joy.

I didn't take lightly or believe it was sheer coincidence that Kimber came into my life at a particularly providential time. In the two years since Cameron passed, I had travelled down a long, winding road of despair and grief. I had begun to heal, but there were still days I struggled and was void of any real joy. I had cut myself off from friends and many times only left my house if absolutely necessary thus isolating myself from the outside world.

In the weeks leading up to the second anniversary of Cameron's birth (and passing), Kimber came into my life. The moment she first put her head on my shoulder, she began to breathe new life and hope into me. We were going on walks and, as a result, I was leaving my house and wasn't so isolated. In the weeks and months that followed, watching her greet every moment with gratitude, joy, exuberant tail wags, and smiles, inspired me. Despite all she had been through, Kimber chose to let go of the past and embrace life and the present moment with sheer, unbridled joy. Simply being with, and around, her was changing me, bringing joy back into my life, and showing me another way to approach my days and life.

I believe Kimber knew from the moment she walked into my life (and home), that I was her person. From our first day together, there was an undeniable connection, an unspoken language between the two of us.

As I sat on my back porch writing this, Kimber repeatedly came over, put her head in my lap, and gazed up at me. I finally stopped writing, put my paper and pen aside, and looked into her eyes. "Kimber, I'm writing your story—our story. It really is a beautiful story, you know." She smiled her precious Kimber smile, then turned, walked over, and laid down next to Ava.

Initially, we had concerns about how Ava and Kimber would mesh. Ava had been an only dog for a lot of years before Kimber arrived on the scene and she could be stubborn and a bit of a princess at times, but it went amazingly well. From the start, Kimber allowed Ava to take the lead and, in turn, Ava allowed her into our family without issue.

We all need best friends who don't judge us, love us as we are, and are by our side through everything life places in our path. Ava and Kimber have truly become best friends. It is especially obvious now with Ava's diminishing eyesight. I watch them from my kitchen window as they walk together in the backyard. They look like two longtime friends out for a casual stroll. Kimber only goes just so far from Ava before she stops and turns to check on her. At times, she walks back and stands beside her; other times she waits patiently for Ava to catch up. She is tender and kind with Ava.

I am grateful that what started out as an act of kindness culminated into bringing life, new hope, and the love, magic, and kindness of Kimber Grace with the Pretty, Pretty Face and the Wiggly Waggly Tail into my life.

# Chapter 5
# FLORIDA

## *Touring the Sunshine State*

ON A COLD, DAMP MARCH MORNING, I FILLED THE TRUNK OF MY Toyota Prius with cases of books and set off for a fifteen-day book and speaking tour in Florida. I arrived at my hotel twelve hours later, completely wiped out, but knowing the worst was behind me. The next day, I only had a few hours left to drive.

My schedule was filled with events for both my Alzheimer's book and my Magical Dogs book, but I made sure to weave in time to visit friends and family. After my first stop in Ormond Beach visiting with Trish, Brian, and their dogs, I pushed on to my cousin, Sharon's house in Punta Gorda. I stayed there for several days since Sharon had arranged for me to speak at the assisted living facility where she worked. Ava's former trainer, Karen, had also arranged for me to do a book signing and fundraiser at the Animal Welfare League of Charlotte County where she now worked. It was fantastic to see Karen again and, to my surprise, another longtime friend, Michele, drove hours that day to join us. My cousins, Sharon and Debbie, were there as well. It was great meeting lots of new people (and dogs), raising money for animal rescue, and also being surrounded by people I already knew and loved.

From my cousin's house, I drove to Key Largo to do an event for Marrvelous Pet Rescues at Founders Park in Islamorada. My longtime friend, Captain Jim, was out of town but he had arranged for me to stay at his house with his girlfriend, Barbie, and their dog, Arrow. While there, I also got to see my friend Patricia whom I had known from our high school days, before pointing my Prius north to begin making my way home. Along the way, I did a fundraiser at the Pucci & Catana pet boutique in Naples, Florida while visiting with my friends, Sandi and Mark. Outside Orlando, I spoke at a branch of the local library about Alzheimer's then, the next day, did a book signing and fundraiser for animal rescue before taking time to visit with my dad's best friend's widow, Barb, and their daughter, Mary, in Kissimmee. My final stop before heading home was a book signing and rescue fundraiser at the Breezeway, a local bar and restaurant in Sanford, where I was able to visit and have dinner with my friend (and former New Jersey native), Marinade Dave.

Because of my busy schedule, it had never been my intention to do any interviews on this trip, but that went out the window during a book signing and fundraiser for the Gulf Coast Humane Society (GCHS). Several people approached and encouraged me to reach out to Ralf and Anke about their dog, Sunset. I intuitively knew I needed to try and make it happen and, after contacting them, they invited me to their home. We spent a wonderful afternoon relaxing and talking in their lanai as Sunset and their other dogs relaxed and slept. When I was leaving I thanked them for taking the time to meet with me and they told me they felt it was meant to be because it was an auspicious day for their family: it was the anniversary of the day Ralf and Anke adopted Sunset. It was additional confirmation for me as well that we were meant to meet so I could tell Sunset's story which you'll read in the pages that follow.

During my travels, I had been given the name of another person to reach out to: Liz. I finally caught up with her many months later by phone and was glad I did because, as you'll see when you read her story, hers is an extraordinary and motivating tale of following your passion and changing the lives of rescue dogs because of a dog named Sammy.

All in all, Florida was a fun, remarkable, but exhausting, trip. In my first few weeks back home, I wondered if I had pushed myself too hard and tried to do too much on the trip, but as time passed I realized how fortunate I had been to have spent time with so many people and how truly precious that time together had been.

Before I left my cousin Sharon's house, she, Debbie, and I made a promise to one another that we would do it again the same time the following year. The plan was for the three of us to get together at Sharon's house the following March. Sharon would take time off from work and I wouldn't plan any book signings or events. We would simply take the time to be together.

A few months after I returned home, Sharon went to the doctor and was diagnosed with pancreatic cancer. Our plan to get together the following year never happened because, instead, the following March, Debbie and I gathered with family and friends for Sharon's memorial.

Sharon had a perpetual smile and a ready, contagious laugh. She was one of the most giving individuals I have ever known and loved everyone fiercely and completely with equal passion, although she did have an extra-special place in her heart for her cats, Jax and Jill (who now happily reside with her sister, Debbie). Sharon would be upset with me if I ended this chapter, and her story, on a sad note because that wasn't who she was or how she lived her life. I believe, more than anything, Sharon would want people to remember the importance of treasuring every moment and every person and to live and love with an open heart.

Ironically, it's the same lesson I was constantly being reminded of, over and over, by every dog who crossed my path. Sunset and Sammy were perfect examples so let's begin our journey in Florida with the story of Liz and Sammy.

Book signing at the Animal Welfare League of Charlotte County
From left: Karen, Sharon, me, Michele, and Debbie

# Chapter 6
# ✦ LIZ & SAMMY ✦
## One Day, One Encounter,
## One Moment Changed Everything

I'VE ALWAYS LOVED ANIMALS. FROM A VERY YOUNG AGE, I brought home stray and injured animals and had countless cats. Even though I loved dogs, and knew several throughout my life that belonged to neighbors and friends, I never had one of my own.

In 2007, my husband, Jim, and I were living in Berks County, Pennsylvania. After deciding to adopt a dog, we started looking at websites for local shelters.

When Sampson, a one-year-old Shiba Inu, came up for adoption at the Berks County Humane Society, I showed him to Jim. Sampson was the right size and super cute, but not knowing anything about the breed, I started doing my research. When I read that they were "catlike," and having loved cats my entire life, I thought it was a perfect fit, so Jim and I went to the shelter to "just look" at the dog.

Growing up in rural Pennsylvania, stray animals had always just shown up at our house so I had never been to an animal shelter. Setting foot in a shelter for the first time, I couldn't believe how many beautiful, healthy, happy animals had been abandoned. I was deeply moved and, without realizing it, my life began to change that day.

Before introducing us to Sampson, Tammy Carannante, the adoption counselor, asked us what we knew about Shiba Inus. I immediately started rattling off everything I had learned: they were an ancient breed, catlike, aloof, independent, and difficult to train. I told her I had also done a lot of reading and research about how to train a dog and the importance of positive reinforcement.

Confident we had some knowledge of the breed, Tammy brought Sampson to meet us and he was crazy! He had a ton of energy, was extremely exuberant, a little nippy—and I loved him from the moment I laid eyes on him.

Knowing this would be my first dog ever, Tammy reminded me, "It's going to take a lot of work. He's still very young and has had absolutely no training."

"We understand," I assured her, confidently, "but I need to ask you something. He's a purebred Shiba Inu. Why is he even here? This breed of dog sells for thousands of dollars."

Tammy looked down at Sampson, "We think he came from a puppy mill."

"What's a puppy mill?" I asked naively.

Tammy grabbed a brochure and handed it to me. I quickly looked at the cover, tucked it in my back pocket, completed the adoption paperwork for Sampson, changed his name to Sammy, and headed home.

Sammy sat calmly on my lap all the way and that was probably the last time he was ever calm. To say he was a challenge would be an understatement. He was aloof, wasn't leash trained, and was reactive to other dogs, strangers, our cat, squirrels, and leaves blowing in the yard—you name it. I had a lot of work to do!

We attended dog training classes but, after two weeks, were asked to not return. According to them, Sammy was disruptive and wouldn't "conform" to what was expected of him, which was fine with me because I didn't want a dog that was a robot. I loved Sammy's free spirit but, wanting to keep him safe from harm, I continued to work with him. In a few short months, we formed a wonderful bond. That bond, however, made him protective of me, which meant strangers had to be on guard, especially in the kitchen. He nipped my aunt on Thanksgiving and my best friend twice—always in the kitchen and always when I was nearby.

We resolved that challenge by having brave strangers come into the kitchen and feed him cheese, his favorite thing on the planet. Eventually, he realized strangers were going to feed him and not hurt him or me. It took well over a year for Sammy to relax, and even though it tried our patience many times, I never once considered returning him to the shelter.

Several months after Sammy's arrival, I came across the brochure Tammy had given me and sat down to read it. It was from an organization called United Against Puppy Mills (UAPM) and the more I read, the more shocked and outraged I became. I had lived in Berks County, which is right next to Lancaster County, my entire life. How was I just now learning that Lancaster County was the East Coast capital of puppy mills? How did I not know any of this was going on?

I phoned UAPM and talked with Jackie Keeney, who started educating me about puppy mills. The following week, Oprah aired a documentary on her show about puppy mills. The minute the show ended, I called Jackie back. "I need to do something. What can I do?"

"That's interesting," she replied, "because someone else from Reading just called who wants to help. Let me connect the two of you and maybe you can do something together to educate people."

The woman, Dr. Erica Oldham, lived two miles from our home. Along with my husband, Jim, we planned a fundraiser for UAPM which was a wonderful event and raised thousands of dollars. More important, we educated a lot of people about puppy mills. The added bonus was Erica and I became very close friends.

In October 2008, Pennsylvania Governor Ed Rendell signed House Bill 2525 into law. Known as the "Puppy Mill Bill," it was aimed at commercial breeders and laid out new criteria for the care, treatment, and sale of dogs. It was a huge step forward for the welfare of the dogs—and Erica, Jim, and I liked to believe we played a small part in making it happen.

I started volunteering at Animal Rescue League of Berks County (ARL), a shelter close to our home, and was astounded at the number of abandoned, abused, and neglected animals that came in on a daily basis. At the time, ARL was taking in over 10,000 animals a year, a staggering number that boggled my mind and hurt my heart. Throwing myself headfirst into animal rescue, I volunteered for the gala and fundraising committees and was elected to the Board of Directors. I learned everything I could because it was becoming very clear that saving animals was my passion in life.

Two years after bringing Sammy home, Jim and I had an opportunity to get another Shiba Inu, a ten-year old male, from New Jersey. Sammy was still challenging us, but thinking another Shiba Inu might

Liz and Sammy

possibly help, a friend and I made arrangements to drive to New Jersey on Mother's Day to get the dog.

For several months, Jim had been having difficulty swallowing and had a doctor's appointment the Thursday before we were scheduled to leave. At that appointment, we learned he had esophageal cancer—and it was terminal.

Stunned, shocked, and depressed, I cancelled my trip to New Jersey, but Jim was adamant that I stick to the plan. "Go get him," he kept telling me. "Please go get him, Liz. We need something happy in our lives right now." So that Sunday, as planned, my friend and I drove to New Jersey and got Josh, who we immediately renamed Saki.

Saki had been living with a ninety-four-year-old woman who was no longer able to take care of him. Initially, Sammy and Saki had a rough time getting used to one another, probably, in large part, because at the time I didn't know how to properly introduce dogs. Since Saki was older, wiser, and calmer, he became a wonderful mentor dog. As Sammy started following Saki's lead, Saki showed Sammy another way to be a dog.

It was comforting for Jim to have the dogs around but, six months after his diagnosis, in November 2009, Jim died. He was only forty-six years old; I was forty-two. At that point, Sammy and Saki became my only true source of comfort. I don't know what I would have done without them. My whole world, other than Sammy and Saki, had changed in an instant. I cried all the time and, while Shibas can be independent, they are also very sensitive dogs. They never left my side and, as a result, were often soaked in my tears.

Between my dogs, fostering, volunteering, fighting for more legislation to shut down the puppy mills, and advocating for dogs, I got through what was the most difficult period of my life.

Every time a Shiba Inu came into the area, people reached out to me for help—and I quickly became known as "The Crazy Shiba Lady." Every time a friend had a problem with an animal or needed advice, they called me. I continued to educate myself on laws, legislation, and dog behavior. I loved my newfound passion.

Then, quite unexpectedly, I met a wonderful man, Bobby Mierzejewski, who loved animals, especially dogs, as much as me and, together with Sammy and Saki, we became a happy family.

In 2011, we were asked to foster a Shiba named Abbey, an escape artist who, over the course of a few years, had been returned to the shelter several times. From the minute Abbey set foot in our house, she ruled the roost and Sammy and Saki calmed down. Abbey never left.

We fostered several Shiba who went on to their forever homes, then in 2014 we received a heartbreaking call from ARL. A nine-year-old Shiba had been brought to a local vet by its owner to be euthanized. The dog had major skin issues and was in terrible pain. She had obviously been neglected for so long that she no longer even looked like a Shiba. The vet took one look at the dog. Infuriated, he looked at the owner. "I'm not going to euthanize this dog simply because you haven't taken care of her."

The owner looked at the vet and, without any remorse or emotion, replied, "I don't have time," walked out with the dog and surrendered her to ARL. Within the hour we picked up Holley. It was the easiest dog integration ever because Sammy, Saki, and Abbey just stood and stared at her. She looked and smelled so awful from infections that our dogs didn't even realize she was another dog. By the time she healed many months later, she was already so much a part of our family that she never left.

With an obvious passion for animal rescue and welfare, I had been educating myself in the various laws, spending time at the shelter, and also studying for my MBA with a concentration in nonprofit leadership. In 2013, Harry Brown, the long-time director for ARL, announced he was going to retire. I applied for, and got, the job. I had never thought about making animal welfare my career, but I was now running the largest open admission shelter in the area and it was truly a major turning point in my life

I learned a lot and eventually became a Humane Police Officer (HPO) and began working on the front lines of animal cruelty and neglect. Animal control is a thankless, extremely stressful function for any animal rescue organization and I have the utmost respect for those who choose animal control as a career.

My friend, Erica, moved to Pine Island, Florida in 2014 and constantly sent us pictures, telling us how nice and warm it was, and how much we would enjoy living there. Finally, at the end of 2017, we decided to make the move.

After settling in Florida, Bobby and I started to talk about my next step. "Rescue is such a stressful business," he began. "Maybe you should just go back to a normal job and volunteer."

I had loved my job at ARL and believed that during my tenure we made important progress toward saving more lives but, after thinking about it, ultimately decided Bobby was probably right. For two months, I did what he suggested—and was sad and absolutely miserable. I missed working in rescue and thought about it constantly. Finally, realizing I wasn't done trying to make a difference, I began searching for job opportunities in rescue.

We were living near Cape Coral and, knowing there were plans to build a shelter there, I reached out to the founder and board President, JoAnn Elardo. She explained they had not yet broken ground so I met with the Executive Director of the Gulf Coast Humane Society (GCHS).

"I know you were an Executive Director at your last job," she said. "But that's my job. The only opening I have is for a shelter manager."

"I'll take whatever I can get," I told her. I meant it and she knew it, so a few days later, I started my new job as shelter manager at GCHS. It turned out to be one of the best decisions I could have made because I learned so much about the day-to-day operations of the kennels, cleaning protocol, controlling infectious diseases, managing kennel staff, and medical concerns for shelter animals. I visited rural municipal shelters in surrounding counties, made amazing contacts, and met so many rescue and animal control officers whom I admired and respected. Since different states have different problems, I also learned how things worked in Florida.

In 2019, they finally broke ground and began building the Cape Coral Animal Shelter & Veterinary Clinic. I threw my hat into the ring for the Executive Director position and got the job. I now had an opportunity to start a shelter from the ground up, along with a full-service affordable veterinary clinic. For me, it was truly a dream come true!

It was a long nine months from the time I was hired until we opened our doors. There were days I walked around while the shelter was still just a shell—no walls, no roof, nothing. I swore I could hear dogs barking and could envision the hustle and bustle of a busy shelter. Many days, I sat by myself planning, preparing, thinking, and praying that I could do the job and also live up to the expectations the community had for the shelter.

Our doors opened in March 2020 just as the world shut down with Covid. We began doing adoptions by appointment. Since it worked so well, we continue doing adoptions that way to this day.

Then, in September 2022, Hurricane Ian made landfall along the southwest coast of Florida. Millions of Floridians were without power and sustained damage from the torrential rain, powerful 160-mph winds, and storm surges. Hardest hit were the cities of Sanibel, Fort Myers Beach, Saint James City where I live, and Cape Coral where the shelter is located.

The shelter averages 100 animals at all times and, the day Ian hit, we had ninety-three animals. We put up the hurricane shutters and gathered whatever food, water, and supplies we thought we would need. For thirteen hours, my husband, the dogs, two volunteers, and I stayed inside the shelter. Even though we got a direct hit, it was new hurricane-resistant construction and built like a fortress, so it only sustained minor damage. We and the animals were safe throughout the storm, but our community was devastated.

Matlatcha, which was known as a "saltwater anglers dream come true" had been washed away by the water. Fort Meyers Beach was swept into the Gulf of Mexico. In our area alone, sixty-one people died and thousands lost everything. The devastation was overwhelming.

With only one way on and off the island where we live, and with the bridge washed out, we were unable to get to our house. We continued to live at the shelter for over a week. While there, we reached out to less fortunate shelters and areas in our community to provide them with pet food and supplies.

A lot of people lost their homes in the hurricane and were forced to move. Many were unable to keep their animals because homeowner's association and apartment complexes prohibited certain breeds. It may be an insurance or liability issue but, regardless, it isn't fair, very sad, and a problem we are going to try and tackle going forward.

Between Covid and Hurricane Ian, animals were being surrendered and all the shelters and rescues were packed. We will never let anyone surrender their animal if it is simply a matter of finances. If they need help with supplies, food, medical expenses, we help. If they are moving and can't take their dog and have no other options, we will find a wonderful home for their pet.

I always joke that a hazard of my job is that you end up with the misfits but, honestly, I wouldn't have it any other way. After Abbey came into our lives, there was Ripley, another crazy Shiba, and many fosters. Every one holds a very special place in our hearts. Although all our Shiba have gone over the Rainbow Bridge, we currently reside with Buckey, an Australian cattle dog/rat terrier; Oliver, a Chihuahua/schnauzer; and Lucy, a very feisty Chihuahua—all rescues, of course, and each with their own wonderful story.

I often think about how Sammy changed my life. Before Sammy, I had been working in sales and for non-profits. The thought of a career in animal rescue had never once crossed my mind. For years, I had negative connotations about rescues and shelters believing they had dogs nobody else wanted. Then I went to the shelter and saw this beautiful purebred dog who had been running loose before Animal Control found him and brought him to the shelter.

Being at the shelter that first time and seeing all the wonderful dogs who just wanted a home, bringing Sammy home, and then learning about the puppy mills drove my passion. I started seeing so many animals that needed help and had no voice. I wanted to help and needed to be that voice.

I am astounded that people still buy dogs from pet stores and puppy mills. We always have purebred dogs—puppies and sweet seniors, large dogs, small dogs, and everything in between—at the rescue. There is always a dog (or cat) that can fit a person's life and lifestyle.

People sometimes come into the rescue and want a certain cat or dog and I wonder if it is the right fit for them, but then I think back to the day we walked into the rescue to adopt Sammy. Tammy must have had the same concerns. One day, laughing, I asked her, "What were you thinking giving a Shiba Inu to someone who had never had a dog before?"

Without missing a beat, she responded, her answer simple and to the point. "I knew before you came to the shelter you had done your homework. I had a feeling you were passionate about helping this dog and would do everything in your power to make it work. I knew he would never come back to us." What Tammy didn't know that day was how much her decision would ultimately help shape my destiny.

The bottom line is, if a person is willing to put the time and effort into an animal and understand the challenges, why not take a chance? It could be life-changing for them just like Sammy changed my life.

Today, as I walk through the shelter, my dream has come true in so many ways. The sound of dogs barking is real, kittens are playing, and people are getting affordable veterinary care for their animals. We have found homes for 3,500 animals and provided care for over 5,000 animals in our clinic. We survived two years of Covid and a CAT 4/5 Hurricane, yet we are still on track to break ground on an addition which will more than triple our capacity. I'm amazed and proud of how well we're doing but that's a credit to our staff, Board, volunteers, and all the people in our community who love and are passionate about animals.

So many people have a passion in their life but are afraid to take that step and follow their dream. I get it. It can be scary, but it can also change your life. Animal rescue isn't the most glamorous job and can be heartbreaking. But when you see an abandoned animal thriving in their new forever home, it's the most rewarding job in the world. I never thought I would have a way to follow my passion and dreams, but it happened. I like to think I'm making a difference in the life of animals, just like Sammy made a difference in mine.

I think a lot about how that one day, one encounter, and one moment changed everything. That day, all those years ago, changed me, and the entire direction of my life and journey.

# Chapter 7

# ANKE & SUNSET

*From Lying in a Ditch*
*to Impacting the World*

RALF AND I HAVE ALWAYS LOVED DOGS. GROWING UP, I WANTED a puppy of my own and, every year, hoped a puppy would be curled up, waiting for me under the Christmas tree. Since my parents didn't want a dog in the house, it never happened.

When I was 19, I moved out and began living on my own. One of the first things I did was get my first dog, Jenny, a German shepherd. She was my companion during my college years and after, when we moved in and out of various apartments. She helped me get over relationships and was my best friend. For almost thirteen years, Jenny and I did everything together and were always there for one another.

After Jenny, Pablo, a white shepherd, came into my life. The following year, I met my husband Ralf. Pablo loved Ralf from the moment they met, and Ralf, who had lost his Rottweiler a few years before, loved having a dog again. Pablo quickly went from being Mama's boy to Daddy's boy.

Pablo got a sibling when Finja, a Rottweiler, joined our family several years later. In 2011, Ralf, Pablo, Finja, and our Siamese cat Picasso, moved to Southwest Florida. We were happy and then, on January 27, 2015, something quite unexpected occurred.

After dinner, Ralf went into his home office to work for a while and I turned on the news. Typically the news is simply background noise and I don't pay attention to it, however, that night was different. When I heard the news anchor say, "Stay tuned for a story about a pit bull found severely injured today. The dog is now in the care of the Gulf Coast Humane Society," I immediately stopped what I was doing and sat down on the couch. Little did I know how the story I was about to hear would change our lives.

As soon as the commercials ended, a dog appeared on the screen. I had seen pictures of injured dogs before, but this was different. Completely different. It was the dog's eyes. I had never before seen eyes so sad and full of despair, fear, hopelessness, and pain. And it felt like those eyes were looking right into my soul.

I sat on the couch paralyzed by the dog and her story. A huge

Sunset

lump formed in my throat as tears began to stream down my face. Ralf came out of his office, took one look at me, and exclaimed, "Good lord, what is going on? What happened? Are you okay?"

"No," I replied, sobbing. "No, I'm not okay, not at all. I just saw this poor dog on the news who has such horrible injuries. They think she was used for dog fighting and then just thrown in a ditch on the side of a road. She was discarded like a piece of garbage, left for dead, all alone and suffering."

Ralf sat down next to me on the couch, took hold of my hand, and we started talking. Even though we had heard of dog fighting, we didn't know very much about it. We weren't sure if this was an isolated incident or part of a much bigger problem. As we continued talking, the dog's picture and story came up on the screen a second time, only this time, Ralf heard it, and was impacted just like I had been.

We immediately shut the news off and tried watching a movie to relax but it was impossible. Our minds kept wandering back to the dog. I laid in bed for hours that night thinking about her and, when I woke up early the next morning, my first thought was: "I wonder how she's doing?"

I turned on the computer and scoured the news station's website for an update, praying the entire time she had made it through the night.

Finally, her photo popped up and, after reading the update, I walked into our bedroom.

Ralf sat on the edge of the bed, searching my face for a clue.

"She's in critical condition but she's still alive."

We got dressed to start our day but, unlike other days, I kept the television on anxiously awaiting news about the dog. Later that afternoon, the station announced they would have an update, so Ralf and I stopped what we were doing, sat down on the couch, and waited. Seconds felt like hours and every commercial was torture. At last, the update came: the dog was still in critical condition but clinging to life. They also gave more information about what had happened.

Paul, a former employee of the Gulf Coast Humane Society (GCHS), had been driving down Sunset Road in Lehigh Acres when he saw a dog lying lifeless in a ditch. Stopping his car, Paul got out to check on the dog. In his own words, he had seen a lot, but this was much worse than anything he had ever seen before. What he saw was absolutely terrifying. The dog was covered with severe bite wounds all over her little body and, despite being in incredible pain, she was still somehow miraculously alive. Paul knew he had to try to help her, so he put her in his car and drove home—a decision that would be the first of many that would save the dog's life.

Based on the extent of her injuries, Paul knew she needed medical attention, but he also knew she faced another problem. Dogs involved in dogfighting are typically not given a second chance. Regardless of the circumstances, they are considered dangerous, and put down. He knew taking the dog to a vet would probably be a death sentence for her so, instead, Paul called his friend (and former boss), Jen, the director of GCHS to ask for help and advice.

Jen listened and immediately told Paul to bring the dog to their facility. Jen, too, knew that based on the dog's wounds, it would be linked to dog fighting and if Animal Control got involved, the dog would be put down.

"I think we're going to go big with this story," Jen told Paul. "Maybe there's a chance something good can come out of this."

After hanging up with Paul, Jen immediately called Wink News, a television station serving Southwest Florida. In doing so, Jen saved the dog's life for a second time that day and it got its second miracle.

Wink News arrived at GCHS a short time later and, from that point on, began providing regular updates on the dog. In one of the early updates, they reported that she now had a name. She had been named after the road where she was found that fateful day: Sunset.

We now began our day checking for updates on Sunset. Several days later, seeing that she was still alive, we decided to visit her. We drove to the pet store, bought a small plush heart that said Life is good!, some soft treats, and drove to GCHS.

Since Sunset was still in critical condition, and GCHS was uncertain she would survive, we weren't allowed to see her. We understood. As we drove home, the thought of making Sunset a part of our family crossed my mind for the first time, but I didn't say anything to Ralf.

Every morning we called GCHS to ask how Sunset was doing. Every day, we were told she was getting a little better. Wink News also continued to provide regular updates. Slowly, Sunset was becoming a celebrity.

On the morning of February 4, just like every other morning, we called GCHS. That day their response was very different: "You can come visit her today if you want."

We ran out, got in our car, made a quick stop at the pet store for more treats and toys, then drove to GCHS. As we pulled into the parking lot, my heart was pounding so hard it felt like it was about to explode but that paled in comparison to how I felt the first moment I saw Sunset.

She was in a large crate, extremely emaciated, and her left front paw was bandaged. It was heart-wrenching to see all her injuries and bite wounds. She constantly turned her head side-to-side to avoid making eye contact with us. I sat down on the floor in front of her crate and reached my hand out to her. After a few moments, she sniffed my hand. Several minutes later, she took a treat and, in that moment, we made our first connection.

Although we were only permitted a short visit, we were allowed to come back the next day and, that day, we filled out an adoption application. As we handed it to them, they told us another family had already put in an application for Sunset. Since applications were handled on a first-come, first-serve basis, we were now second in line to adopt her. I tried to remain calm, but I was worried.

We went back the next day, the next day, and the next. We visited Sunset every day for weeks. We spent time with her in an outside playpen and brought her treats and toys. Sunset loved lying down next to us and often stayed snuggled up to us for hours as we talked quietly and gently petted her.

One day we arrived at GCHS and, as soon as they brought Sunset out to the playpen and she saw us, her tail began to wag. A few days later, she kissed us for the first time. We were bonding with her and, slowly, she was also starting to trust us.

In the meantime, Sunset had undergone numerous medical procedures. She had surgery to fix a split left front paw and while they initially thought it might have to be amputated, the paw ultimately healed. Amputation was also considered for a severe wound on her tail but it, too, healed. A part of her upper left lip was missing, ripped out by another dog, so she had dental surgery for the wounds inside her mouth, cheeks, and lip.

After learning that Sunset had been used as a bait dog, and not knowing exactly what that meant, I began to do my research and that's when I found out the true horrors of what Sunset had been through. Bait dogs are chosen based on their temperament. They are usually docile, amiable dogs who don't want to fight, so they are used to train other dogs to fight. They tie the dogs' legs together and tape their mouths shut so they can't defend themselves. Then they let the other dogs loose. Dogs like Sunset get mauled and, when they are done with them, they are typically thrown away like trash. Sunset had also been used for breeding and had given birth to a litter not too long before she was found. Unfortunately, we don't know what happened to her puppies.

On March 7, we arrived at GCHS and, as always, when they brought Sunset outside to the playpen, she laid down between Ralf and me, and snuggled herself to sleep. A woman and two children walked up to the playpen but, after seeing us, stopped as if they were unsure what to do. A GCHS employee walked over to them and, as they talked, they constantly glanced in our direction. At that point, I realized who they were. This was the family who was ahead of us for Sunset's adoption.

My heart began to race and I felt nauseous. Looking down at Sunset, peacefully sleeping between us, I knew I had to stay calm. Before long, the family entered the playpen so I got up to say hello and Sunset woke up. She didn't move but stayed cuddled up at Ralf's side. The kids approached Sunset and, eventually, she got up. She was very calm but stood, motionless. Fifteen minutes later, the family left so we sat back down and Sunset laid down between us again. I looked at her, my eyes filling with tears, and whispered to Ralf, "I don't want Sunset to go home with that family."

I knew it was selfish on my part but I also instinctively knew they weren't the right fit. I could tell they were nice people and a nice family but I didn't think Sunset would do well with two young kids. I didn't think it was what Sunset needed but ultimately it didn't matter what I thought because it wasn't my decision.

Ralf and I drove home in silence. The realization that we might not be the ones to adopt Sunset left me heartbroken and terrified.

A few of Ralf's friends were in town and they planned to go out that night. Knowing how I was feeling, Ralf was hesitant but I encouraged him to go. I knew it would be good for him, but I also needed time alone to pull myself together, sort through my emotions, and figure out how to handle what was happening.

After Ralf and his friends left, I completely lost it. I couldn't imagine life without Sunset. As I lay curled up on my bed, sobbing uncontrollably, I got a text from Jen that simply said: "Check your email."

Shaking, nauseous, and certain Sunset had gone home with the other family, I opened the email and, through my tears, began to read. When I finished, unsure I understood what I had just read, I took a deep breath, wiped away my tears, and read the email again.

The other family had reached out to Jen. After seeing how comfortable and safe Sunset felt around us, and how much she trusted us, they believed Sunset belonged with us. I read the email again to make sure I hadn't misunderstood. I hadn't. At the end of the email, Jen asked us to reach out and schedule a meet and greet between Sunset and our dogs Pablo and Finja.

I immediately called Ralf. It was so loud where he and his friends were that he couldn't hear me, so I hung up. A minute later, my phone rang. "Sorry," Ralf apologized, "I had to come outside to hear what you were saying. What's up? Are you okay?"

I was yelling and talking so fast that Ralf finally broke in, "Babe, I can't understand what you're trying to tell me. Calm down!"

I took a deep breath and started again but all I could get out was "We got her! They're letting us adopt Sunset!"

It was already 8:30 p.m. While I typically don't call people that late, I couldn't help myself. I dialed Jen's number and, to my surprise, she answered. "I'm sorry to be calling so late, Jen, but I just wanted to make sure it's true. We can adopt Sunset?"

Jen laughed. "Yes, it's true, Anke. We're happy for all of you."

Hearing those words felt like the weight of the world fell off my shoulders and I could breathe again. I hung up and started to cry again, only this time they were tears of absolute joy and relief.

The next day we took Pablo to meet Sunset. We had gotten Pablo as a puppy and made sure he was properly socialized with people and other dogs. We had brought him to a puppy play group, and had taken obedience training. Pablo got along with everybody until one day when we were out for a walk and he was attacked by a dog who was off leash. The owner had no control over his dog, so as Pablo began to defend himself, I started kicking the other dog, and eventually it ran back to its owner. A few weeks later, the same thing happened with the same dog and owner only this time I reported it to the police. From that point on, Pablo still adored the ladies but was no longer a fan of other male dogs. I was positive he would love Sunset but was concerned how he would react to the other male dogs at the shelter.

As it turned out, there was no need for me to worry because as soon as Pablo met Sunset he loved her! Pablo had a blast playing in the playpen, loved all the attention he and Sunset were getting, loved everything and everybody, and thought it was the coolest thing that he got to meet so many people and other dogs. He didn't bark at one single dog whether it was male or female. Once again, Sunset had worked her magic.

The next day was Finja's turn. Just like Pablo, we had gotten Finja as a puppy and done all the same things with her: puppy playgroup, obedience training, and socialization. She was amazing and very smart, however, other than Pablo, she wasn't a fan of dogs she didn't know. She mostly ignored them and, since Finja was extremely obedient, I didn't anticipate any issues. I also didn't anticipate that Finja would have a difficult time at the shelter because of all the other dogs barking.

When Sunset and Finja met in the playpen, Sunset immediately sensed Finja's discomfort (long before any of us did). She calmly allowed Finja to sniff her and then they ignored each other. Confident everyone would be fine at home, we agreed to pick Sunset up the next day.

I walked Sunset back to her kennel one last time. She still had to wear a boot on her front left paw whenever she was outside and, as I leaned over to take it off, our eyes met. I was flooded with overwhelmingly intense feelings of love and trust—and could sense the feeling was mutual.

As I took a photo of Sunset, she continued to look at me with those soulful eyes. I told her we would be back in the morning to bring her home but it was incredibly hard for me to walk out and leave her behind. Morning couldn't come quick enough.

On March 10, 2015, Sunset came home with us. She was overjoyed to see Pablo again, happy to meet Picasso, and Finja was much more relaxed than he had been at the shelter. Welcoming her into our family and home was easy and without issue.

Later that day, I called Jen to update her and she asked if we would be willing to meet at GCHS two days later for Sunset's official adoption ceremony. With Wink News and other news channels following and regularly reporting on Sunset's recovery, she was somewhat of a celebrity. Now, everyone wanted to cover her adoption because everybody needed (and wanted) a happy ending to Sunset's story. We agreed without hesitation.

We had brought the bed Sunset slept on at the shelter home with us and placed it in our bedroom next to Pablo and Finja's dog bed. We also set up a large crate and put a nice bed and cozy blankets inside for her. The first night, Sunset chose to sleep in the crate and it was a deep, intensely relaxed sleep that let us know she felt safe and knew she was home.

Two days later, we started to get ready for Sunset's official adoption ceremony by putting on the new collar we had custom-made with her name on it. We were incredibly happy for her. At the same time, I was nervous. I had never done television interviews before, but there was another reason for my concern. Sunset's case was still an ongoing police investigation. While we remained hopeful that whoever had done this to her would eventually be caught, I had lingering concerns they might come after Sunset, or us.

On the other hand, I knew the day would also provide us with an opportunity to be a voice for Sunset and all the dogs impacted by dog fighting while also honoring and celebrating everyone who had been part of Sunset's rescue, healing, and story—including us. Pushing my fears and concerns aside, we drove to GCHS.

When we arrived, I was speechless. The parking lot was overflowing with cars and people were everywhere. Knowing we couldn't back out now, we got out of the car, reminding ourselves over and over to, "Be her voice."

Within seconds, three different news teams spotted us and approached us for an interview. The first interview wasn't terrible, but when Jen told me, "Great job! You're a natural!" she gave me the confidence I needed to continue. The second and third interviews went much better. After that, we started talking to all the people who had come to the event. Everyone was happy to see Sunset and to see how wonderful she was doing. In the midst of all the people was Paul.

It was our first time meeting Paul in person and his first time seeing Sunset in weeks. We hugged and sat down on the floor with Sunset. Paul began to pet her, her tail wagged non-stop and, through tears of joy and gratitude, we talked about how grateful we were that Sunset had gotten a second chance in life.

People began to gather in the conference room to watch a slide show an employee of GCHS had made, and we got up and followed. As soon as the slide show started, I was overcome with emotion and ran to Jen's office to try and pull myself together. I was finally able to watch it the next day. Without question, it is beautiful and I am forever grateful to the lady who made it. But to this day, I have a hard time not crying when I hear the first few seconds of the video.

Sunset, on the other hand, was a champion. She remained very calm and you could tell she recognized people she had met before. She was extremely happy to see Jen and Paul again, along with the shelter manager, veterinarian, and vet techs who had taken care of her in those early critical days.

It was a fantastic, but emotional, day. That night, exhausted, we all crawled into bed early and watched Sunset's adoption story air repeatedly on all the news channels. We were so proud. Sunset and her story put a spotlight on the harsh reality that dog fighting was a problem in our area.

Having conducted my own investigation and research, I knew Sunset had gone through hell and that I owed it to her to continue bringing awareness to the public about the evils of dog fighting. While she didn't have a voice, I, along with a village of amazing people, did. Together, we became her voice and began educating the public and reminding them to remain vigilant for signs of possible dog fighting in their neighborhood or backyards. Sunset's story had only just begun yet she was already starting to change the world. Jen's vision of seeing something good come out of what had happened to Sunset was becoming a reality.

In her first few weeks with us, it was obvious Sunset had never lived inside a house. The day after we brought her home, she was lying on the couch next to Ralf when he turned on the television. Sunset was completely mesmerized and couldn't take her eyes off the screen. Everything was new and there were so many exciting firsts, but there were also many things that scared her.

She refused to go on walks unless one of our other dogs came along. We wondered if she had possibly been kept together with other bait dogs and when she was taken somewhere alone it meant something terrible was about to happen to her. A squeaking door resulted in long periods of fearful barking. Again, we wondered if the door squeaked where she had been? Any time we brought our broom from the garage into the house and got close to Sunset, she would flinch and cower down, especially if Ralf was holding it. It wasn't hard to imagine the reason behind that reaction, but the truth is we'll never know for sure. Like so many other things about Sunset's past, we will never know all she went through and perhaps that's a good thing because, instead, we focused on working to help her recover and thrive.

Since Sunset had immediately bonded with Pablo, it was from him that she learned how to be a normal dog, including what to do with a toy. The first thing she paid any attention to was a red Kong chew toy. I spent the entire afternoon sitting on the floor with her, trying to convince her it wouldn't hurt or attack her but it wasn't until Pablo came over and showed Sunset the Kong was safe that she finally touched it with her nose.

Every morning, as Ralf got dressed, the instant he started to put his socks on, Sunset wanted to play. Soon it became their morning ritual to play whenever Ralf put his socks on.

In the weeks that followed, we learned that part of Sunset's personality included being unbelievably caring and empathetic to others. One day, while Ralf was sitting on the couch, he took a sip of water and started coughing. Sunset immediately ran over to the couch and stayed by his side until he was fine. Another day, Pablo laid down on the floor and started scratching his ear. Concerned something was wrong with him, Sunset ran over and stayed by his side until she was sure he was okay.

Anytime we were out in public with Sunset, people always stopped and asked, "Is that Sunset? How's she doing? It is such an honor to meet her in person. Thank you for opening your heart and home and giving her the life she deserves."

Her story had touched so many people's hearts and they constantly asked for updates so Ralf decided to create a Facebook page. To this day, Sunset's Facebook page still has over 3,000 followers.

As the face of the Southwest Florida Anti-Dogfighting campaign, we started taking Sunset to anti-dog fighting events as well as to events at GCHS and adoption events for local rescues. Initially, she was fine but over time we noticed Sunset withdrawing into what I called "her survival mode." People came up to pet her or take a photo with her but she just stood, motionless, not engaging or involved in what was happening around her.

Realizing Sunset no longer enjoyed going to the events, we immediately stopped. The only place we continued going was to GCHS and that was because she loved it. She was always overjoyed to see the people she had spent her first days and weeks with after she was rescued. She knew they were the people who had saved her life.

As Sunset continued to overcome her fears, she became a silly, goofy, playful pup. She preferred staying home with us. It was her safe haven. Outside our home, in unfamiliar surroundings, she was unsure and would stop and stand still. The minute we were home, she was back to being our happy girl who loved being with her family and her pack.

And, yes, our other dogs were her pack and she was their leader. She loved and cared for her pack and always made sure everybody was safe and happy. She ended disputes between our other dogs by stepping in between them and acting like a barrier. She never had to bark, nip, or bite because her mere presence immediately ended any dispute.

On the one year anniversary of Sunset's adoption, Wink News called to see if we would agree to a follow-up story. Despite the passage of time, people were still interested in Sunset and were continuing to follow her Facebook page. Knowing we were her voice and that continuing to educate the public about the menace of dogfighting was her—and our—mission, we agreed.

In the summer of 2019, we began talking about leaving Florida. The temperatures and humidity during the summer had become unbearable for us. It was too hot to even go in our pool. As a result, we spent months on end in our house. Having already gone through Hurricane Irma, every year we worried about the possibility of going through another hurricane with our dogs. When I had a basal cell carcinoma on my leg and a precancerous spot on my face removed, that sealed the deal. We decided it was time to move.

We wanted to live in a place with four seasons. Taking both personal and work reasons into consideration, we decided to relocate to New York State. I sat on the couch with Sunset lying by my side, and as I began to tell her about the move, she looked up at me. "We're going to have a huge fenced-in backyard where you and your pack can run without anyone having to be concerned about suffering a heatstroke. I promise you, Sunny." She continued to look at me then, smiling, put her head down, and went to sleep.

Those were our plans, but God had other plans for Sunny.

In July 2019, Sunny passed after a relatively brief illness. We were devastated. With so many people following her story from the day she was rescued, I knew it was important to tell them what happened. As soon as I posted on her Facebook page, people immediately blew up her page with heartfelt condolences. We were deeply touched and found great comfort in the compassion and sympathy shown to us from around the world.

Wink News asked if we would do an interview. While it was the last thing I wanted to do, I agreed because, once again, I wanted to be Sunset's voice. One hour later, they were at our house and, once again, our baby girl made the evening news.

At the end of July, a crowd gathered at GCHS for Sunset's memorial service. While a part of me dreaded the day, I was extraordinarily proud of my baby girl and all she had achieved. We had T-shirts with Sunset's paw print on them and the money from the sale of the shirts was donated to GCHS. Jen spoke. I spoke. I gave interviews to the local news channels because, once again, I could be Sunset's voice.

Sunset's story didn't end with her death because, the truth is, her story is (and will always be) about her life. It's the story of how she changed people's minds and perceptions about her breed, created awareness to the horrors of dog fighting, and the impact she had in the world. Even though her life on earth may have been too short, it is still a story with a happy ending.

We heard from a lot of Sunset's followers who told us they adopted pit bulls because of her and her story. Through Sunset, people learned the truth about these remarkable dogs and, because of Sunset, a lot of dogs were rescued, adopted, and got their own happy ending.

Sunset did a wonderful job of showing the world how resilient, loving, forgiving, and strong a dog can be even when humans have treated them with absolute disregard and hatred. She showed the world that regardless of what they are forced to do by evil humans, with love, care, and patience, dogs can heal and become incredible companions.

And Sunny *was* incredible, a true soulmate, a one in a million. Despite being dog people, she taught us so much about dogs (and about life) and we experienced things we never would have without her. Seeing and being a part of her amazing recovery was one of the most rewarding things that ever happened to us. It changed us, and our lives, and I am forever grateful I had the honor to meet Sunset and be "her mom."

Sunset is the reason we will continue to rescue dogs as long as we can. Dogs that deserve a second chance in life just like Sunset. Without Sunset, there would be no Alaska, Dozer, Blue, Gracie, or Rambo who are with us to this day. Chances are Dozer and Blue wouldn't even be alive today because, without Sunset, we never would have started adopting dogs, particularly pit bulls, that nobody else wanted.

Even though I knew Sunset would want us to carry on her legacy and be there for dogs who needed help, initially, I didn't think I had the strength to do it. Then, a few weeks after Sunset passed, she gave me a sign and the strength.

I am a paramedic and was at work resting between calls. Scrolling through my Facebook feed, I saw a post about a dog that had been found as a stray in Miami. The dog was in deplorable condition. At the exact moment I saw his picture, I felt a sudden sharp pain in my stomach as if somebody had punched me. It startled me because nothing like that had ever happened to me. Before I could think about it any longer, our team of paramedics headed out on another call.

Several hours later, we returned to the station and I went back on Facebook and saw there was an update about the dog. As soon as I started to read it, I immediately felt the same sharp pain in my stomach. I'm not one to normally believe in things like that but this was unmistakable and I knew with absolute certainty it was Sunset telling me she wanted me to help this dog.

The post had been made by Haley, the person from whom we had adopted Alaska and Dozer, so I reached out to her to learn more. "I thought of you guys," Haley said quietly, "but didn't want to bother you so soon after Sunset's passing. The pup needs a foster but again I don't want to rush you."

I told Haley what had happened to me when I saw the post. She listened and simply replied, "Again, Anke, it's up to you and Ralf. If you want to give it a shot, we can get the dog to you tomorrow morning and you can foster her. Think about it."

I assured Haley I would talk to Ralf and let her know either way. That night, Ralf and I went out to dinner and talked. On one hand, we were hesitant because it had only been a month since Sunset left us and we wondered if it was too soon. However, a larger part of us felt like Sunset wanted us to do this to carry on her legacy. Finally, I looked across the table at Ralf and said, "Sunset went through so much in her life yet she was so strong. I think she wants us to be strong now."

Ralf nodded his head in agreement so we went home and called Haley. "We'll take her. I know that's what Sunset would want us to do."

The next morning, Gracie came to our home. There was no need to keep the dogs separated like we normally do with new additions to the pack. From the moment Gracie arrived, it felt like she had been with us forever. She also helped fill the emptiness and void left by Sunset.

I knew Sunset saw how much Ralf and I were struggling—and that her boys were lost without her. Alaska and Blue, had essentially been raised by Sunset and had been having a very hard time without her. They both instantly fell in love with Gracie and I knew Sunset had sent her to us. Five years earlier, we saved Sunset. But, on that day, she saved all of us. For me, in some ways having Gracie was like a part of Sunset had returned.

We left Florida in November 2020, and moved to New York State. It was an adventure moving thousands of miles with five pit bulls and a Siamese cat but we enjoyed the trip and moved into a great home near Buffalo, New York. It has the huge fenced-in backyard I had promised Sunset, and I think of her often when I'm sitting there with our pack. I know she would have loved the yard.

I also know she's watching over us and loves everything she sees because every once in a while, in her own unique way, Sunny lets me know she's still by my side. It happened not too long after we moved here.

We were driving to Niagara Falls when, out of nowhere, a sign appeared that read: Rainbow Bridge. Having no idea in advance that one of the bridges between New York State and Canada was named the Rainbow Bridge, I was unprepared to see it and burst into tears.

As we pulled into the parking lot at Niagara Falls, I was still struggling to pull myself together. Drying my tears, I opened my door and stepped out of the car and there in front of me across the entire sky was the most beautiful brilliant rainbow I had ever seen. I knew it was my baby girl telling me she is always with us and was okay.

# Chapter 8
# UTAH

## *Buzzing Around the Beehive State*

IN *MAGICAL DOGS: LOVE AND LESSONS FROM OUR CANINE COM-panions*, you met Rudy, a mutt who had been returned to a Utah shelter multiple times by multiple people. Rudy's future looked bleak until the day Corinne walked in and decided to take Rudy home and give him a chance. As Rudy learned to trust and settle into his first real forever home, Corinne took a sabbatical from her job as an international flight attendant and began painting and writing children's books using Rudy as her muse. Together, they changed each other's lives.

The day Rudy crossed over the Rainbow Bridge, Corinne reminded everyone that "Rudy would want you to remember to Celebrate Life! and Enjoy The Ride!"

Corinne and I spent hours talking on the phone, laughing and reminiscing about Rudy. During one phone call, she asked if I would consider coming to Utah for a visit.

"Actually . . ." I began, and went on to tell her about my idea of writing an "on the road" dog book. "What do you think?"

"What do I think?" Corinne said excitedly. "I think it's a great idea and I have people I would love you to meet. Please come!"

Early one May morning, I left New Jersey, boarded a plane in Philadelphia, and five hours later landed in Salt Lake City. Corinne was waiting at the airport and we talked non-stop on the drive to her home in Park City. At the mention of Rudy, she sighed. "One day I'll get another dog, but not now. Not yet."

Corinne has a big heart and I knew when the time was right, she and her next dog would find one another. She knew it, too.

That night, we made dinner together, and continued to talk nonstop.

Rise Above It!
Courtesy of www.corinnehumphrey.com

Afterwards, we cleaned up and, with cups of tea in our hands, sat down to relax. Corinne looked at me and smiled. "I reached out to two of my favorite local rescue organizations and arranged for you to meet people from both," she paused. "Starting early tomorrow morning,"

Exhausted from a long day of traveling, that was my cue to excuse myself and head to bed. Hanging on the wall over the bed in her guestroom was one of her colorful, whimsical paintings of Rudy calmly sitting and watching her fly overhead in a hot air balloon. On a nearby mountain ledge stood a bighorn sheep. The name on the painting was "Rise Above It!" Smiling, I shut off the light, crawled into bed, and blissfully drifted off to sleep.

Early the next morning, as promised, a car pulled into the driveway, honked its horn, and thus began my adventure in Utah.

My first day I met Cathy and learned more about her organization, Canines with a Cause (CWAC). She introduced me to Cameron and Brianne, two individuals whose lives were hugely impacted by CWAC. That weekend, Corinne and I did a book signing at the Nuzzles & Co adoption center in Park City before heading to their main location in the Wasatch Mountains to meet with Claire. From her, I was introduced to Jennifer whose life was changed thanks to a very special program run by Nuzzles & Co.

In the midst of all this, a very special dog unexpectedly entered the picture for Corinne.

As you'll see in the stories that follow, my days in Utah were filled with remarkable people, organizations, and dogs who had overcome circumstances, adversity, and challenges and fully embraced the concept of rising above it!

# Chapter 9
# CATHY & CANINES WITH A CAUSE
## *We Give Second Chances*

IF WE TRACE BACK, CANINES WITH A CAUSE (CWAC) ACTUALLY began in Paris. Although, in reality, Paris was just the starting point for me. This is a story that gradually unfolded over time—and the end result was CWAC.

My career began in the fashion industry. I was living and working in Paris for well-known designer Patrick Kelly. I loved the work and had a fabulous life but, after Patrick died of AIDS, I moved home to San Diego. I was lost and had no idea what to do next, so I began traveling with the hope that I could find an answer.

In 1995, while living and working on St. Thomas in the U.S. Virgin Islands, Hurricane Marilyn struck. When all was said and done, over eleven thousand people were homeless and there was over $2.5 billion in damage. The island was essentially decimated and went into lockdown. After the government evacuated, people began looting until the National Guard came in and restored some sense of normalcy.

One afternoon, while driving around looking for basic essentials and supplies, I saw a couple walking along the side of the road. I stopped to talk with them and found out they were on their honeymoon and were walking to the airport to try and get a flight home. I drove them to the airport. When we arrived, one of the first things I saw were stacks and stacks of crates filled with dogs and cats. The military wouldn't allow the animals on their planes. Since the animals had no health certificates, they were essentially stuck with nowhere to go.

Knowing something needed to be done, I rallied my troops. Friends and acquaintances on the island came together and we transported the dogs and cats back to the small island shelter that was still habitable.

For the next three months, my first thought every morning was, I love this! I had unexpectedly found my calling. So, when I left St. Thomas and moved to Park City, Utah, I began volunteering for Best Friends Animal Sanctuary.

That led to becoming the Executive Director of Friends of Animals, Utah (FOAU). We were rescuing a lot of dogs from high-kill shelters and those dogs changed me. To look into the faces of dogs who had no hope, who were essentially saying, "Please, get me out of here," and knowing we were giving them that hope was life-altering. It brought me so much joy and further confirmed what I already knew. I had finally found my passion: animal rescue.

Over the years, people told me various stories of how their dogs had helped them through sad, difficult, or traumatic situations. One woman told me: "My husband passed and I was so sad. I was crying all the time and never left my house. Then I adopted a dog and now I'm out walking every day." A mother shared, "My son has autism and the dog brought him out of his shell."

After hearing story after story like that, I realized we were doing a lot more than rescuing and adopting out dogs. We were healing and changing lives. We were bringing joy to people.

Unfortunately, the truth is there are only so many places for dogs. There are only so many fosters, families, and homes, so I started thinking outside the box for other ways to rescue dogs and connect them with people.

Having recently learned a great deal about Post-Traumatic Stress Disorder (PTSD) as well as animal-assisted therapy, I approached the Board with an idea.

"I've been thinking about starting a program where we would place rescue dogs with veterans who have PTSD," I told them. "What do you think?"

Glancing around the table, I saw heads nodding. The Board unanimously agreed it was a great idea and that is where and how CWAC began. In the early days, we were part of FOAU and focused on training

Cathy and CWAC pups

dogs and placing them with veterans as comfort animals. We partnered with the Veterans Administration (VA) to learn the best way to work with the veterans. Over time, as the program grew and evolved, we ultimately became our own organization and moved to a small facility in Salt Lake City.

Then the final piece of the puzzle fell into place: the prison connection. After pulling dogs from shelters, they were sent to partner prisons in the areas where we are located. Inmates, who had undergone a rigorous application process followed by weeks of positive reinforcement training, began working with and training the dogs.

Since the dogs are with the inmate 24/7, they are trained virtually around the clock and it also gives the inmate an opportunity to really get to know the dog's personality. We recognize that not every dog is a good fit for the prison program or to eventually be partnered with a veteran. Dogs in that situation have gone on to become search-and-rescue dogs or avalanche dogs, while others were adopted out to the public. The dogs who stay in the prison system and pass their Canine Good Citizen (CGC) certification move on and are matched with a veteran.

CWAC is currently in three states: Utah, Idaho/Eastern Washington, and Nevada, which may seem like odd locations but they are all quite intentional. A lot of veterans prefer living in small rural towns versus a city. Living "in the middle of nowhere" allows them to "disappear" and makes it easier for them to deal with the symptoms of PTSD. Therefore, we have chosen locations where veterans tend to congregate and live. Each location is also close to a VA hospital as well as a CWAC-partner prison.

Our program is based on the philosophy of "training the trainer." Once a veteran is matched with a dog, they attend weekly classes at one of our locations. Learning to train their dog and meet goals is therapeutic, builds confidence, achieves success, and allows them to gain independence—all major factors in the recovery and healing process. The weekly classes also provide the veteran with opportunities for socializing.

There are so many facets to what we do. Consequently, the result is something much bigger. It's no longer just about finding a dog a home or helping a veteran. While it still begins with rescuing a dog, the dog then goes on to become an integral part of an inmate's life. During that phase of the program, dogs help the inmates gain a new skill, purpose, and sense of achievement. It also allows inmates to give back to the community outside the prison walls.

Once the dog is paired with a veteran, it becomes part of their healing process to help them get back to school, work, connect with their family, or whatever else the veteran needs to get over that bridge to having a life again. In some cases, the dogs have been the link that prevented suicide, ultimately keeping the veteran alive.

The dogs, and our program, also support the veterans' partners/spouses and families. Keep in mind that a spouse or child may not have had a lot of contact with the veteran during their deployment. Now that the family is back together, they may feel detached from one another or have difficulty finding common ground. The dog becomes that common ground and provides them with an opportunity to connect.

We also have mental health professionals who, if a veteran is struggling or lacks a support system, will step in and make sure they get the support they need.

The bottom line is we stand by our motto: We Give Second Chances. Whether it's a dog, a trainer who is incarcerated, or a veteran, CWAC gives them that second chance because we believe everyone—every single being on the planet—deserves a second chance.

# Chapter 10

# CAMERON & ROMEO

## *God in the Form of a Dog*

AS A MEMBER OF THE U.S. ARMY INFANTRY, I ENDED UP IN A TERrible location: the Korengal Valley in eastern Afghanistan. It was called the "deadliest place in the world" because more people were dying in that one place than anywhere else at the time.

I spent a year in the Korengal Valley before returning to the States and Fort Carson, Colorado where I was stationed. I was suffering from fairly severe PTSD but tried hiding it by numbing myself with alcohol every day.

After being honorably discharged, I returned home to Utah where I continued down the same self-destructive path. Between hard-core drinking and PTSD, I was getting myself into a lot of trouble, which ultimately culminated in a major fight at a bar downtown where I hurt a guy pretty bad. I was facing some serious charges and looking at prison time. Luckily, the VA stepped in and wrote letters to the judge talking about my case, me, where I had been, and all I had been through. The judge ultimately decided to put me on probation rather than locking me up which was great, but being on probation meant no drinking or drugs. I was supposed to be a "good boy", but I wasn't and continued drinking and doing drugs.

For quite a while I had been thinking about getting a dog, telling myself it would be nice to have a hiking partner. In retrospect, the larger truth was that even though I didn't love myself or anyone else at the time, I wanted love and thought maybe I could start with a dog.

One day, while searching for dogs on my computer, I came across Canines With a Cause (CWAC). Their program for veterans seemed like a great option for me, so I reached out to them. Later that day, Cathy called me. We talked and she explained the program in greater detail, got some of my basic information, and promised to get back to me. A few days later, she did.

"Hey, Cameron," she said. "We have a dog we want you to check out. There's no commitment. Just come meet him."

I couldn't wait to meet him. On the drive over, I was nervous, excited, happy, and scared. Walking in, I immediately spotted him. He was chasing a ball, but as soon as he saw me, he stopped, walked over, smelled me, then went back to chasing the ball.

He was a two-year-old yellow Labrador retriever named Romeo

Romeo

who had belonged to a Sheriff and his wife. When they got divorced, neither of them wanted Romeo so he ended up at a shelter. For months he was repeatedly overlooked until, finally, the University of Utah Veterinary school offered to adopt him to "train" their students. That would have essentially resulted in his death but Cathy stepped in, rescued him, and called me.

Without hesitation, I told Cathy I wanted to take him home and she agreed we could give it a chance. The instant I loaded Romeo in my car, I fell in love.

As part of the CWAC service dog in training program, we started going to classes at their training center on a regular basis. Even though Romeo was only two years old, he was so smart. He listened and learned quickly. As we continued to learn and train together, our bond grew stronger. It didn't take long before I told Cathy I wanted to keep him.

I had a dog!

As smart as he was, Romeo remained somewhat aloof and acted like he wasn't that "into" me. I knew he loved me and that his aloofness was tied to abandonment issues. Afraid I was going to leave him or walk away from him like the other people had done, he refused to take his eyes off me. Everywhere I went in the house he followed me. He wanted to make sure he wouldn't get left behind again.

I, on the other hand, was dealing with my own issues. I was still drinking and partying. Despite all that Romeo was going through, every night I went out and left him. And every time I did, something happened. He pooped in the house or got into the garbage and spread it all over the house. Once he even figured out how to open my freezer and ate every piece of meat I had in there!

While I loved Romeo, I started seriously thinking about giving him back to Cathy. Not having a dog would allow me to continue drinking and partying and doing what I wanted rather than what Romeo needed or wanted me to do.

Before making my final decision, I had a heart-to-heart talk with my dad. He reminded me I had made a commitment—a commitment that now involved another life that depended on me. I hung up the phone and looked at Romeo. He came over and sat down next to me. We sat together for a long time with me quietly petting him, buried deep in thought and reflection. Finally, looking into his eyes, I knew. Giving up on Romeo would also mean giving up on myself.

That one decision and choice to keep Romeo completely changed my life. I was no longer going out, partying, or drinking. Anytime people invited me out, my answer was always the same: "I can't. I have a new dog and if I go out, he's gonna act a fool and do something stupid."

Trying to keep Romeo from doing something stupid ultimately kept me from going out, doing something stupid, and getting myself into trouble. He saved me.

From that moment on, we went everywhere together. We became a unit. We went hiking in the mountains and swimming at the lake. In the summer we went to Snow Basin and took the gondola to the top and hiked around. He loved being in the car so we made long road trips to Oregon and southern Utah. We went to the VA hospital and to Weber State University.

Everywhere we went, everybody loved him. It's easy to love Romeo because he's always happy and constantly has a smile on his face which makes him extremely approachable. Since he wears a "Service Dog" vest, people always ask me first if they can pet him. But, once I agree, Romeo immediately rolls onto his back so they can rub his belly. Watching people pet Romeo's belly and see the smile on their faces, made me happy.

Romeo was just being himself and showing the world that he was loving, happy, and kind. People started talking to me and asking me questions about Romeo. As a result, I started opening up to people. In doing so, it helped me let my guard down and I quit isolating. Through Romeo, I realized that not only are people good but that it's good to connect with them.

Romeo was showing me a new side of life and a new way of being. He was showing me I no longer needed to be so angry or shut people away. Instead, I could be open and happy. Romeo was also showing me a new way of approaching life that I had been unable to do through therapy or the well-meaning advice of family and friends.

There is my life before Romeo and my life after Romeo because getting him was, without question, a turning point.

At the time he came into my life, I was completely self-destructive and upset with my life. The Korengal Valley was freaking crazy and I had so much PTSD from that period. Adding drinking on top of that made me suicidal. Even though the alcohol made me not care about myself, I still craved it. Every time I drank, I overdid it. As a result, I was extremely poisoned by alcohol. My life was heading in a bad direction: I had legal things going on; I didn't have any healthy relationships; my family had pushed me away; I felt nobody loved me; and I was drinking and driving all the time. I had reached a point where I didn't care about myself, anything, or anybody. I was at the point where I wanted to die—and probably would have if Romeo hadn't come into my life. If I didn't get Romeo, I probably would have taken my own life, but every time I looked at him, I thought, "We are totally dependent on one another. If something happens to me who is going to take care of him?" Ultimately my love for Romeo outweighed my desire to destroy myself and I learned to love myself because I loved him.

In his own unique way, he also kept me out of relationships that probably wouldn't have been healthy for me. There were times when I met a woman, brought her to the house, and after we left Romeo tore things up. Since it was out-of-character at that point for him to act that way, I knew it was his way of telling me the woman wasn't good for me and that I couldn't be with her.

One woman, after watching Romeo and me together, said, "I guess I can't ask you to choose between me and the dog?"

She already knew the answer, but I still looked at her and answered anyway. "Don't ask me that because I will choose Romeo." And it's true. I will always choose him.

There was one girl Romeo liked. I ended up marrying and having a child with her. The first day I brought my son home, I held him up for Romeo to see. Romeo's ears perked up and he walked over, smelled him, and licked his face. It was so special. They have been best friends ever since. My son doesn't know life without Romeo.

She and I have since gotten divorced because, although she was good for me at the time, we ultimately grew apart. After the divorce, I moved into an apartment which didn't allow dogs so a friend started watching Romeo for me. I thought I would be okay living alone in the apartment. After all, I had lived alone before, but now my life was no longer about being alone or toughing it out. It was no longer about "I've been through war so I can get through anything." My life was now about something and someone else. It was now about my dog and my son, so I got my act together and bought a house with a big yard for them.

In the process of making a better life for Romeo and my son, I made a better life for myself. I cared so much for them that I got to bask in the rewards. My love for them bounced back to me and it became this full circle of love.

Romeo has been with me through thick and thin. Through the worst times in my life, he was by my side. He has also been with me through the best times of my life probably because he is the best thing that has ever happened to me. Through him, I noticed my dark patterns and was able to change them. The nights I wanted to go out and drink, I chose instead to take him for a long walk and clear my head. He became a tool for self-improvement and my life has continually gotten better since I got him.

From the moment he stepped into my life, Romeo was always excited about everyone and everything: "Let's go meet this guy." "Let's talk to this person." "Let's go over here and see this." Because Romeo has a perpetual smile on his face, I find myself smiling more now. As a result, I've met strangers I never would have because of him.

The people in my neighborhood know and love Romeo. He inspired my neighbors to get a dog and, because of what we have been through in the CWAC program, I was able to give them pointers on exercise, staying active, and training. So now, Romeo is changing life for other people—and other dogs.

I have a neighbor, an old-timer, who met Romeo for the first time and started telling me about a dog he once had that looked just like him. He started coming over to see Romeo, always bringing him treats, and he's now my best friend in the neighborhood. I never would have made a friend like that without Romeo.

When I moved here, I never walked and wouldn't talk to anyone. But now, because of Romeo, I'm friends with my entire neighborhood and they are all friends with Romeo.

Romeo is just a pure gentle soul who saved my life, but the truth is he would do that for anyone. It's who he is. I'm just thankful he's mine.

Early on, Romeo kept me from going out to bars. While I wasn't fighting or hurting people, I was still able to get alcohol and bring it home. Slowly over time, I worked my way into AA and am now clean and sober. I take Romeo to AA meetings and people love him. Some people don't want to talk or share at a meeting, but Romeo walks right up to them and rests his nose on their lap. When they look down at him, I tell them, "You don't have to look anyone in the eyes or talk to the group, but you can look into Romeo's eyes and tell him what's going on." And they do. I've seen it happen over and over.

Romeo is that dog. When Romeo gets close to you, it's as if his eyes look into your soul and he can sense what a person is going through and is able to get them to open up. He breaks a person's old shell off and whatever they were feeling goes away. Whatever a person wants to be or do, Romeo is able to look into their soul, see what's inside, and bring it out. He doesn't want a person's shell; he wants the beauty, love, and kindness that's inside.

I remember looking at him shortly after he came into my life and thinking, "I need to be open and happy like this dog". All of a sudden, I found myself talking, smiling. I was open and happy, just like Romeo.

And because of him, I now know love—real, true, pure love—and to feel loved like that is amazing. I've also learned when you get love, you give love. All of these amazing lessons and changes, and all because of this dog in front of me.

Romeo has been a part of my life for twelve years. It breaks my heart to see him limping now when he walks and makes me emotional thinking about the fact that he is getting older and on the downslope of life, but I've had so many amazing moments and memories with him. I will always have the memories, the love, and the gratitude that Romeo came into my life and saved me.

A few months ago, I told Cathy I wanted to get another dog so Romeo's knowledge could be passed on. Now, Romeo and I have Duke, a chocolate Labrador retriever. They are buddies but what has been amazing is seeing my son with Duke. They clicked, just like Romeo and I did, and love each other so much. It's beautiful to see my son want to train Duke just like Romeo is trained.

My life is so different now. I'm not alone anymore. I'm not a drunk anymore. I'm not destroying my life anymore. I'm a much better version of myself. Anytime someone asks me, "How did you do it?" my response is always the same: "It's because of CWAC, a dog, and time and effort."

I have a friend who lives in Southern Utah. We were stationed together in Afghanistan. He was having a hard time so one day I mentioned CWAC. "Dude," I told him, "get a dog." He did and his dog did the same thing for him that Romeo did for me: she calmed him down and changed his life.

Somehow, all those years ago, Cathy knew these dogs would save veterans. I don't know how she knew, but she did and I'm forever grateful because this program straightened me out. CWAC gave me a reason to love myself because I had to love this dog. I couldn't be a dirtbag with a beautiful, hyper dog. I had to stay out of trouble, I had to hike more, walk more, I had to be better and that's what the program does for people. It shows them "You're worth it. Look at what you're doing. You're training a dog!"

I'm sure Cathy hears all the time that she and CWAC are saving lives—and it's true. I'm not sure I will ever be able to find the words to properly thank her or explain the impact this dang dog has had on my life—and all for the better. This program saved my life and opened me up to be happier, quit being so hard on myself, and know that I deserve and can have love.

You get a dog and realize life isn't about social media, your ego, trying to look good, or even what's going on in the world. It's about hanging out with your dog and being happy and, for me, whatever makes my dog happy, makes me happy. That has been my life for twelve years.

Romeo and I are never apart. Everywhere we go and everything we do it's Cameron and Romeo . . . Romeo and Cameron. We have become this unit; this one being of light. Our light and energy have grown brighter and stronger because we have each other. He'll never be alone again, he'll never be abandoned—and the same is true for me.

We were sitting together at the VA hospital waiting for my appointment one day when a guy sat down next to us and started petting Romeo. After a few minutes, he turned to me and said, "Do you know what you got with this dog?"

I looked at him, confused. "Spell dog backwards," he said. "*That's* what you got with this dog."

And it's true. The day Romeo and I met a new presence came into my life. God came into my life. For me, it was in the form of a dog.

# Chapter 11

# BRIANNE & CRICKET

## *Don't Let Your Past Define Your Future*

I WAS THE YOUNGEST OF THREE GIRLS IN MY FAMILY AND ALWAYS wanted a dog. In an attempt to dissuade me, my parents told me I could get a dog when both my sisters moved out. I believe they thought I would forget. I didn't.

When I was seventeen, my oldest sister got married and moved out. The following year, my middle sister followed suit. The next day I came home with a Rottweiler puppy. My parents took one look at him, then at me, and said, "What is that?"

"It's a dog," I declared.

"You're not going to have a dog in this house."

"You told me when both of my sisters moved out I could get a dog. They're gone. Here's my dog."

And that was that.

I named the puppy Jagger T. Clause. I loved the name Jagger. The T stood for Thumper since he thumped his back leg whenever I petted him and Clause because, at the time, Christmas was my favorite holiday. I had gotten him from a bad section of Ogden, Utah. One of the first things he did was destroy a bean bag chair before moving on to chew the leg off an end table my parents had received as a wedding gift.

In the years that followed, I had a boxer, a German shepherd, a puggle, and many other dogs.

For several years, I worked as a vet tech, but ultimately my career was in education and teaching. I had been working as a high school English and health teacher for ten years when, in 2015, my life took a complete 180-degree turn and I ended up in the Utah State Prison.

Many of the inmates were there for drug-or gang-related offenses. For many, their lives outside of prison was difficult so, to some degree, being incarcerated gave them a break from that life.

That wasn't my story at all. I wasn't the typical inmate. I came from an affluent family and had a Master's degree. I had a husband, a family, and children who were thriving. For me, being in prison was awful. I was miserable and lost. To not see my kids, to no longer have a job, and (even though it may sound trivial) to not have a cell phone, was difficult.

I immediately decided to search for something I could do that would make my time there beneficial in some way. Within a month, I became a unit coordinator and oversaw all the other inmate's job assignments. A few months later, I was offered an opportunity to work with dogs through the Canines With a Cause (CWAC) program in the prison.

Initially, I was nervous but I knew it was an opportunity to learn something and pass that knowledge on to other people. It would also bring a sense of normalcy to my prison life. And there was something else: trust. Being offered the opportunity meant that both CWAC and the prison trusted me. I'd been through a lot of scrutiny and personal attacks on the outside before coming to prison. I'd been destroyed in many ways, but this meant there were still people who had not entirely written me off. For me, that was huge and I didn't want to do anything to screw that up.

I began shadowing other inmates and their dogs until, three months later, I got my first dog. CWAC volunteers came in a few hours every week to train us, but it wasn't easy for the dogs or us. Some corrections officers had issues with the fact that the dog handlers got extra privileges like going outside the building to take their dogs potty. If there was a problem on campus and we went into lockdown, no one (including the dogs) was allowed out of the building. There were times when we were in the building over twenty-four hours with our dogs. It wasn't an easy environment for any of us but the inmates and CWAC did our best and always kept the dogs uppermost in our minds and focus.

I loved being part of the program and caught on pretty quickly. Within a year, I was a Senior Trainer which meant that along with training dogs, I was also training other inmates in the program. I was also assigned to work with dogs who were having a difficult time transitioning or learning. Once I got them to the point where they were well on their way and comfortable, I handed them off to another trainer and moved on to another dog.

Throughout my time there, I probably worked with fifty to sixty dogs. Sometimes I only had a dog a few days while I assessed them. Other times, I had a dog for several weeks until they were ready to be handed off to the next trainer. I loved all the dogs, but when you're working with that many dogs, it's difficult to get attached to any one dog in particular—until Cricket.

Cricket, a border collie-bull terrier puppy, came into the prison when she was ten months old. Initially, she was assigned to another handler so I didn't have any interaction with her. Once everyone was confident in her abilities, she was discharged and went to a veteran, but before long, she came back to the prison for rehabilitation. It hadn't worked out with the veteran who had struggled with the positive reinforcement aspect of the training. Cricket came back with a ton of fears.

While Cricket was with the veteran, I was working with a Red Heeler named Stella who came to us straight from the shelter. She had mange and worms, was sick, scared, and, barely able to lift her head, so I began feeding her by hand. After three months together, Stella was healthy and started learning some behavior modifications which were key to her working through her fears. She was so eager to please and ended up being a great dog and was ultimately adopted into a loving home. It was amazing to be a part of her journey.

By the time Stella left, Cricket had already come back but I had been assigned another dog. However, Cricket's handler wasn't confident she could give Cricket what she needed, so I relinquished my dog to another trainer and took Cricket. I knew she still had a shot at becoming a service dog for a veteran, so I worked with her for the next two months. She passed her Canine Good Citizen certification and went to another veteran. Once again, due to several unfortunate circumstances, it didn't work out with him and she came back.

Cricket came back two more times. Every time she came back to me, there were new fears we had to overcome. She was afraid of so many things: leather, men, shoes—you name it. She couldn't get her footing and people kept giving up on her too quickly.

In 2019, knowing I was supposed to be released in six or seven months, I told CWAC I would continue training other trainers but wanted to keep Cricket with me because, after my release, I hoped Cricket would leave with me. Three months later, CWAC told me they had an adopter for Cricket and took her.

The following month, Cathy, from CWAC reached out to me. "Brie, I would hate to lose you as a trainer so, if you're interested, when you get out we'd like to offer you a job."

I was stunned and in awe that Cathy had that kind of trust and confidence in me. I didn't know anyone at that point who had transitioned from prison into a job working with dogs. I assured Cathy I was absolutely interested and, for the remainder of my time in prison, I continued working with dogs.

I was released in September and it was amazing to be home and surrounded by my family. Even though there were boxes piled everywhere in my house, I didn't think about unpacking. I just wanted to spend that first day being with everyone. That night, we were all hanging out on the floor in my living room when there was a knock on my front door. At first, the sound startled me because it had been quite some time since I even had a door, but I got up off the floor and opened it. Standing on my front stoop was one of the CWAC trainers—and Cricket.

"Here's your dog," she said, handing me Cricket's leash. I looked at her and at Cricket, confused, and unsure what to say. She explained, "One of our volunteers offered to keep Cricket until you were released. We wanted you to continue working with other dogs so we told you she had been adopted out."

Although I was chomping at the bit to start working with CWAC, I wanted to take the next few weeks to unpack and get settled while also giving Cricket time to feel comfortable being in my home and with me.

Cricket was forty-five pounds of solid muscle that could fly through the air like she was seven feet tall. She became my jogging buddy. She loved to swim and was completely obsessed with balls to the point where I had to hide them so she could focus on other things. Her love language was simple and basic: "Come play with me!"

Cricket helped me transition to being home again. Nights were difficult (and sometimes still are). I had been living in a tiny little space—almost suffocatingly small—and now I was in my master bedroom. Since I don't allow dogs on my bed, for the first week, I slept on the floor next to Cricket because I needed to feel her next to me. It was where I felt safe.

I was living alone and anytime Cricket got up and stood by the door, my heart and mind raced. Wondering what or who was out there, I cautiously peeked out only to see a deer standing in my backyard. Cricket gave me the companionship and security I needed to begin feeling safe in my home and in my life.

Leaving the house was still problematic for me. Since Cricket wasn't a service dog, I couldn't take her everywhere with me. Going to the grocery store was especially difficult. In prison, any time a voice came over the speaker it was for something bad. In the grocery store, whenever a voice came over the speaker, it triggered me and sent me into a panic. I had to call my sister and she would talk me out of the building. "Your car is in the parking lot, Brie. Leave your cart and go to the exit." She would continue calmly talking until I was back in my car and able to head home.

Finally, in October 2019, I started working for CWAC shadowing other employees. In early 2020, I began working with veterans. I had gone from training dogs in prison to training veterans how to train their dogs. Once again, I was teaching and back in my element. Obviously, this was a different setting and environment and, while none of it had been planned, it all came together perfectly.

In 2021, I became the Adoption Coordinator for CWAC. I find fosters for a dog until it is adopted out, and also do some boarding and training at my house, but the majority of my job is devoted to training veterans to train their dogs.

I use Cricket to assess dogs for any type of reactivity or aggression. She's so good at working with other dogs. She corrects them softly and is equally amazing with any puppies I bring into the house.

The veterans in our program come in with PTSD. Even though I had a different scenario play out in my life, what happened to me sometimes allows me to connect with and relate to them. I know what it's like to be told what to do, and I make sure they know that I'm not there to boss anyone around. The majority of veterans have no idea what I've been through, but there's an unspoken understanding that just naturally occurs.

The veterans are very appreciative of the fact that they're getting trained for free and all they have to do is show up. They receive support from every angle and the majority of those who go through the program are an absolute pleasure to work with. It's amazing to watch a veteran's transition from the beginning of the process to the end. It's remarkable how much they change. While it's a credit to them, it also speaks volumes about CWAC. This organization

Cricket

has helped so many dogs and so many people in a variety of life situations.

I never imagined this is what I would be doing with my life. I never imagined my life would take the path it did. But, when it did, there were so many lessons and blessings along the way. Early on, the prison pushed back and didn't want me to be part of the program, but CWAC had my back from the first day I entered the prison program and they continue to do so to this day. To have that kind of support is life-altering. It makes you believe in yourself again.

And then there was this dog named Cricket who had been abused and had so many fears. I had my own fears, but together we faced and overcame them. We never let our past define us. Instead, we forged ahead and created a brighter, happier future—together.

# Chapter 12

# CORINNE
# & ADOBE

## *Living and Loving the Life of My Dreams*

I'M LIVING THE LIFE OF MY DREAMS IN THE PLACE OF MY DREAMS. Looking back, I'm not sure any of this would have happened were it not for two dogs that unexpectedly came into my life, starting with Rudy.

For twenty-five years, I'd been working as an international flight attendant for a major commercial airline. Since I was away from home for days (and sometimes weeks) at a time, it wasn't feasible for me to have a pet. However, when an imminent company bankruptcy brought an offer to take an extended leave of absence, I jumped at the opportunity and applied for a five-year unpaid sabbatical. I had been craving more creativity and deeper meaning in my life as well as the time and opportunity to take painting classes and to get a dog.

Enter Rudy, a skinny, scarred, English pointer mix who had been in and out of various shelters and foster homes for over three years. Many of his teeth were cracked, broken, or missing and the vet suspected he had been chained up and mistreated or attacked by other dogs. In the beginning, it was challenging to work through his fears, but Rudy ultimately became my much beloved pet and companion.

During our eleven years together, my life took some unexpected (and wonderful) turns. Rudy became my muse and the inspiration and star of all my paintings, prints, and five children's books. Every piece of wisdom in my books came from Rudy: Take a Closer Look; Let Yourself Be Loved; Follow Your Heart; Don't Be Afraid to Leave the Path; and Life is Filled with Magic and Joy!

After Rudy passed, I was consumed by overwhelming and unending waves of crushing grief. I felt his absence in every aspect of my life and could no longer muster the energy to paint or sketch. The next "Roaming with Rudy" book project was pushed into the far recesses of my closet—and mind. I forced myself to take advantage of my freedom and began traveling. I hiked at a local dog forest hoping that by watching the antics of other people's dogs I would somehow feel better. I borrowed friends' dogs to try and fill the hole in my heart (and life) that had been left by Rudy. Even though I knew the time wasn't right for a new companion, I looked at PetFinder several times a day. Somehow seeing pictures of Rudy-lookalikes made my sadness less strangling.

One day while scrolling through Facebook, a post from Canines with a Cause (CWAC) popped out at me. They were in need of an immediate foster for Sarge, a yellow Labrador retriever, whose owner had a prolonged three-month hospital stay. I immediately reached out and agreed to foster Sarge. He was a seventy-five-pound bucket of love and the perfect temporary solution for my sadness.

Shortly after Sarge went back to his owner, my friend, Patti, came for a visit and to conduct interviews for a new book. One day, we were out meeting people and dogs from Canines With a Cause, when we crossed paths with a sassy blue heeler/border collie mix named Adobe. He was in the CWAC prison program and had been paired with a female inmate. It's an incredible program but not a perfect fit for every dog. According to the inmate, that was what happened with Adobe.

"He's an absolutely beautiful dog," she told me, "and completely falls in love with his person, but he doesn't love this environment. Prison conditions are challenging for us, so it's understandable that it can be challenging for the dogs. Gratefully, the dogs let us know fairly quickly if this is the right environment for them. After two and a half weeks, Adobe let us know this environment was too stressful. He began to bark a lot, especially at night when the guards came around with flashlights every hour to do bed checks. Adobe needs a calmer setting. He needs to be moved into foster care where he can continue his training."

Pausing for a moment to compose herself, she continued. "I fall in love with every single one of the dogs I work with quickly. Even though Adobe was only with me for a short time, it still hurts to see him go."

Realizing CWAC needed a foster for Adobe, I agreed to bring him

Adobe on his chair by the fireplace
(Note Corinne's painting of
Rudy on the wall)

home to decompress until he could be adopted. Later that day, Patti and I headed to the CWAC training center to pick him up.

Adobe was super smart and eager to learn and please. I, on the other hand, was a bit overwhelmed by his non-stop energy and independence, which was a stark contrast from sweet Sarge and senior Rudy. I thought he was snappish and bored, but Patti connected with him immediately. She adored him and, as she continued to watch us interact, told me, "He loves you, Corinne."

I wasn't convinced but I didn't think or worry about it too much because I was just fostering him. I knew this handsome black-and-white speckled herder would have no trouble finding a permanent home.

Before Adobe came into my life, I had planned several vacations so I made arrangements for Adobe to stay at a CWAC-approved boarding facility while I was away. When I came home, Adobe and I went camping, to dog parks, and shopping at Home Depot. We began training classes at the local Petco, which got me out and re-energized once again. It also helped keep Adobe's mind engaged, which I hoped would ultimately support CWAC's original plan for him to one day be a therapy dog.

One morning, Cathy, the director of CWAC, called. "We've decided Adobe is a little too 'busy' to become a therapy dog in our program so we're putting him in our adoption program."

"You're giving up on him too quickly," I told Cathy. "He's smart and has really mellowed out. He's such a great dog!"

"Corinne, trust us on this. We need to get him settled, and he's not the kind of dog who will lie by someone's feet for hours while they work."

"Well, what do you want me to do?"

"We want you to keep him!" she laughed.

Before starting CWAC, Cathy was the director of the animal shelter where I had gotten Rudy years before. Back then, Cathy saw something in Rudy that I didn't: a perfect match and a lively new companion and muse for me. Was it possible Cathy now saw something in Adobe?

Unsure and unconvinced, I continued to vacillate a few more weeks. I made a list of the pros and cons of adopting Adobe. He was fun, but he wasn't very cuddly. He wasn't Rudy or anything like Rudy but maybe that was better? It certainly wasn't an instant love affair, but it hadn't been an instant love affair with Rudy either.

Since Patti had spent time with the two of us, I called to share my concerns with her. "What if I'm not busy enough for him? Would he be happy here with me, a single woman in her late fifties? Maybe he'd be better off with a bunch of kids that would match his energy level? Wouldn't he be better off with a family?"

Patti listened and, when I finished going through my long list of concerns and apprehensions, she couldn't hold it in anymore. "Corinne," she sighed, "you and Adobe *are* a family! People with kids don't have time— they're constantly running to school, soccer practice, scouts, work, and errands—they're never around." Other friends agreed with Patti, pointing out everything I had already done to plan my days and life around Adobe.

In the meantime, Adobe seemed restless and unsettled while I continued weighing my options. Then one day, I woke up, looked Adobe in the eyes and knew. "Adobe," I quietly began. "I've made a decision. You're mine. You're home."

Adobe stared at me with an intensity that assured me I was making the right decision and that he knew, understood, and was happy.

Once Adobe knew he was here to stay, he immediately staked his claim on the chair by the fireplace. At long last, I went back into the studio to begin sketching my new speckled mutt. We traveled in my camper van and had amazing vacations in southern Utah's red rock country, Lake Tahoe, and drove all the way to the Oregon Coast. In Oregon, Adobe saw the Pacific Ocean for the first time and experienced the freedom of running down wide, endless beaches.

The more time I spent with Adobe, the more I realized just how funny, handsome, and smart he was. Unlike my initial impressions, he also turned out to be incredibly cuddly and intuitive. On my not-so-great days, he climbed onto my lap, placed his paws around my neck, and fixed me with a steady gaze that clearly told me exactly how he felt: "We're in this together. Everything is going to be alright."

As we settled into our life together in Park City, I began painting in earnest with Adobe as my new muse and inspiration for an ever-growing collection of popular paintings and children's books.

Because of Adobe's capacity and enthusiasm for learning, we engaged in all kinds of activities from Rally and Agility to Canine Good Citizen training. We took tracking and nosework classes as "research" for a potential children's picture book and it turned out that Adobe enjoyed that, too. Everything we did together strengthened our bond.

With my sabbatical at the airline officially over, I began planning my flying schedule around Adobe's classes. I started flying less and only working one-day trips because I was happiest being home and hanging out with my constant companion.

For most people, the Covid epidemic changed their lives. It changed mine as well, but for me, it had a silver lining. With travel restricted and discouraged, the airline parked over 800 airplanes. As a result, they needed to reduce staffing and offered me a generous retirement package. After forty-plus years of flying, I had had enough and jumped at the chance to close that chapter and focus on other things like art, writing, and my dog. I was also antsy to move and discover the next best place.

Adobe became my faithful assistant. Together, we scouted different locations in Oregon, California, and Washington ultimately settling on a small seaport town on the Olympic Peninsula.

The process of selling my house, packing everything up, and moving to a new, unknown place was stressful for me and Adobe. He paced and whined and worried about being left behind despite my constant reassurance that there wasn't a chance that would happen.

The area where we live now is a far cry from the rugged high desert and harsh winters of Utah, but Adobe and I took to it immediately. We enjoy the beaches, mountain trails, mild weather, and the incredible art scene. We found a new trainer who specializes in Nose Work and Tracking—and Adobe is a star! He aced his first Odor Recognition Trial and is now learning to do underwater and vehicle searches. Not only is it great for him, but I'm learning to be a better handler. This experience is also evolving into a new children's book, *Making Sense of Scents: A Dog's Nose Knows.*

As part of a vibrant community of artists, one of the first things I did was set up my new studio. Adobe's sassy personality emerged onto the canvas and his messages were a bit different with themes like: Snap Out of It!; Live a Colorful Life; Bloom Where You're Planted; and Be On Top of Your Game. Within a year, the paintings were accepted into the North-wind Art Organization's Hospital exhibit as well as their Showcase Gallery.

Adobe has added unexpected and immeasurable richness to my life. He's seen and supported me through break-ups, big life changes, multi-state moves, and career changes in a way humans couldn't.

There is a saying that "Anyone can teach their dog to sit, stay and speak, but did you ever stop to think about what your dog could teach you?" It always makes me pause and reflect on my life and how it has evolved. To this day, I am amazed that two dogs came into my life and "spoke" to me, prompting me to create (and thrive), succeed beyond my wildest imagination, and live the life of my dreams.

# Chapter 13
# CLAIRE &
# NUZZLES & CO.
# PURPLE PAW
# PROGRAM
## *Stopping the Cycle of Violence*

MY PASSION FOR ANIMALS AND MY LIFE'S MISSION IN ANIMAL WEL-fare is a result of growing up in a home where pets were respected, loved, and treated like family members. They were my siblings.

I was also born with a need to be of service to others. As a young Girl Guide (the Canadian version of the Girl Scouts), I participated in an event where my group went to a home for the blind to read to their residents. Each Guide was assigned a resident and a dog from a local shelter. I can still picture the woman, comfortably seated in her recliner relaxing while I read to her and she petted the dog. It didn't matter if I was reading her a book or the newspaper; what mattered was that she had company and she was petting the dog.

That experience, and dog, had a lasting impact on me. It made me understand a dog's incredible compassion and healing powers and ultimately led me to my work with Purple Paw.

In Utah, one in five men and one in three women have experienced Intimate Partner Violence (IPV). Those who are fortunate to have never personally been a victim of IPV, typically know someone who has: a family member, a friend, or a coworker.

Many times, IPV is hidden. Initially the victim may not recognize that they are being abused. It can be physical or emotional, and typically escalates over time.

Abusers frequently use family pets as a means of threatening or controlling their victim. Unfortunately, threats to harm or kill an animal aren't always idle or imaginary. Many times, abusers follow through on their threat. As a result, 70% of victims hesitate or refuse to leave an abusive situation for fear of leaving their pet behind. By staying in a dangerous situation, the victims further expose themselves, their children, and their pets to more violence and even death.

Since most domestic violence shelters can't accommodate pets, victims often seek refuge in a family or friend's home, or even in their car. For a variety of reasons, they aren't always viable options and, if they are, don't last.

The Purple Paw Program began in 2012 after Nuzzles & Co. received a request from a local domestic violence shelter to temporarily board a pet. The pet's owner, an IPV survivor, was unable to take their pet with them to the shelter. Realizing how much we helped that survivor by simply caring for their pet, we knew we needed to develop a program to help more people. We began by partnering with the shelter, offering to foster or board pets for however long their client needed in order to get their life back on track. The partnership was so successful that we expanded the program to offer our services to all domestic violence shelters in Utah.

When I was offered the Purple Paw Program Director position, I was excited because it was an opportunity for me to help people and pets, a perfect match for me.

Not long after, in Salt Lake City, a woman escaped her abusive home. but had to leave her pets behind. She went back regularly while her husband was at work to care for them. One day, she and a friend drove to the house thinking he was at work, but as soon as they got out of the car her husband walked out with a gun. He began firing, shooting both women multiple times. He then grabbed his wounded wife and dragged her into the house while her friend lay injured and bleeding in the street. After barricading his house, he continued to injure and traumatize his wife. The abuse went on for hours until a SWAT team was finally able to talk him down and rescue her.

We received a call from the Sheriff's office saying there were dogs in the house and wondered if we could help. I drove to Salt Lake City and rescued the two dogs. Several days later, a cleaning crew discovered a cat hidden in the house. In all the chaos, the survivor's family had forgotten the cat, so I went back and got it.

That episode made us realize we weren't reaching all the victims who needed our help so we expanded our program once again and partnered with any organization or professional who assisted survivors (including law enforcement and health care providers).

Since the program's inception, we've provided services to almost 400 pets and assisted 200 survivors. A pet can stay with us for as long as it takes the survivor to get back on their feet, which can be several days or several months. The longest stay has been eleven months, but the average stay is eighty-five days.

In addition to boarding and fostering, our Certified Veterinarians and Technicians provide the pets with physical care: examinations, dental care, vaccinations, spay/neuter, treatments, and surgery in our fully-equipped Veterinary Suite. Our Certified Animal Behavioral Specialists and Trainers provide emotional and behavioral rehabilitation while our staff and volunteers provide an abundance of love and playtime. We also provide supplies such as food, crates, and anything that will enable pets to remain with their families. Everything in the program is offered at no cost to the client. We're supported entirely through donations and grants and rely heavily on the generous services of our volunteers.

The only requirement asked of the survivor is weekly communication either by phone, email, or text. I send them photos or tell them stories and funny anecdotes about their pet. I often Facetime or Skype with them and also encourage and facilitate visits as often as they want and for as long as they want. My goal is to keep them engaged and remind them their pet loves and needs them.

Once a survivor is reunited with their pet, I typically don't hear from them, although there are a few survivors who stay in touch and keep us updated.

In some instances, it may take several attempts for the victim to permanently escape the control and violence. We assist them as often as they need until they have successfully resettled and started a new life.

Several months ago, I got a call from a Utah Domestic Violence Shelter asking if we could temporarily board a client's dog. The woman had been severely beaten and I was warned that her dog may have suffered injuries as well.

I was shocked when I saw the woman's wounds, but I was also deeply touched by her emotional struggle when she released the dog to me. She had fought to save her dog's life. I reassured her we would take excellent care of her dog and that they would be reunited again. She cried. I cried. It was heart-wrenching.

Our vet examined the dog and while his physical wounds healed, he remained depressed and fearful. Our staff and volunteers took extra time to comfort him. Shortly thereafter, a wonderful foster took the dog into her home where he began to thrive. Before long, he was back to being a normal, happy dog.

In the beginning, the woman called me daily for updates but gradually her calls became less frequent. I also noticed a change in her spirit. One day, she shocked me when she asked if we could find a new home for her dog. She was still struggling to find her way and was not sure she would ever be able to take him back.

My heart sank. I felt like we had failed both her and her dog. This wasn't how their story was supposed to end. I reminded her that her dog was being well-cared for and told her to take whatever time she needed. She remained unsure whether she would ever be able to take her dog back, but I continued to reassure and encourage her.

Slowly, she got healthier. After her abuser was sentenced and incarcerated, she finally felt free and able to start her life over again with her beloved dog.

The majority of pets we board and foster are reunited with their family, but that's not always the case. Although initially, I found it hard to accept, over time, I realized that every situation is different. Ultimately, what we offer those we serve is the opportunity to escape the violence along with the time they need to consider their options and make the best decision for themselves and their pets.

Keep in mind that it's not just people who are the victims of Intimate Partner Violence. Many of the pets have also been abused, either physically or emotionally, or have witnessed the abuse and are affected by it. The impact of the abuse or trauma comes out in the animal's behavior—typically as fear or aggression. Our amazing volunteers and staff pour love into them. They spend lots of time talking, touching, and playing with them and patiently rehabilitate and nurse them back to complete health.

A boxer once came in with a broken jaw. Since it was impossible for the dog to eat, the dog was slowly starving to death. Our medical team performed surgery on the dog's jaw and, while it was a tricky surgery (along with the risk of possible complications), it was successful. The dog was finally able to eat without pain and began to thrive.

Contrary to what many would assume, it wasn't the abuser who had injured the boxer—it was the survivor's adolescent son. He had kicked the dog in a moment of rage.

Children exposed to violence are more likely to have increased emotional, behavioral, and social difficulties. If children aren't taken out of that environment, statistics show they will often repeat the learned behavior. By enabling the survivor to escape an abusive situation, we are also helping to save the children and breaking the cycle of violence.

The Purple Paw program began with one request and has since grown into an incredibly important and successful program that saves the lives of IPV and sexual abuse survivors, children, and pets. It also allowed me to follow my personal mission and passion of helping people and saving animals.

Claire with her dogs, Denver and Aspen

# Chapter 14

# JENNIFER, COOPER & LYLA

*Everything is So Much Better Now*

I GREW UP IN A SMALL, RURAL FARMING COMMUNITY IN NORTHeast Utah. My father and brother had hound dogs, which were common in our area since they helped get rid of the raccoons that constantly plagued the farmers.

Even though our dogs had a doghouse, they essentially lived their lives chained in the backyard. When I was young, the concept of a dog living in a house was unfamiliar and foreign. It wasn't until I was much older that I saw dogs living in someone's home as part of their family.

In my 20s, I was married, happy, and living what I believed was an ideal life. I kiddingly called myself a "desperate housewife" based on the hit show at the time about a group of women who were living a seemingly perfect suburban life. In many ways, my life mirrored that show. We had two homes, nice cars, and my husband was extremely successful. I worked as a dental assistant, but as my husband became more successful, we decided I would quit my job in order to be more available to entertain his clients, travel, and attend company outings, and events.

One night, while playing Bunco with a group of ladies, one of them said, "I have two Shih Tzu puppies that are almost twelve weeks old. I'm desperately trying to find them homes, so if you know anyone who might want one, let me know."

Since I wasn't working and felt I had time to devote to a dog, I asked her to come over that Saturday morning with the puppies.

My nieces, who were five and eight years old, were visiting us at the time. While we loved both puppies, we agreed I should adopt the puppy named Diamond (because of the diamond-shaped patch of fur on his chest). We decided to change his name and I gave my nieces the honor. One chose Monte; the other Cooper. We invited friends and neighbors over to vote and later that day we shared the results. His new name would be Cooper Monte.

It was a joy to have a puppy in the house. My nieces doted on Cooper, wrapping him up in blankets and carrying him around like a baby. He loved every bit of it. Every year, when my nieces visited, we had a birthday celebration for Cooper complete with party hats, balloons, a cake, and a trip to the pet store where we bought whatever he touched with his nose.

Cooper quickly became the love of my life. Initially, I tried to crate train him. But every time he cried, I took him out and put him on the bed with me. I didn't really know what I was doing, so we enrolled in puppy classes and got the basics down. On graduation day, Cooper and I wore graduation caps and posed for pictures at the commencement ceremony. From that point forward, I spoiled him rotten. People constantly told me I was spoiling him. I simply smiled, nodded, scooped Cooper up, and loved him even more.

My husband traveled frequently for work so, most of the time, it was just Cooper and me. We went everywhere together and became a dynamic duo. He was the one constant in my life, and for several years we were happy. Then my life took a drastic turn.

I had begun to suspect my husband was being unfaithful. One night, I looked at his phone and confirmed my suspicions that he was having an affair with his secretary. The next morning, after he left for work, I packed his things up, put them on the porch, changed the locks, and sent him a message telling him what I'd found out and that we were done. Later that day, he moved into our second home with his secretary.

He was my high school sweetheart and I was devastated. For a while, we shared custody of Cooper but that became increasingly difficult for me. Eventually, I decided it was healthier if we cut ties completely. While the divorce was difficult, I got through it. In the years leading up to the divorce, my husband had rarely been home. Now, with Cooper by my side, I was ready to build a new life.

Then the bottom completely fell out.

One morning, I woke up to the news that my husband's businesses weren't entirely legitimate and that he was part of a $14 million Ponzi scheme. We had been married for eight years and that entire time I had been completely unaware our life was a façade. It was devastating to see how his actions were now hurting a lot of people and causing a lot of damage. Embarrassed and ashamed, Cooper and I didn't leave the house for several weeks.

When I finally emerged, people asked me, "How did you not know?" "You may not believe me," I told them, "but, honest to God, I didn't."

It was true. I was a young woman who had everything she wanted. Whenever I questioned where the money was coming from, he gave me a vague response or talked in terms that made no sense or that I didn't understand. I never questioned why I was never allowed to drop by his office or why my name wasn't on any accounts. In hindsight, I'm lucky it wasn't because it meant I didn't have any ties to his fraudulent businesses.

Soon, people started showing up at the house to take cars and other possessions. Then the heat was shut off. Finally a foreclosure notice was tacked to the front door. I packed up my things, and Cooper and I moved to a small rental home south of where we had been living.

I couldn't believe this had become my life. I despised what my ex-husband had done and felt like an idiot for not knowing better. My initial embarrassment and shame turned to extreme anger. Not knowing how to deal with the emotional turmoil, I turned to drugs and alcohol to cope.

Eventually, I moved back to my hometown to be closer to my family, hoping it would pull me out of the unhealthy habits I was developing. I started dating someone I knew in high school. He was a dog lover and Cooper got along great with his two dogs: a golden retriever and a cock-apoo. He lived in the country and had a lot of land where the dogs could run and play. Cooper loved chasing rabbits and countless times I tracked him down on the four-wheeler, only to find him face covered in dirt stalking a rabbit hole. We took the dogs with us everywhere: to the lake, the mountains, and on countless camping trips. During the harsh winter weather, he, I, and the three dogs cuddled up by the fireplace. We were enjoying life and, as an added bonus, I was clean and sober.

There is a lot of truth to the saying that "You can take a girl out of the city, but you can't take the city out of a girl." As much as I enjoyed living in the country, I longed to be back in the city. I loved city life, plus there were more job opportunities for me there. Eventually, Cooper and I moved into an apartment in the city. I hadn't lived in an apartment for years and Cooper missed having open space to run and play so it was an adjustment for both of us. Just like we had always done, Cooper went everywhere with me and my nieces came for their annual weekly visit to spoil him and give him extra love and attention.

Eventually, I rented a home, Cooper and I met and befriended a few of the neighbors, and slowly, we fell into a routine. Life, once again, began to feel normal.

Every spring, our community has a clean-up day where people pile yard waste and bulky items at the curb. One rainy spring night, while sitting on my front porch, I spotted a cat darting between traffic and all the items piled at the curb. Knowing it was in danger of being hit by a car, I began to chase after it. Several blocks away, I finally caught up to it and realized it wasn't a cat but a very malnourished dog in extremely poor condition. There were areas where her hair was thin and almost non-existent, while in other areas, her hair was severely matted. It looked as though someone had attempted to cut away some of the matting, and in the process, her skin had been cut. The hair on her ears and in her paw pads was very long. She was soaking wet, shivering, and panting. I scooped her up and carried her home.

The following day, we went to a low-cost veterinary clinic who determined she was a Shih Tzu-Yorkie mix between three and five years old. They recommended I feed her every two hours since she was so malnourished. For the next week, I stayed home from work to take care of her. She was extremely lethargic, slept around the clock, and never made a sound. Cooper was excited to have a friend, but she was so tired and weak, she didn't pay much attention to him.

I called her Little One, knowing if I gave her a name, I ran the risk of getting attached to her. I put posters up to try and find her owners, but after several weeks, no one came forward to claim her. Considering the condition she was in when I found her, I was relieved. I didn't want her going back there.

After Little One put on a few pounds and regained her strength, she became a real spitfire. I named her Lyla after a character on the Showtime series, Dexter: a British woman who, just like Lyla, was scrawny, skinny, scrappy, and definitely in charge.

Lyla, the dog who never made a sound, found her voice. In fact, she barked so much that my neighbors began to call and complain. Whereas Cooper loved everyone and wanted to be everyone's friend and gave kisses freely, Lyla didn't care for people. Her focus was on loving and protecting our home and me. She also loved (and inhaled) food—probably a carryover from her days of living on the streets.

Unfortunately, even though I had been doing really well and had remained clean and sober, I started using again. As a result, life became a rollercoaster for the three of us. I had reconnected with someone I dated in the past. One weekend, we went away with several others to San Diego. We were staying in a beautiful house on the beach. The back of the house faced the ocean and was a solid wall of glass on all three levels. Over the course of the weekend, the man and I had a huge disagreement. While the others were on the top floor dancing and having fun, I was on the middle floor, running terrified in a desperate attempt to get away from him. When he finally caught up to me in a bathroom, he began to beat me. He got on top of me, slammed my head against the tile floor then reached up, pulled the towel bar off the wall, and stabbed me in the knee.

The police were called, and they took me to a friend's house. The next day, my knee was red and hot. Unable to bend it, I went to the emergency room.

As a result of the injury, I was in constant and excruciating pain and my substance abuse intensified.

The only thing in my life that brought me any joy or semblance of normalcy were Cooper and Lyla. They were two peas in a pod. Even though they didn't play together a lot, it was obvious they loved one another. They always slept together and waited together at the door for me to come home. Their love and devotion to me never wavered regardless of what I was doing and they were the only things in my life I could count on.

I met and began dating a wonderful man with a six-year-old son who was hearing impaired and fell in love with both of them. His son had an extraordinary connection with Lyla. I'd never seen anything like it. I felt this was my chance to finally have a happy family, and desperately tried to get my life together for them, Cooper, Lyla, and myself.

For six months, I hid the severity of my addiction. Every morning, I put on scrubs and pretended to go to work at a dental office but, in reality, I was hanging out at my drug dealer's house. When my boyfriend learned the truth, he told me I could no longer come around or be anywhere near his son. Out of love (and with the best of intentions), he also alerted my parents and landlord that I was spiraling out of control.

My mother came to help but she didn't know what to do—and then I got a three-day notice to vacate the house. As the difficult reality sank in that I no longer had a home for myself, Cooper, and Lyla, I started taking phone calls from my prior abusive boyfriend. I told him because he had hurt me so severely that night at the beach house, he was the reason for my addiction. I told him I was desperate, needed help, and that he needed to help get me into treatment.

"Come home," he said. "We'll figure it out."

I believed him. With no other options, Cooper, Lyla, and I moved into his house. He had three bigger dogs—two Boxers and a 140-pound African Boerboel—but the dogs meshed well. Lyla, the tiniest of all the dogs, acted like she owned the place and took charge of all the other dogs, including his Boerboel.

A few nights later, while we were out to dinner, he reached across the table and took hold of my hand. "I'll get you all the help you need," he said. "I'll put you on my insurance, and we'll get you into treatment, but in order to do that you need to marry me."

I had tried Alcoholics Anonymous (AA), outpatient treatment, and even tried going cold turkey. Nothing I tried had worked. I knew I was a very sick person and believed I was a terrible partner, an awful dog mom, and a selfish piece of garbage. I feared being alone and, knowing I couldn't do it on my own, my immediate response was, "Okay, great!"

Two months later, despite still being very much in love with the man and his son I thought would be my forever family, I married the man who had abused me. We had a beautiful wedding in a stunning location. Once again, I was living in a big fancy house on top of a hill with a beautiful view.

There is a saying in AA that, when you keep getting involved in the same type of dysfunctional relationship, "Your picker is broken." Let me tell you, my picker was definitely broken because one month after our wedding, my new husband was arrested for securities and exchange fraud and taken to jail.

The money that had been earmarked for my treatment and rehab now went for his legal fees. Frustrated, my drug use began to accelerate and things continued to spiral downhill. As he prepared for his upcoming trial, his anger flared and he began abusing me again. I left several times but had no place to go. While I technically had a home, it wasn't a safe place for me so it became a vicious cycle of staying until the abuse became unbearable. I would leave, and then, because I needed financial support and had no place to go, I would return.

My other concern was Cooper and Lyla. They were my life and sanity and I was afraid to leave them behind in that house of horrors. One night, fearing for their lives and mine, we ran out of the house, absolutely terrified, and never went back.

Trauma and domestic violence had led to a life on the run—a life that was one long, chaotic nightmare filled with substance use, drinking, risky behavior, and criminal charges. I was no longer the person I once was, making decisions and doing things I never would have done in the past. I constantly put myself and my animals in dangerous situations, continued using drugs, and was arrested several times. To say I hated myself is an understatement.

Despite all the chaos and dysfunction, Cooper and Lyla, even on my worst days, never gave up on me. When I felt I couldn't push through the maze, they showed me how to be resilient and what it looked like to keep going. When I felt I had completely lost my way, they provided consistency and showed me a path.

With no money, no job, and nowhere to go, I went to see my former boyfriend and his son. He told me I couldn't stay, but seeing how much I was struggling, he offered to keep Cooper and Lyla for me from time to time. Whenever I turned down his road to drop them off, Cooper and Lyla immediately knew where we were going and would get so excited. Some nights, I slept in my van across the street from his house so I could wake up and walk the dogs with his son, whom I had fallen in love with three years earlier.

By that point, I'd been in and out of five different domestic violence shelters. Only one had allowed me to bring Cooper and Lyla. I knew I needed to figure life out, not only for myself but for them. An important part of that was getting into treatment and getting the help I desperately needed. But I also needed to figure out what to do with Cooper and Lyla. They weren't safe with the man I'd married. He had threatened to hurt them in the past and I knew he was fully capable of carrying out his threat.

In addition, Cooper's health had begun to decline. Over the years, despite not being able to afford much for myself, I always continued to pay for a health plan for Cooper because I never wanted him to go without. I became obsessive about taking him to the vet. At our last appointment, I told the vet I would sell my soul to the devil if Cooper could live forever and it was true. He was undeniably the love of my life, and I couldn't imagine life without him. We had been together for nearly fourteen-and-a-half years , and while many of those years had been rough, we always had each other. At times when I felt broken, Cooper's unconditional love and devotion made me feel whole. On the days when I didn't feel like living, Cooper gave me a purpose and reason to keep fighting. Ultimately, he didn't care where we went or what we did as long as we were together.

While researching resources for the three of us, the local YWCA told me about the Nuzzles & Co. Purple Paw Program and suggested I reach out to Claire. I called her and explained my situation. I was upset, scared, and sad, but Claire listened intently and spoke softly and sweetly. Her entire demeanor was very calming. If there's one word that describes Claire it is: angelic—and she truly became an angel in my (and our) life.

I found a twelve-step based retreat house for women and, on a windy, snowy day in mid-December, Cooper, Lyla, and I headed to Nuzzles & Co. to meet with Claire.

I explained to Claire that I was trying my best, but the dogs hadn't been getting the care they deserved. Cooper was on medication and I was struggling to make sure he got what he needed when he needed it. Despite feeling like I'd consistently failed them, I was afraid to leave them with Claire. In some way, it felt like I was giving up on them. I was also apprehensive about Lyla because she wasn't friendly or fond of new people and places. She'd bitten a couple of ankles over the years so I was concerned how she would respond and what would happen to her in the program.

On the other hand, I had no choice. I was unable to sustain any type of normalcy and refused to be unsheltered for another winter. Things needed to change for the three of us, fast.

As I continued sharing our story with Claire, I started to cry. She sat quietly and listened. When I stopped talking, she placed her hand on my shoulder. "Jennifer, do you realize what you're doing for these animals? You're bringing Cooper and Lyla here to give them a better chance at life. You're caring for them in a way that, right now, you can't. You're giving yourself and them a chance at a better life which, without question, makes you their hero and the hero of this story."

And, with that, I dried my tears, gave Cooper and Lyla a kiss, Claire a hug, and left.

Every day, Claire sent me cute emails along with pictures of Cooper and Lyla. It was obvious they were adapting to their new surroundings and Lyla was doing surprisingly well. She had started to bond with a man who worked at Nuzzles & Co. and he was working on improving her manners. The girl at the front desk kept Cooper with her and gave him the bacon off her cheeseburgers. Cooper loved bacon so I knew he was being spoiled and loved. They both were. Claire assured me Cooper was getting his medication and the staff loved and pampered him. She also told me he snored *really* loud and even sent me a recording of him snoring. Little did I know that would be the last time I would hear him.

Two days after Christmas, having already left the treatment program, I was staying at my friend's house when I got a message: "Jennifer, it's Claire. Call me. It's important."

I had left Cooper and Lyla on December 14 and thought they were doing fine. Clearly confused, I picked up the phone and called Claire.

Before she was able to even say hello, I blurted out, "Please don't tell me one of my dogs is dead."

"I'm so sorry, Jennifer."

"Which one?

"Cooper."

I screamed, fell to my knees, and started cross examining her, "What happened? What went wrong?" And then I stopped and listened. Claire was crying, too.

"Jennifer," she continued, "I'm so sorry. He was fine here. He was comfortable and everybody loved and spoiled him. His passing was very peaceful and, when they found him, Lyla was next to him, and he looked like he was sleeping."

"I want to see him," I said.

A friend agreed to drive me to Nuzzles & Co., a forty-five-minute drive each way over snow-covered roads. I was inconsolable the entire trip.

When we arrived, my friend encouraged me to take as much time as I needed. Even though he had multiple sclerosis and used a wheelchair, he sat in his truck for nearly five hours while I stayed with Cooper's body and Lyla. He was such a kindhearted person and never once complained.

Knowing Claire was grieving along with me, I brought her flowers and thanked her for her love and compassion. I also came clean with Claire about where I was in my life.

"Jennifer," she said, "you now have two choices. You can use your grief and sorrow as an excuse to fuel more poor choices, or you can use it as motivation to change your life and honor Cooper and his life."

Honoring Cooper sounded like the obvious and only choice, so I left Lyla with Purple Paw. In mid-January, I made it into another treatment facility. Once again, after a week, believing I had a handle on my problem, I left. This entire time, I'd never addressed my current grief or past trauma. No matter how badly I tried, I was unable to stop using drugs. I knew I was ruining my life, but still felt incapable of stopping.

A few weeks later, I visited Lyla at Nuzzles & Co. It was the first time I felt happy in a very long time, but it was short-lived. Leaving her broke my heart and sucked me back into the same old patterns.

After hearing about a thirty-day clinical trial for a medication that blocked the effects of the substances I was using, I decided to give it a shot. As an added bonus, every participant received $7,200. I signed up and used the money to get an apartment. In April, I went to Nuzzles & Co. and picked up Lyla.

Jennifer with Cooper (left) and Lyla (in her lap)

The entire staff told me how much they enjoyed having Lyla, but I was overjoyed and grateful to be leaving with her and to have a safe, secure home for us. Taking her home was the beginning of a new and beautiful life. It felt amazing to have her warm furry body sleeping next to mine and I was determined to never again take her presence for granted. I started going to church and we settled into a normal, healthy daily routine of taking several walks a day and enjoying our home and each other's company.

As much as my life had turned a corner, I was still having trouble finding (and keeping) a steady job. In addition, since I hadn't yet fully dealt with the trauma of my past, the ever-present strong pull of substances remained.

Shortly after moving in, I was trying to move a sofa into my apartment by myself when a short Italian man approached me in the hallway. "Do you need help?" he asked.

"Yes, I do."

After we moved the sofa in, he extended his hand. "I'm Paul. My wife, Betty, and I live down the hall. Please let us know if you ever need help."

Over time, Paul and Betty started building a friendship with Lyla and me. One night, knowing I hadn't been completely honest with them, I explained I was struggling with using substances and was hoping to get help. They were completely non-judgmental, loving, and supportive.

Not too long after that discussion, I was arrested for substance abuse. The day I went to court, I called Paul. "I made a mistake and have a feeling I may be going to jail. Lyla is at my place and the key is under the mat."

Paul immediately went and got her.

After being incarcerated for thirty-two days, I was sent to a treatment facility for the next five months. Paul and Betty took care of Lyla the entire time. They visited me regularly and many times brought Lyla. Every time I looked at Lyla another level of determination kicked in. Here was this innocent little life that wanted to be with me (and I wanted to be with her). As much as I wanted this to work for me, I needed to finally make it work for Lyla, too. To do that meant diving headfirst into the complex trauma that was part of my life story to uncover not just *what* I was doing but *why* I was doing it. I needed to address all the things I'd avoided for far too long.

During a particularly difficult day at treatment, I recalled something that had happened many years before. I was twelve years old, laying on the floor kicking and screaming and having an absolute fit. My dad sat down next to me, looked at me, and calmly asked, "Why?"

I looked at him, incredulous. "What do you mean *why*?"

"Why are you so upset?"

"Because I'm having a bad day," I said matter-of-factly. "Don't you ever have bad days?"

He looked at me and shook his head. "I haven't had a bad day since November 6, 1970."

"What's so important about that day?" I asked.

"It was the day I left Vietnam," he said quietly. "I've had hard days since then, but I've never again had a bad day."

That memory and moment put things into perspective for me. For me, the date is December 9, 2019, which is the day I went to jail and the last day I ever used. Since then, I have had hard days and quite a few sad days but I haven't had a truly bad day. I was also able to get out of my addiction alive, which is a privilege denied to many.

In June 2020, I returned home in the midst of a pandemic. The entire world had shifted on its axis, but one constant remained in my world: Lyla. I immediately went to Paul and Betty's to pick her up. With the world essentially shut down, Lyla and I had uninterrupted time together.

I focused on reconnecting with her, and myself, and staying clean and healthy.

Months later, Betty and I were standing in their house talking, when she looked at me and said, "I wondered if you would have the capacity to care for Lyla when you came home. Paul and I thought there was a very real possibility Lyla might stay with us permanently." Tears filled her eyes, as she continued, "But the day you came to pick her up and knocked on our door, the moment I opened it, I knew. All doubt left my mind. The love and connection between you and Lyla was undeniable and I knew, without any doubt, Lyla needed to be with you."

While I was away, Lyla had become a part of Paul and Betty's family. They enjoyed her company and quirkiness and loved her—and I knew she loved them, too. It has resulted in a beautiful friendship between the four of us. I refer to Paul and Betty as Pappy and Grandma and there are very few days when we don't see each other.

During her time with Pappy and Grandma, Lyla had gotten used to having someone around all the time, so when I started a new job at a residential substance use treatment facility she didn't do well. A neighbor complained that she "barked for hours." Without hesitation, Paul and Betty swooped in and started to doggie sit Lyla while I was at work. Betty sent me updates throughout the day. When I traveled recently to see my family, Paul and Betty took Lyla for her routine checkup and dental cleaning at the vet. That day, I received this update:

*Hi Mom,*

*Looks like you pulled a fast one on me this morning. Do you know what they did? I don't know because they gave me some medication for nausea in addition to that sleepy stuff . . . I'm so groggy I can't keep my tongue in my mouth or walk straight. I sure can't wait to get home. Do you know they didn't even offer me lunch? They told Pappy and Grandma I did okay and would probably feel sleepy for the rest of the evening. Well, that's about all I have to say.*
*Love, Lyla*

Another one of my favorites came the following day:

*Hi Mom,*

*Happy Sunday! Well, Grandma says I'm back to normal, and I think she's right! Phew!! I'd still like to know just what they gave me. I couldn't keep my eyes open, let alone hold my head up or walk straight. Did I mention that too? I already ate my breakfast and I'm looking forward to a walk, but Grandma says it's spritzing rain and snow. Is my warm winter coat at home? Tell my uncle that we are thinking of him and his family. Give him our hugs. Mom, have I told you lately what a good person you are? Always willing to help. Plus, you're a great mom and take such good care of me but you can stop with the dental care anytime!!! Oh, and they did that personal invasion thing again . . . you know looking for worms and parasites. Well, I could have told them I didn't have any of these and I was right!*

*Love, Lyla, Pappy, and Grandma*

Betty is an amazing cook and the four of us get together regularly for family dinners. Lyla and I are blessed and grateful for their unending love and support. Every day after work when I pick Lyla up, she is typically sitting or lying next to Betty enjoying a belly rub. She always has one paw resting on Betty's thigh to let the world know: She is mine. Paul enjoys taking Lyla with him to run errands, explore new parks, or to go on adventures.

Lyla is a little sweetheart with her own unique personality. She makes me laugh all the time. Just like Cooper, she doesn't care where we go as long as we go together. She is just happy to be along for the ride.

Looking back, I realize my life began to change with Cooper. I became one of "those people" who had a wardrobe of coats and jackets and, ultimately, a stroller for their dog. I never thought I would do that, but I didn't care. I had this dog who loved me with every ounce of his being and if he was cold and shaking it only made sense to get him a coat or a sweater. He loved going for walks. When he could no longer comfortably go on long walks, it was a simple decision: "By God, I'm going to get him a stroller so we can keep going for walks together."

In the years after Cooper came into my life, so many relationships came and went and our situation was constantly changing. We were always moving, I was unemployed, relationships with my family were strained. Yet Cooper, and his unending, unconditional love was the constant I could always count on.

Everything in my life is so much better now. The colors in my life are brighter, my relationships are healthier and stronger. My family and I now have a healthy relationship and genuinely enjoy being together. My abusive ex is in prison so I no longer have to constantly look over my shoulder.

Lyla is now considered my emotional support animal. I've recently returned to school and she often accompanies me. She's always on her best behavior and provides me great comfort when we cover difficult topics in the social work program. Mornings, when Lyla is the most playful and cuddly, are my favorite time with her.

Claire, the Purple Paw Program, Nuzzles & Co., and Paul and Betty are, without question, my heroes. So much of this would never have happened if not for their encouragement and support of me, Cooper, and Lyla.

Cooper and Lyla came into my life and ultimately made me face my demons, believe in myself, and become the best version of myself. Regardless of what was happening around us, they always looked at me like I was their hero. Sometimes I think back to the day I left them with Claire and she told me, "Jennifer, you are their hero." That day, walking out of Nuzzles & Co. (and for a very long time afterwards), I didn't feel like anyone's hero. At long last though I finally understand what Claire meant.

# Chapter 15
# ✧ ON THE ROAD ✧ AGAIN
## *Two Humans, One Dog, Four Wheels, and 1,800 Miles*

AFTER MY RETURN FROM UTAH, ROBB AND I SAT DOWN TO TALK. He, Ava, and I had missed one another during my solo trips to Florida and Utah. Since my travels for the book weren't over, we decided to switch things up for the next trip. Rather than me continuing to travel solo, the three of us would travel together in our motorhome.

First, let me tell you a wee bit about our motorhome. Many on the road these days are mammoth-sized motorhomes or massive fifth wheels sporting several bump-outs and luxurious, cozy interiors. If that's what you're picturing our motorhome looks like, you need to wipe that image from your mind.

When the RV craze hit America back in the 1970s and 1980s, motorhomes and campers of all shapes and sizes were introduced with the major players battling over maximum trailer length, interior square footage, and comfort. Toyota got into the mix with its own unique vision. Deciding to keep things small and compact, they cornered the market on the affordable and practical—and that is where and how we entered the world of motorhomes.

Ours is a 1992 Toyota Rockwood, a Class C micro-mini motorhome. Google it. The pictures you'll see are probably a fairly accurate depiction of what ours looks like, since for all intents and purposes, it looks pretty much exactly as it did the day it rolled off the production line. It still has the original trademark turquoise and white interior and exterior; and all the cabinetry and woodwork is original.

At only twenty-one feet in length, it's easy to drive and compact enough to squeeze into some of the tightest and smallest camping and parking spots. Its compact size also means it's not very spacious so we have to pack thoughtfully and minimally.

The main cabin has a kitchen, kitchen table with bench seats, and a couch which converts to a queen-size bed. Once converted, it covers the narrow aisle and bumps into the kitchen table meaning the only way to reach the bathroom or refrigerator from the cab area is to walk on top of the bed. There's another queen-size bed over the cab.

There is a bathroom in the back which is separated from the main cabin area by a vinyl accordion-style door. It contains a small sink, toilet, and shower but since the shower is too small to make it practical for any form of bathing, we use it for additional storage.

What our motorhome lacks in space, it makes up for in character. Its quirky, retro vibe separates it from the majority of campers and motorhomes you see on the road or at campgrounds. It's unique, reliable, dependable, and a little offbeat—a bit like Robb and me.

When planning our trip, I decided we would be gone for two weeks, making it manageable without over-taxing the motorhome, Robb, Ava, or me. We would leave New Jersey in mid-June and head to South Carolina, our southernmost destination on the trip. From there, we would begin working our way north, making stops in North Carolina, Tennessee, Virginia, and Maryland, before arriving home on July 4th weekend. I was excited to be back on the road again, together.

# Chapter 16

# SOUTH CAROLINA

## *In The Heart of the Palmetto State*

OUR FIRST DESTINATION IN SOUTH CAROLINA WOULD BE DANNY & Ron's Rescue outside of Camden. From there, we would spend two days at Dreher Island State Park before visiting our friends Bill and Mary Ann, and their dog, Emma, in Salem.

When scheduling my visit with Danny & Ron's Rescue, I was forewarned that, due to the busy and sometimes unpredictable nature of their lives and the world of rescue, there was no guarantee either Danny or Ron would be there the day we arrived. Based on their calendar, it seemed the best possibility of catching them at home was if we arrived around noon on Tuesday, June 20.

On Monday, June 19, we pulled out of our driveway. We typically prefer the more scenic and relaxing backroads, but knowing we needed to be at Danny & Ron's the next afternoon, we decided to stick to Interstate 95 through Pennsylvania, Delaware, Maryland, Virginia, and into North Carolina.

Road construction on the interstate turned our seven-hour trip into a nine-hour journey, but we arrived at the Rocky Mount KOA in North Carolina long before nightfall. We checked in and before setting up, took a walk around the campground to shake off some of our road weariness. There were only a few other people at the campground. Since Ava was the only dog, she had a blast running around the fenced-in doggie play area. As dark clouds began to gather in the distance, we decided to walk back to our motorhome, set up, and have dinner. That night, a gentle rain lulled the three of us to sleep.

Day One back on the road couldn't have been more perfect.

The next morning, we still had a four-hour drive ahead of us, so we were on the road by 7:30 a.m. I crossed my fingers and said a prayer that either Danny or Ron would be home when we arrived.

My fingers were still crossed when we pulled off the quiet country road and up the driveway toward their brick and white clapboard house. The sprawling front yard and surrounding flower gardens were well-manicured and in full bloom. As I got out of the motorhome and approached the house, I heard dogs barking.

A man, with a warm, captivating smile that lit up his face, came out of the garage and walked toward me, hand outstretched. "I'm Ron," he said. "Welcome to the Doghouse."

Ron led me through the garage into a multi-purpose room (part mudroom, part laundry, and part pantry). From that vantage point, I could see into the kitchen and living room, which were filled with dog beds, crates, toys—and dogs. Dogs of every size and shape occupied every conceivable nook and cranny. I stood there, stunned and speechless, when another man approached me with an equally warm, welcoming smile. "I'm Danny. Welcome. Let me show you around, but keep in mind," he said, his smile getting even bigger, "there's no place in this house that's off-limits to the dogs."

I finally uncrossed my fingers, grateful that both Danny and Ron were home and for the opportunity to spend time visiting and talking with these extraordinary men about their life together, the Doghouse, and Danny & Ron's Rescue.

Afterwards, we headed to Dreher Island State Park in Prosperity where we relaxed and I began working on the draft of Danny and Ron's story while it was still fresh in my mind.

From Dreher, we drove two-and-a-half hours to Bill, Mary Ann, and Emma's house. I've known Bill since high school. He has always been one of the "good guys" and just a great human. I was excited to see him again. There's something about being with a person you've known for what feels like forever: a comfort and an ease. The minute Bill and I saw one another and started talking, the years melted away. His wife, Mary Ann, and their dog, sweet Emma only added to the magic of the day.

But let's begin with the moment I uncrossed my fingers and headed into the Doghouse.

# Chapter 17
# DANNY &
# RON'S RESCUE
## A Day in the Doghouse

RON: BOTH DANNY AND I GREW UP LOVING ANIMALS: CATS, DOGS, turtles, fish, and lizards. Virtually every kind of animal found their way into my childhood home outside of Chicago, Illinois and the same thing happened at Danny's family home in Wilmington, North Carolina.

We didn't meet until many years later, while working as trainers in the hunter/jumper world of horses. At the time, Danny was one of the leading hunter riders in the nation.

Long before we dreamed of starting a rescue, we went to the local shelter regularly, chose three or four dogs scheduled to be euthanized, and brought them home. After getting them acclimated, socialized, and healthy, we found them new homes in the horse community.

When I bought this house, it was never with the intent of turning it into a rescue. At one point, it really was a normal home and we lived here for many years with only a few rescue dogs. All of that changed in 2005 with Hurricane Katrina.

After Katrina hit, our first thought was how to help the people who were displaced from their homes. We were in Florida at the time and after learning a lot of people from Louisiana had been moved to a racetrack in Boca Raton, Florida, we reached out to our customers and contacts in the horse world for donations. We bought staples needed for everyday life. While delivering them, we learned how disconnected the people felt from the outside world. Without televisions, they couldn't see what was happening and it also limited their ability to locate loved ones, so we went out and bought sixty televisions for them.

And then we saw the desperate conditions the dogs in New Orleans were living in. They were stacked in airplane crates in warehouses. With no one handling the massive influx, we realized they would remain in the crates until they were either rescued or claimed by their owners. We immediately switched gears. Our mission now was to get some of the dogs out of there.

We filled a horse trailer with dogs and brought them back to our home. Many of them were covered in feces, urine, and dirt, so we cleaned them up and took care of any medical or other problems they had before adopting them out to our horse community. We ended up taking over 600 dogs from the Katrina catastrophe. Keep in mind that, at the time, this was still a normal home and we weren't set up for dogs like we are now.

As word spread, the media caught wind of what we were doing and stories began to appear in newspapers and on television. One day we got a call from Danielle, an attorney in Michigan, who had heard about us and wondered how we were funding the work we were doing. After explaining that we were taking money out of our retirement fund, she suggested we consider forming a 501(c)(3) so we could begin accepting donations and preserve what remained of our retirement. She also volunteered to do the paperwork for us.

In 2008, we obtained our 501(c)(3) status and Danny & Ron's Rescue was officially born. As everything continued to grow, we began to expand and switch things around. In the process, we turned our home and life over to the dogs, literally and figuratively. Every single room and space was converted into a place for dogs. Every room—from the kitchen and pantry to the living room and bedrooms—was redesigned to accommodate an office, a grooming area, a quarantine area, and living spaces for dogs. Couches, chairs, crates, and dog beds were placed everywhere for the comfort of the dogs. The original wood flooring was replaced with Italian stone since it is both durable and easy to clean.

DANNY: As the rescue continued to grow, there was also an increase in the calls we got and the number of dogs we brought in. We were getting a lot of dogs with injuries or who were heartworm positive. The policy in Camden (Kershaw County) used to be that any dog who tested positive for heartworm was automatically euthanized. Thankfully, they have since reversed that policy, but back then we were going to shelters to pull dogs off the euthanasia list.

Our home exists solely for the enjoyment, comfort, and safety of the dogs who come here—regardless of what brings them in or how long they stay.

As you saw, the master bedroom is on the main level. We share that room every night with almost twenty dogs. The bedroom upstairs is where guests stay so they can have some peace and quiet. But we need to stay downstairs so we can listen and keep an eye on the dogs in the event they need us at any point during the night.

We have cameras throughout our home, as well as in the outside fenced areas, which allows us and our staff to keep an eye on the dogs. Dog doors and ramps provide easy access to the outside fenced-in areas so the dogs can run and play.

Neither of us draw any salary from the rescue. We earn our living by working with horses. What we do for the dogs is very much a labor of love.

RON: One of the biggest misconceptions is that because the world of horses is often a very wealthy community, people think we're a wealthy rescue. The truth is we struggle month-to-month to survive. This house is my personal home and it was paid off until I had to re-mortgage it to keep the rescue going.

DANNY: One of the reasons we struggle is because from the moment we sign onto a dog—or they sign onto us—they are treated like family. Every dog that comes to our rescue is considered an individual and, as such, is treated on an individual basis.

The things that happen to dogs are in no way due to any fault of their own. They happen because of neglect or bad situations created by people who simply don't care or don't want to learn how to properly care for a dog. These dogs are perfectly beautiful animals who have their own stories and lives. They have a right to live. It's one thing if a dog has an incurable disease, but many of them have diseases that can be cured. We do the same for them as we would for a human family member. They know that through both good and bad we will stick by them.

We treat every dog that comes in as if it were our personal dog. Take

Danny (left) and Ron
Photo courtesy of www.photosbyjuliep.com

for instance, a dog who has been hit by a car. It may have a broken leg—
or worse. If that was my personal dog, would I put it to sleep simply because it was hit by a car? No. I'm going to fix it, so that's what we do. We
send it to the orthopedic vet knowing the cost may be $1,000 or $10,000.
We are different from most rescues in that respect. Other rescues, if the
cost is over a certain amount, will automatically euthanize the dog and
use that money to go out and get other dogs.

RON: We promise every dog who comes here that we will care for them
to the best of our ability. If we have any say in the matter, they'll never
be in a shelter again. To keep that promise, we have very strict policies
and procedures.

First, every dog is microchipped and the microchip is registered in
the name of the rescue. That way, if the dog is ever brought to a shelter
or is repeatedly picked up by Animal Control, we're the first ones to be
called.

We also have a very strict adoption contract. The dog can never be
given away to anyone else—even a family member—unless we have pre-
approved it. Should someone ignore the terms of the contract and give

a dog away without telling us, they are subject to a $5,000 fine as well as the possibility of a lawsuit.

We are fortunate to still have our attorney, Danielle, working for us pro bono because we've had people ignore that policy and we've taken legal action against them. We want to keep our promise to the dogs that they'll never end up in a shelter again. The only way to do that is to know where they are.

DANNY: All any of these dogs ever ask of us is to be loved so we do everything in our power to make sure that's what they get.

RON: As the rescue has grown so has our staff. What started as a small operation with a staff of one where I vacuumed and mopped twice a day, we now have twenty-five people on staff as well as people who clean and maintain the home and yard. At this moment, someone is on the computer communicating with a veterinarian's office while someone else is giving a dog a bath to prepare him for his adoption later today. Two other people are cleaning every inch of the home.

Other staff left here at 5:00 a.m. this morning to take a dog to an eye clinic. The dog came to us from a horrible home situation and is completely blind because of juvenile cataracts. Today he'll have surgery. Tomorrow, when he comes back here, he'll be able to see.

We got a call last night about a dog who had been caught by Animal Control. The dog had no vaccines and the owners couldn't afford the fines so the dog was scheduled to be euthanized today. We were told we could have the dog if we picked it up between 1:00 p.m. and 2:00 p.m. today. Unfortunately, in the past, even when a shelter knew we were coming to get a dog, the dog was euthanized before we arrived. When we ask why, they tell us it takes less time and effort to stick a dog with a needle than it does to fill out the paperwork. Therefore, a staff member left to make sure they would arrive well in advance of the 1:00 p.m. deadline. We'll pick the dog up and take him straight to our vet. Every day somebody is going somewhere to do something.

Abuse cases are the worst. A nine-month-old Boston terrier kept pooping in the neighbor's yard. After the neighbor asked the owner to keep the dog out of his yard, the owner took a screwdriver and poked both of the dog's eyes out. His solution was to blind the dog so it couldn't find its way into the neighbor's yard.

The court awarded us the dog and when the court case came up, the Animal Control officer told the Judge that the other dog seemed okay. The Judge looked at him, questioningly. "Other dog?"

The Animal Control officer explained that when he picked up the dog, another dog, a dachshund, had been in the house. The judge immediately ordered him to get the other dog and awarded us that dog, too.

When we brought the dachshund into the house, the terrier started howling and screaming. Even though the terrier was totally blind, he could sense the dachshund was here. When we put the dachshund down, she immediately walked over, leaned into the terrier, and the two of them went out the door together, like two dolphins swimming side-by-side. Apparently, she was his sight dog. They were both adopted by a couple in Atlanta and still go everywhere together, side-by-side.

DANNY: It's true that one of the worst things in the world of rescue are the abuse cases. To think a human being has done something purposely to an animal is one of the hardest things to handle emotionally and creates immense doubt and disappointment about humans.

The other difficult thing is puppy mills. We see so many people who get a dog and think they're going to make a profit by breeding it. They make $150 and start using the dogs for their livelihood. The dogs are bred repeatedly, don't get proper veterinary care, and end up spending their lives in cages without any human interaction.

Do you see that little dog sleeping soundly on the fireplace hearth? That's Hilde. She was a puppy mill dog. Prior to coming here, she essentially had no contact or interaction with people so, even though we've had her for a year and a half, it's still difficult for anyone to touch her.

A few years ago, we got three puppy mill puppies. They were almost four months old and couldn't walk. They were incredibly wobbly so we took them to the vet to make sure it wasn't anything neurologic. It wasn't. It was simply that they came from a puppy mill and had never been out of a crate or been given an opportunity to walk.

RON: We've also had some incredible things happen through our rescue work. See the dog laying on his dog bed next to the fireplace? That's

Taryn. Seven years ago, someone posted a video on Facebook of Taryn. She was in the back of a kennel at a shelter shaking uncontrollably. People kept tagging us in the video asking us to please save her, but we explained the dog was in California and we were in Florida. We certainly had no shortage of dogs to save where we were, but people continued to ask us to help. Finally, we said if they could help us get the dog from California to Florida, we would save it.

That's one of the great things about Facebook. People came together and a fellow horse trainer and animal rescue person had a customer who flew Taryn from California to us. When she arrived, she was absolutely traumatized.

At times, we work with an animal communicator named Kathy. She has the ability to connect intuitively with animals, regardless of where they are, and has been amazingly accurate time after time. We decided to ask her about Taryn.

Taryn told Kathy she was living with total guilt because she hadn't been able to save her owner. When Kathy asked Taryn what she meant, she explained, "There was so much blood, blood everywhere, and I felt bad I couldn't save her. Then people came and took me to this cold place with all these barking, noisy dogs and I was so scared." Again, she told Kathy she still felt guilty that she hadn't been able to save her owner.

None of this made any sense to us, so I immediately called the shelter and asked if they had any history on Taryn. They told me Taryn's owner had been murdered and that it had been an extremely brutal murder. Afterwards, Taryn was taken to the shelter.

Taryn has been with us for seven years and she still doesn't allow strangers to pet her. You can only approach or touch her on her terms. We decided she's already been through so much and doesn't need any more changes or adjustments, so Taryn will live here with us for the rest of her life.

DANNY: After the floods in Louisiana in 2016, we started seeing scenes very similar to what we saw with Katrina. People were being displaced along with thousands of dogs. The shelters were completely overwhelmed and running out of space. As a result, they only held a dog for a few weeks before they were forced to euthanize them to make space for other dogs. We loaded up our bus with $30,000 of supplies and headed to Baton Rouge to help.

We made the rounds to smaller rescues and brought them Frontline, heartworm medicine, and antibiotics. People had donated food, but what they desperately needed were medical supplies. When we pulled in, you would have thought we were giving them the world. To many of those dogs, we were. We pulled twenty-eight dogs from Louisiana and loaded them up in the bus and brought them back.

The bus was a welcome, and necessary, addition to the rescue. In the beginning, we used our two personal vehicles to transport dogs from disasters or puppy mills, but we never had a vehicle big enough to take as many dogs as we wanted. When a fundraiser finally got us out of the red and ahead of the mark, we invested in the bus. It can comfortably fit thirty dogs in crates. We had special heating and air-conditioning systems installed so if we're ever stuck or stranded in bad weather, the systems still function. We also had special hospital flooring put down so it can be easily cleaned and disinfected.

The bus is also a wonderful advertisement for the rescue. We've had people who see the bus driving down the highway, write down our number, and adopt a dog from us. When we pull into a horse show, we're like the ice cream truck. Kids and people go crazy and run over to meet the dogs.

RON: We typically take fifteen to twenty dogs to a horse show and have truly been blessed by the horse community and their support of us and our dogs. Since horse people are animal lovers, that's where the majority of our dogs have gone and, since we personally know them, it makes the adoption process much easier.

Other adoptions begin when people see a dog online and fill out the application. Once an application is received, our Adoption Department begins researching the applicant by contacting their veterinarian, family, friends, and references. One of the requirements is that the applicant must have a fenced-in yard.

We had a man who wanted to surprise his girlfriend with a dog but we won't adopt dogs out as surprise gifts.

If someone refuses to sign our adoption contract, we won't allow them to adopt a dog. Some people are offended if they don't meet our requirements and aren't allowed to adopt a dog. But, again, our promise to every dog is if they can't live a life as good (or better) than they do here, they don't leave.

We aren't a shelter; we're a rescue. We can tell you about every single dog. We can tell you what makes them happy. We can tell you if they are nervous or fearful. One of the hardest things to get through to people is the need to be extra cautious in order to keep the dog safe. We explain that their home is a new place and they need to be especially careful around doors because if the dog gets out, they will run. We get so many calls from people who have only had a dog a few days when an elderly relative comes to visit and, because they are slow getting in the door, the dog gets out and takes off.

A case in point is a puppy mill dog named DeeDee who had lived for several years in a cage. After living with us for two years, DeeDee was ready for a home. A very nice young woman adopted her. The day she came to get DeeDee, we explained that, since puppy mill dogs are frequently frightened by the smallest thing, DeeDee would probably always be a flight risk.

The woman said she understood and, after getting DeeDee settled in her car, drove less than a mile down the road to show her parents the dog. As she and DeeDee were leaving her parents' house, the door slammed. DeeDee got scared and, in the ensuing confusion, the young woman dropped DeeDee's leash and DeeDee took off. The woman immediately called us and everyone stopped what they were doing to look for DeeDee.

For the next few days, people spotted DeeDee darting through the woods before losing sight of her. Humane traps were set and a bloodhound was hired to track her.

Then, one afternoon while we were riding in the truck with the man and his bloodhound, our Marketing Director, Kim called after speaking with our animal communicator, "DeeDee told Kathy she is sitting in the woods watching three boys playing basketball."

We had literally just passed a house where three boys were playing basketball, so we immediately turned around and went back. The bloodhound picked up DeeDee's scent, but was unable to locate her, so we set up a coyote-size trap. Every morning, we checked the trap and left behind shirts the rescue staff had worn, hoping DeeDee would pick up the scent. Every morning, even though the trap was empty, it was obvious DeeDee had been there and had moved the shirts around. After three weeks, DeeDee finally went into the trap.

We brought her to our house and DeeDee walked in like she had never left. She was cool, calm, and collected. We decided to keep her—not because the woman was a bad owner, but because it had been so emotional for everyone here at the rescue for so many weeks. We wanted to make sure none of us—including DeeDee—would ever go through anything like that again.

DANNY: Before a dog can leave our safe environment and be comfortable in the next home or environment, they have to gain enough trust and confidence in themselves and in humans. The process can't be rushed. For some dogs it can take a matter of months. For others, especially dogs who have been abused, it can take years. Others will never leave our home.

John is a perfect example. He was found living in the back of an abandoned car in Key West, Florida. The car had no roof or windows and the owners chose to chain and leave John inside it and occasionally throw food out to him. For years, John lived, chained in that car, in his own feces and urine.

Even after coming to us, John remained a dog you couldn't pet. Gratefully, he didn't bite and was fine during his baths. But, other than that, you couldn't get close to him. The closest you could get was to hand him a treat. When my sister met him, she felt that possibly a lot of one-on-one time would help, so she took him home to work with him. John really liked (and bonded with) my sister, but after she died, John came back to us.

When he came back, you could tell he had come a long way. He was so much happier. Now, first thing in the morning, John jumps up on the bed and wakes me up. As soon as I sit up, he puts his paws on me and we begin our day with me petting him. If I were to go up to him on my own, he would walk away, but at various times throughout the day when I am hanging out, John comes up to me. Because he's already been through enough, we're going to keep John here with us.

RON: Anytime the shelter gets a dog who is critical or in a dire medical condition, they call us. That was the case with Milton. Animal Control found Milton wandering and brought him to the shelter. His legs were completely matted together making it impossible for him to walk. The shelter explained their vet could neuter him but he was unable to do the extensive medical work they believed the dog required. We picked him up and took him straight to our vet, Dr. Fulmer. He called an hour later to tell us they had cut the mats to free his legs and found the bones and tendons on his legs were exposed and full of maggots. In addition, his temperature had dropped so low that they believed he was dying. They asked if we wanted to try to save him or euthanize him.

"Is he acting like he wants to live?" I asked them.

"He is."

"If he wants to live, let's go on with it."

In an attempt to raise his body temperature, the vets heated bags of fluids and surrounded him with the bags. They cleaned out the maggots and performed several surgeries to repair his legs. At that point, they didn't know if the skin would grow back or if he would require skin grafts.

To this day, Dr. Fulmer cannot believe Milton lived. His temperature was below what it should have been for a dog to live. His organs had been shutting down, but he rallied so hard. Even on his bad days, Milton still wagged his tail. He now lives in Washington, D.C. and has a wonderful life.

DANNY: This little white poodle standing next to us is Cotton. A lady brought him into the shelter with a towel wrapped around him like a diaper and told the person at the intake desk she didn't want the "damn dog" because she couldn't do anything with him and that he should just be put to sleep.

When we got him, he was extremely emaciated and so sick that our vet didn't think he was going to live. His rectum was so caked with feces that it was completely closed off and he was unable to go to the bathroom. We honestly didn't know what color he was for the longest time because his entire body was completely covered and caked in urine and feces. It took two years before he began to look like a dog again.

Since we feed all the dogs in our bedroom in crates, Cotton learned to come in and eat with the other dogs. He would get up on the foot of our bed but, if you moved, he raced off. He was absolutely petrified of being touched. Occasionally, he would get near our pillows or we would find him under the covers if we weren't in the room and, as long as you ignored him, he was fine. Occasionally, we would feel a lick on our face but, again, we had to lie very still and pretend we didn't see him. This went on for months and months until, very gradually, we were able to touch him.

Through it all, Cotton had a way of looking at you as if he were saying, "Please be patient with me. I'll get there." It took him a long time but, eventually, he did.

Cotton has his own dance where he twirls and kicks his back leg. We call it The Cotton Dance and, despite everything he went through, Cotton has never stopped dancing. Every morning before breakfast, he jumps up on the bed and does The Cotton Dance. We decided a long time ago that we could never put him through any kind of fear again, so he'll be here with us for the rest of his days.

RON: There can be so much pain and heartache in rescue but when you look at these precious dogs you know it's all worth it. Our life is so far from normal. We essentially live in a doghouse and, every night, eighteen or nineteen are dogs under the covers of our bed with us. Occasionally, a spat will break out among the dogs, but it's very short-lived. They live as a pack so well and they do it with incredible harmony.

DANNY: To us, they are more than a pack of dogs. Every day, we feel immensely blessed in so many ways.

We've also been very blessed by our horse community and everyone who supports our rescue. We could pull dogs from the euthanasia list or court cases or wherever but the reality is we can only house so many dogs here. If people didn't believe in us and our mission, the wheels would stop.

It can be frustrating when we think of the millions of dogs and cats that are euthanized every year in shelters and think we haven't done enough. But we've also been immensely blessed. Because of our rescue, over 14,000 dogs have found new homes and new lives.

Magical connections have been made like Maggie, a three-legged dog, who was adopted by a woman who was an amputee. Honestly every connection and every report we get keeps us afloat mentally.

Every night we look around this house and count our blessings—and the blessings just keep coming.

# Chapter 18
# BILL, MARY ANN, KATIE TO EMMA

*From Fear to Love and Respect*

MARY ANN: I MET MY FIRST DOBERMAN IN THE MID '80S WHILE vacationing on Martha's Vineyard. While out for a bike ride, I came across the local Humane Society and decided to stop and see if any dogs needed to be walked. The woman immediately pointed to a red Doberman. It was the first Doberman I'd ever seen in person and all I knew about them was what I'd seen and heard on television: they were fierce and would turn on their owners. I stood there, terrified, but decided to push past my fear and take her for a walk.

We headed down a dirt road. By the end of our walk, I didn't want to leave her. When I went back to Connecticut, I couldn't get her out of my mind and started researching Dobermans. Eventually, I got my first Doberman, a sweet puppy I named Katie.

When I put Katie in the back seat of my little Toyota Celica for the trip home, she put her front paws on the console and straddled the hump between the seats like she was riding a horse. She had a big old ol' round belly, one floppy ear, and I was in love. Katie and I went through a lot together including moving from Connecticut to Rhode Island to South Carolina back to Connecticut and then, in 1990, to New Jersey. She was a sweet, smart little girl and truly became the love of my life.

As often happens with a dog, Katie led me to other people, rescues, and eventually other Dobermans. Because of Katie, I reached out to a woman named Sharon at the Delaware Valley Doberman Pinscher Assistance (DVDPA) who had a four-year-old red Doberman named Jessie.

A young man had adopted Jessie when she was a puppy. After getting married, he and his wife got pregnant. Even though Jessie had never shown any signs of aggression, when his wife told him to get rid of the dog, he did.

I met Jessie Thanksgiving weekend. Even though I was a stranger, she was friendly and welcoming. When I went to take her, the young man had tears in his eyes. It was obvious he was devastated—and Jessie was clearly confused—so it was a tough separation for both of them.

From our first day together, I could see that Jessie was heartbroken and also had severe separation anxiety. We went for long walks to help her get acclimated. Over time, we became friends, but it wasn't until Bill came into our lives that things really shifted for Jessie. Having a man around helped because Bill was a rough and tumble playmate and Jessie took full advantage.

Just like with Katie, Jessie was with me through a lot of changes in my life, from being single to getting married to moving back and forth between houses. She never hurt a flea and was extremely good with children. My nephew RJ used to lay on her like she was a pillow and she loved it. Jessie also welcomed and found so much joy playing with Bill's children, Dallas and Bill II. Every night, as we all settled into our beds, Jessie made the rounds, going bedroom to bedroom to make sure everyone was safe before she went to sleep.

Jesse's tail was so short that when she wagged it, her entire back end wagged. We credited her short tail for her world class farting ability because simply sitting down was sometimes reason enough for her to pass gas. Bill would just laugh and say, "Good shooting."

There were only two things Jessie didn't like: rain and mornings. All day long, she dragged her pillow and chased sun spots around the house so she could relax and lay in the sunshine.

Shortly after Jack passed, we learned about Selena. She was being used as a breeder dog and had already had numerous litters by the time the SPCA got her. They asked DVDPA to take her. After they did, Sharon called us.

We went to meet Selena at a kennel outside New Hope, Pennsylvania, and she was absolutely stunning. She was black and rust with a beautiful face and ears—and teats that hung down to the ground. We were afraid she would be anti-social, but she was fine.

BILL: Actually, the whole adoption process with DVDPA and this dog was amazing. It was very thorough and controlled. Based on all she had been through, they wanted experienced Doberman owners for her. At our first meeting, we went over to her pen and she walked up to the fence and wasn't the least big aggressive.

We brought her home and initially she was prone to falling down the small set of stairs in our home. As a breeder dog, we were unsure if she'd ever been out of a crate or had the chance to walk down steps before, so we started working with her and eventually she got it. We also changed her name to Gracie (short for Graceful) and began exercising her every day just like we'd done with our other dogs.

MARY ANN: Gracie was an amazing dog and ultimately she (and Sharon) led us to Reba, a very small, stunning, red and rust Doberman. We were told she was reactive to men but she never had a problem with Bill. We don't know for sure what happened to her before we got her, but the only problem we ever saw was if you had a broom or long stick she would slink down. It was sad.

BILL: Of all our dogs, Reba was the hardest to get to know. She was very clingy, but we didn't know if she would bolt, so we always kept her on a leash. At the time, we had a large wooded area behind our house which is where we took her to go to the bathroom by giving her the command: "Woods." She never pulled on the leash and always went out and came back into the house without a problem. Finally, we started walking her out without a leash and she always went out and came right back in.

One day, we came home and opened the door to let her out. Immediately, she took a hard right and was gone. She ran like a greyhound and before I could call out her name, she was 100 yards away. Our first thought was, now what? I hopped in the car and, luckily, it wasn't long before we got a phone call.

In a matter of minutes, Reba had covered almost two miles before being spotted by someone. They stopped, opened their car door, and Reba hopped right in. The people took her to a kennel in a nearby town where we'd taken our other dogs at various times.

When my phone rang, I picked it up and the girl on the other end said, "We have a red and rust Doberman here. Are you by any chance looking for one?" Even though we'd never brought Reba to the clinic, they knew we were Doberman people so we drove down and picked her up.

Afterwards, we discovered that Reba had an accident in the house while we were out. She obviously knew she'd goofed. Concerned we might have been mad, she decided to take off.

MARY ANN: Reba was the first dog we ever picked up directly from the transport vehicle. The second happened four years later with a dog named Coors that we'd agreed to foster. Since Bill was working, I drove down to meet the transporter, Jack.

Without a doubt, Coors was the biggest Doberman I'd ever seen. A male Doberman typically weighs between seventy-five and one hundred pounds, but Coors was 130 pounds. He was absolutely huge and, at the time, my transport vehicle was a small four-door Infiniti.

I got Coors situated in my backseat. Driving up Route 32, all I kept thinking was, "There is a massive black Doberman I just met sitting uncaged and taking up my entire back seat. What if he tries to come into the front seat? If he does, what do I do? What is Bill going to think? What have we gotten ourselves into? I hope he's nice."

Sharon advised us to introduce Reba and Coors on neutral ground. Rather than taking him to our house, Bill and I decided I would bring Coors to the parking lot at his job and he would have Reba with him.

BILL: I was at work and when Mary Ann got Coors out of her car, I was amazed. He was an absolute sweetheart, but he was huge! Although Reba and Coors were initially cautious of one another, they got along, so we put them back into our respective vehicles and drove home.

When we got there, Reba wasn't happy and bared her teeth to put Coors in his place. Over time, Reba relaxed and Coors brought out the puppy in her. He taught her how to play again and a side of her we'd never seen emerged.

Every time we left the house, we could see Coors's silhouette sitting and watching us leave. Every time we came home, Coors howled—a long, deep howl. Over time, he somehow got Reba to start singing too, which meant we always walked into a wonderful duet going on.

MARY ANN: Every morning at sunrise, Coors woke up ready to go and had one thing on his mind: food. The minute he heard movement upstairs he ran from the den to the kitchen and sat, patiently waiting for us with a big smile, to let us know he was ready for breakfast.

I always fed Coors and Reba before I sat down to eat. Without fail, Coors would come over, lean into me, place his head on my thigh or my chest, and watch me eat. We used the fact that he was food-motivated to our advantage to train him, but it also meant that he ate things. Once, he ate a pair of Bill's underwear and, more than once, he ate my hair scrunchies.

BILL: We knew Coors was also a runner so we always took him out on a leash.

A lot of bicyclists use our road and one day when Mary Ann took Coors out, he spotted a guy riding his bicycle off in the distance. He snapped the leather on his leash and took off after him. Mary Ann immediately called me. Since I was working nearby, I hopped in my car and went screaming in their direction.

The bicyclist saw Coors coming and sped up before making a fatal mistake: the road he turned onto had a sharp ninety-degree turn before coming to a steep hill. He probably made it about a half mile when he realized he wasn't going to outrun Coors, so he stopped and put his bike between them.

Coors ran up and sat down right next to him. When I arrived, I got out of my car and walked over to the two of them. Coors was sitting there smiling at the two of us. The guy had been prepared to meet his end but, instead, here was Coors sitting there smiling at him. He was a nice guy and very relieved.

Coors never left. We were foster failures and decided he was going to stay with us.

MARY ANN: Coors was the only male we ever had. He was adorable, cuddly, and the biggest love muffin. We always had to make sure his pillow was close to us when we sat on the recliners because as soon as I sat down, Coors pulled off my shoes and immediately started licking my feet. Bill couldn't stand it, but I was in heaven.

Coors had a heart the size of Texas. He truly was a gentle giant, sweet beyond words, and the most affectionate Doberman we ever had. He always wanted to be near you, touching you, every second. He loved us completely and totally.

And then, Emma came into our life.

Little Miss Emma went through quite a period of transition with us. We were in the process of moving from New Jersey to South Carolina. A few weeks after we got her, we left New Jersey and stayed at our beach house in South Carolina for a week before moving into a local bed and breakfast where we stayed until we finally closed on our house. We were happy the day we finally started to move in and looked forward to settling into our life and new home with Emma.

Two days later, we got a call that Bill's mother passed so we got back in the car and drove to New Jersey. While still in New Jersey, we got a call that a high school friend of mine had died of a heart attack so we drove from New Jersey to my parents' home in South Carolina for another funeral. By now it was the end of August and literally all Emma knew was the backseat of our car and the Interstate.

BILL: When we finally got home to South Carolina, Emma wanted to be anywhere but here. We've been through training with her and she will come, sit, heel and do everything right. She's also managed to get loose a couple of times – and when that happens, the race is on. She'll take a couple of laps at full speed around the house before jumping over the ditch and then she's gone. A couple of times she ran down to the end of the road, stopped, turned around, and stood quietly waiting for us to chase her.

The funny thing about Emma is despite her strong desire to get away from us, her separation anxiety is pretty significant. If you aren't including her in whatever you're doing, she cries and carries on.

She's beautiful, truly show quality. She has tattoos and has been microchipped. God knows why her original owners wanted to get rid of her. They tried to sell her on Craigslist and, luckily, were unsuccessful. It turns out that we're actually Emma's third owners, but this is where she'll stay. I love her to pieces. The best way to describe Emma is that she's like

Emma

a cat. She can be very stand-offish and doles out love and affection on her own terms.

MARY ANN: Since we were now settled in South Carolina, I began searching online for Doberman rescues in our area and found the Georgia Doberman Rescue (GDR). Since we're both retired, we now volunteer doing transport for them.

Ollie was our first transport for GDR and, of all the transports we've done, he's the one who completely stole my heart. We met up with a woman named Tracy in Anderson, South Carolina, and out came this sweet large dog with big floppy ears. We got him comfortable on the backseat of my car and hadn't gone very far on Interstate 85 when he came up behind me and put his head on my shoulder. He was a lovebug, just like Coors, and wanted to have a person near him.

We recently transported Bart, a four-month-old Doberman puppy who had been found on the street in Georgia. After spending some time at a local vet's office, he was released to GDR and we agreed to foster him. Based on our foster failure history with Coors, I think the only reason Bill allowed me to foster Bart was because he was already scheduled to go to his forever home the following week. After Bart's adoption was finalized, we transported him to his new home in the Atlanta area. Letting him go wasn't easy but knowing he had a good home made all the difference.

I love doing transport work because I know that when the dogs get to where they're going happiness, joy, and a better life, is waiting to welcome them.

I'm the type of person who not only loves, but needs, a dog. I was diagnosed with MS in 1986 and, in all sincerity, I believe the dogs are keeping me healthy. I told myself years ago that I'm not going to end up in a wheelchair, so I walk my dogs every day. By exercising them, I get exercise as well which is keeping me healthy and happy.

I think back to the first time, all those years ago, when I walked into the Humane Society and saw that Doberman. Although my initial reaction was fear, I'm grateful I gave that dog a chance because it resulted in a great love and respect for the breed and has also filled our lives and home with a lot of dogs. Every Doberman has been unique and we have truly loved them all. We've been blessed because, individually and collectively, they've made our lives richer and our hearts fuller.

# Chapter 19

# NORTH CAROLINA

*Switching Gears in the Tar Heel State*

FROM SOUTH CAROLINA, WE WERE DRIVING TO ASHEVILLE, NORTH Carolina, approximately three hours away. Our first stop was going to be at Warren Wilson College in Swannanoa, just outside of Asheville. I graduated from Warren Wilson in 1979 and wanted to go back for a visit.

After that, we were going to park the motorhome at a campsite and switch gears for a few days and stay at the Aloft, a pet-friendly hotel in the heart of Asheville. I had heard about a unique program they were running and was curious to learn more.

While still visiting with Bill, Mary Ann, and Emma, we'd noticed one of Ava's eyes was red and tearing. Bill and Mary Ann immediately reached out to the nearest veterinary clinic, but they didn't have any availability to see us. We decided to push on and call veterinary offices from the road until we found one that could squeeze us in.

An hour outside of Asheville, the Charlotte Street Animal Hospital said they had time to see Ava and to come directly there when we got into town. It was a beautiful facility and the staff was warm, welcoming, and professional. Gratefully, Ava only had a minor irritation in her eye and, after providing us with eye drops to soothe and heal it, we proceeded to the front desk to check out.

When Sarah, the young woman at the front desk, realized we were from New Jersey, she asked where we were headed. "We've been traveling in our motorhome," I explained, "but we're taking a break now to stay at the Aloft."

"Oh, my gosh!" Sarah said, clearly excited. "You're going to love it. It's beautiful. I adopted my dog Rocco through the Aloft program!"

Without hesitation, I told Sarah one of the reasons we were going to the Aloft was to find out more about the program. I also told her about my book and asked if she'd like to talk to me about Rocco. She wrote her contact information on a Post-It, handed it to me, and I promised to reach out.

Daisy

The Aloft was all we had hoped for, and probably more. Everything—from the accommodations and room service to the staff and downtown location—was exceptional. However, it was their program with the local rescue that, for me, pushed them over the top.

Before checking in, Robb, Ava, and I walked over to meet the current dog wearing an "Adopt Me" vest: a chihuahua mix named Daisy. With her big brown eyes, easy smile, and friendly, cuddly disposition, Daisy was positively adorable. She and Ava really liked one another, so for the next few days, between interviews and sightseeing, we hung out with Daisy.

During our stay at the Aloft, I interviewed Laurie who had participated in the program at the Aloft. During the course of her interview, I discovered that she and Sarah knew one another, and together had been part of Rocco, Sarah's dog's journey.

People often ask me how I find the dogs and stories for my books. My answer is always the same. I don't. The dogs find me and this was a case in point. My plan was to simply learn more about the Aloft program. But, once again, dogs (and their people) found me and it all came together perfectly—and magically.

# Chapter 20
# ✦ DAVID, EMMA ✦
# & ALOFT
## *Everything Happened for a Reason*

DAVID: OUR INITIAL REASON FOR STARTING THIS PROGRAM AT THE Aloft was two-fold. First, as a business, we are extremely dog friendly and, second, as a hotel, we do a community service project every quarter. At the time, I was the Aloft General Manager, Emma was Assistant General Manager, and Christine was our Sales Director. As the hotel executive leadership team, we started talking about the possibility of the hotel fostering a dog. I love dogs and loved the idea, but none of us were sure the company would allow it or if we could find a rescue or agency who would work with us.

EMMA: When I began working at Aloft, I loved that they were pet-friendly and didn't charge their guests a pet fee. I loved meeting the guests' dogs and making every dog feel special while they were at the hotel. It was also wonderful to have my daily work environment filled with all these furry, lovable, little beings.

One day, while talking with my boss, David, I casually mentioned getting a hotel dog. I never dreamed he would agree, but David looked at me, and said, "Let's talk about how we could do that."

Originally, our plan was to get a dog that would be a mascot at the hotel. We continued to throw ideas around and then everything changed the day I boarded a plane for Tampa.

DAVID: The next thing I knew, Emma returned from a business trip and told me she met a man on a flight to and from Florida who might be able to help us with the program.

EMMA: It was actually quite remarkable how it played out. I was heading to Florida to interview for another position within our company. On my flight, I chatted with the gentleman seated next to me. Rick, I learned, was the President of Charlie's Angels, an animal rescue located just outside of Asheville. We immediately took out our cellphones and started sharing photos and stories of our fur babies.

When we arrived at the airport in Tampa, we exchanged business cards, shook hands, and headed off to our appointments.

The next day, I boarded the plane back to Asheville and, once again, found myself sitting next to Rick. We laughed and continued our conversation about dogs. Only this time, I told him about our hope to get a hotel dog which evolved into us sponsoring one dog at a time at the hotel. By the time our plane landed, we had put together a rough scenario of how the program might work and agreed to get together a few days later.

DAVID: When Rick and Kim from Charlie's Angels Animal Rescue came in, they brought along one of their dogs that was up for adoption for us to meet. We began talking about the various possibilities for the program. Understandably, they had questions and concerns: Did we have a place to walk the dog? Where would the dog sleep? Who would care for it? After answering all their questions, we decided to do a three-month trial.

We set up a doggie playpen in the lobby and put water and food dishes, a dog bed, and toys in it. We made up a chart to keep track of how often the dog was to be walked, fed, and pottied and who would be taking responsibility. A few days later, our first dog, Gabriel, arrived.

EMMA: When David got the staff together and explained the program to them, every single staff member was on-board and incredibly excited. With people coming and going all day long at the hotel, we knew not every dog would do well in that kind of environment. So we placed a crate in the back office to allow the dog twenty-four hours to get acclimated and comfortable. That also gave us time to get to know the dog and see how they were adjusting to the environment.

In August 2014, Gabriel became the first dog we had at the Aloft. Our initial goal for the program was to get one dog adopted per quarter, but

Gabriel was adopted in three days. The first two years, over eighty dogs were adopted through the program.

DAVID: We were surprised at all the interest the program was generating with our guests and the media. It never occurred to us when we were initially planning the program that it was something no one had ever heard of, or done, before. We simply wanted to do a community service project.

When an article appeared in the Associated Press about the program, other news media outlets picked up on it. Before long, newspapers and television/radio stations around the United States, Europe, and South America began running stories on what we were doing. It was rewarding to see the dogs being adopted, but it was equally rewarding to have other hotels calling us because they were interested in starting a similar program.

While we suspected our guests would like the dogs, we honestly didn't know how much. The feedback from our guests has been overwhelmingly positive. It's not uncommon to see a guest arrive at the hotel and, before checking in, immediately go over to play with the dog. The dog helps create a unique and memorable guest experience.

EMMA: Dogs make people feel at home and this has translated to our guests. It's great to see the guests interact with and react to the dog and it becomes part of a person's (or family's) vacation experience.

The entire staff was excited to have the dogs at the hotel and really stepped up to the plate. Front desk personnel, breakfast people, night staff, and bartenders all took turns walking and feeding the dogs. The breakfast team, who already comes to work really early, wanted to be the first ones here so they could take the dog out. To have the first part of your work day be about a dog makes the rest of the day go better.

We maintain a log for everyone to use when they take the dog out. There is space for them to write the dog's name, where they walked, how long their walk was, and what the dog did in terms of pottying.

Charlie's Angels made the process easy for us, but they also do a phenomenal job of ensuring the dog goes to the right home. If someone is interested in a dog, once they fill out the application, Charlie's Angels begins a thorough and strenuous review process: checking references, contacting their veterinarian, and doing home visits. In the case of guests from other states, extra levels of reviews and inspections kick in. We've had guests leave only to come back after the review process is completed to get the dog. Absolutely everything is done to ensure the dogs go to a happy home.

DAVID: I'm not sure any of us really thought the program was going to work. After the three-month trial, we expected to stop the program. Fortunately, that didn't happen. We're now in our ninth year. To date, over 250 dogs have been adopted from the Aloft program. It's incredibly rewarding and heartwarming to know we've been part of getting that many dogs to their forever homes. I couldn't be happier—for our employees, our guests, and most important, for the dogs.

EMMA: It's tough to stop myself from taking all the dogs home with me because they are all so sweet and some of their stories are so sad.

Ladybug was a sweet, shy four-year-old beagle-pointer mix who came into the hotel wearing a tiny rain jacket with a hood. When they took her rain jacket off, she looked like a miniature Dalmatian. She'd been living with a family who also had a black Lab. For some reason, the family decided they no longer wanted dogs, so they tied them up outside, took their photo, and posted on Craigslist: "Free dogs. Come pick them up."

Charlie's Angels has people who monitor for things like that because often dogs in those situations are picked up and used as bait dogs for dog fighting. Gratefully someone from the rescue saw it and went and got them.

Ladybug came into the hotel wearing her little "Adopt Me" vest and wagging her tail. She was absolutely the sweetest little girl. She was also incredibly shy. Anytime someone approached her, she tinkled a little on the floor, so the staff began working with her to get her out, socialize her, and make her feel more comfortable.

Her first adventure out of the hotel was with Christine, our Sales Director, and me. Asheville is a very pet-friendly town so we took her to a local outdoor bar. Everyone immediately began making a fuss over Ladybug. We took off her leash. As we turned around to order drinks, Ladybug walked over to the next table, jumped into a stranger's lap, and ate his entire meal in under thirty seconds. There sat Ladybug, smiling, content and completely at-home with a belly full of deep-fried macaroni and cheese.

Christine profusely apologized to the man as she went to take Ladybug back, but he just laughed. "I didn't know what to do. She was so cute and I didn't want to yell at her."

Every morning, Ladybug jumped into my office chair and waited for me to get to work. I was falling in love with her, but one thing stood in the way of adopting her: I've always been a one-dog person and I already had a dog. My other dog, Butters, was everything to me and, not wanting to jeopardize my relationship with him, I decided to take the weekend to think about it before making a final decision.

Monday morning, I walked into work and another dog was standing in the lobby wearing the "Adopt Me" vest. I panicked. "Where's Ladybug?"

A coworker told me someone had filled out an application for her. Since it looked like the application was going through, Ladybug went to stay with a foster parent until the adoption was finalized.

I was devastated. That quickly turned to heartbreak and, finally, acceptance that I had simply waited too long and it wasn't meant to be.

The next day, a local news station in Charlotte was doing a segment on the program. When I arrived, Kim from Charlie's Angels walked over to me. "Someone on staff said you were interested in Ladybug. Her adoption fell through. Are you still interested?"

"Absolutely!" I assured her. This time I wasn't going to hesitate and miss my opportunity so I immediately filled out the adoption application and waited anxiously while they went through the review process.

After being approved, I picked Ladybug up from her foster mom and brought her home. I had her bowl of food ready. After briefly glancing around the room, she walked over, ate her bowl of food, as well as Butters' bowl of food, then laid down to take a nap. I knew—and more importantly, she knew—she was home.

To think back on who Ladybug was the day she walked into the hotel, so shy and looking so forlorn, to where she is now is amazing. Everyone agrees that she is the happiest little girl and, just like Butters, completely spoiled.

Any time we arrived for work at the hotel, she knew where we were and immediately ran to the stairwell and toward the back office to see David. She loves seeing David and he loves seeing her. He considered adopting her, but he was in the middle of building a home so it wasn't the right time. Lucky for me.

Ladybug (left) and Butters

With Butters getting older, it's been wonderful for him to have another dog around. It also helps with his anxiety. Butters and Ladybug are the best thing that could have ever happened to me.

I know of several other employees who adopted a dog through the hotel's program with Charlie's Angels. People who, just like me, didn't know they needed doggy love until the dog showed up and picked them.

When I look back, it was magical how it all came together. I realize that getting on the plane that day to Tampa was about something so much bigger than a job interview. I believe the true purpose was for me to get on the plane, meet Rick, and get this program going. Everything happened for a reason.

# Chapter 21

# LAURIE, CASEY & ZOEY

## *We Needed One Another*

I WAS NEVER MUCH OF AN ANIMAL LOVER—THAT WAS MY SISTER, Ellen. She loved all animals, especially dogs, and was always caring for a lot of dogs at the same time.

Shortly after turning forty-one, all that changed. I'm not exactly sure why, but for some reason I decided I wanted to adopt a dog. As soon as I told my sister, she started looking for a dog for me.

One day, shortly after I got home from work, Ellen came over. "I need you to see something," she said, holding up a picture of a dog. "He's with the rescue I volunteer with. Let's go meet him, Laurie."

I looked at the picture and agreed. We reached out to the woman fostering him and set up an appointment for the next day. Driving to the woman's house, I was excited, but as soon as we started walking up to her door, I froze. "Ellen," I began, hesitantly, "I'm not sure I'm ready for this."

"Let's just meet the dog," she said calmly. "And see how it goes."

The woman invited us in and brought us downstairs to her finished basement to meet him: a beagle mix approximately two years old. Ellen sat down on the floor so I followed suit and he came right up to us wagging his tail. He was incredibly friendly and loved the attention.

Seeing that the three of us were getting along, the woman quietly opened the sliding glass door in her basement and slipped out into her yard, closing the door behind her. We continued to play with him for another fifteen minutes, when I finally looked at my sister and asked, "What do you think?"

"What do I think? I think he's amazing! I think he's friendly and relatively calm. I think if you don't adopt him, someone else is going to take him in a minute."

I felt the same so I got up off the floor, walked over to the sliding glass door, opened it, and walked out. I was so excited that I left the door open. The puppy followed me out and began walking around her yard sniffing all the unfamiliar scents.

"I'll take him," I told the woman.

And that's where it all began.

The first night, fully confident he would curl up and quietly sleep in his crate, I put him in and shut the door. He immediately started whining. I listened to him whine for about five minutes, opened the door, and took him out. That was the first—and last—time he was in a crate!

Since he came in as a stray, not only did we have no idea what his background was but the poor little guy didn't yet have a name. My family and I put our heads together and ultimately decided to name him Casey.

Casey loved to hike and I loved having him along with me on hikes and everywhere I went. I learned relatively soon that Casey loved squirrels—or at least loved chasing them. A few times while we were out for a hike or a walk, I wasn't paying complete attention when he saw a squirrel and took off after it. The leash flew out of my hand, and Casey ran, barking, after the squirrel. Both times, when he heard me yelling his name, he stopped, and came back to me, but only after making sure the squirrel was no longer in easy reach.

For the most part though, Casey was well-behaved and we settled in really well together. However, with no real experience with dogs, I decided (for both of our sakes) to take Casey to obedience classes. Since he was treat-motivated, he did incredibly well, caught on quickly, and really seemed to enjoy it.

The place where we were taking training classes also offered agility training. Once we finished obedience, I decided to give that a try with Casey. He loved it and proved to be quite the character during class!

Casey occasionally became completely full of himself and started doing zoomies around the house which I found both entertaining and hysterical. At our third agility class, he must have gotten a surge of that same overwhelming confidence because he started doing zoomies around the agility yard. The other dogs stopped and watched Casey. One by one, they started to follow him. Before long, all the dogs were running and chasing him. We all stood there laughing.

Casey taught me a lot: how to be with a dog, how to train a dog, and mainly what it felt like to be loved by a dog.

Because of Casey, I adopted two more dogs: Corey and Molly. For me, three dogs was enough. Despite knowing I was at my limit, I continued looking into other options.

I began volunteering with a local rescue that had implemented a program at the Aloft in downtown Asheville. Aloft kept a dog at their hotel 24/7 hoping a guest or visitor at the hotel would see the dog and adopt them. Since the hotel was only two blocks from where I worked, I went there on my lunch hour, got the current dog, and together we went for a walk. We always made sure we stopped at my office because my coworkers loved meeting the dogs. The dogs loved it too because my coworkers showered every dog with lots of treats and love. Being in new situations and surroundings with new people, also provided a great opportunity to socialize the dog.

After leaving my office, we visited other offices in the building including the office where my friend, Sarah, worked. I knew Sarah was looking for a dog, so I made sure I always introduced her to every dog.

One lunch hour, I brought a somewhat shy Chihuahua to meet her. While she wasn't initially sold on the dog, before long, she fell in love with, and adopted, Rocco. To this day, she sends a Christmas card every year with Rocco's picture on it.

Next, I considered the possibility of fostering. My sister had her own dogs, but also fostered dogs, and I saw how much she enjoyed it. I also saw how much it helped the dogs get ready for their forever home and family. Believing fostering might be a perfect option for me, I decided to give it a try.

While searching various rescues in my area on the internet, I saw a dog listed with a foster-based rescue in Asheville. She was a beautiful black and brown beagle mix they estimated was somewhere around seven years old.

The minute I saw her picture, and looked into her eyes, I knew I wanted to help her. I went to the rescue, signed all the paperwork to fos-

Zoey

ter her, and brought her home. The second we walked into the house, she froze. Every little noise scared her. For days, she hid behind or under furniture, trying to be invisible, and stay as far away from me as possible.

Deciding she needed a name so I could talk to her, I again enlisted the help of my family and together we decided on Zoey. Since she'd been found as a stray, no one had any idea where Zoey had been or what she'd been through. I knew it would take time and patience and that it could be a very long road.

So as not to overwhelm her, we began in baby steps. If she was laying on her bed, I sat down next to her without ever touching or looking at her. I knew going too far or too fast would only set her back but, over time, I ramped it up a bit by spending longer periods of time next to her, talking to her, and calling her by name. Eventually, I was able to pet her.

Two other things helped Zoey and me. The first was my sister. Ellen came over and, because of her years of experience with dogs, gave me tips and suggestions which were helpful for Zoey and me.

The other thing that helped was my other dogs. Zoey felt welcomed and safe with them. Simply watching and being around them for a few weeks helped her relax and come out of her shell.

Zoey came home with me in August and the rescue kept reaching out asking if she was ready to be listed for adoption. Finally, in November, I realized she might still have a bit of a rough road, but I told them they could try listing her. Almost immediately, a woman reached out wanting to meet Zoey.

We met the woman at a nearby park. While Zoey was timid, she let the woman pet her and didn't try to run away.

I told the woman everything I knew about Zoey, stressing repeatedly that she needed to, "Give her time. Have patience with her."

"I can do that," the woman said confidently.

Honestly, my gut feeling was that she just wanted to adopt a dog. It didn't matter if it was Zoey or another dog. That concerned me, but, for Zoey, I needed to trust the woman was doing this for the right reasons.

The next day, Zoey and I met the woman at the rescue. She signed the adoption papers and left with Zoey. I left in tears. It was very difficult to let Zoey go but I also knew that finding her a forever home was the reason I had initially brought her home with me. Now she had that home.

The next morning, the woman called. "Zoey has been under my bed since I brought her home. She won't come out."

"You need to give her time," I reminded her. "One night isn't enough."

She listened to me explain again that it often takes a dog a while to get used to a person, a home, the household, and routine. When I finished, she simply said, "I can't do it."

I was overjoyed! I immediately called the rescue, explained what happened, told them I wanted to adopt Zoey, then raced over to the woman's home to pick her up.

After filling out her adoption papers, I brought Zoey home. I now had my first official "foster failure" under my belt—and couldn't have been happier!

Although she'd already been with me and in my home, Zoey continued to be timid. I had to be extremely mindful of the smallest things. She loved going for walks, but every time I put her harness on, I had to quietly close the plastic clasps on her harness because the clicking sound when you closed them made her tremble. Loud noises still scared her. Everything still scared her.

While out for walks, if she saw another dog, Zoey immediately started pulling on the leash and barking. We began working on having her focus on me, rather than the dog. As soon as she did, I gave her a treat. Even now, if we're out walking and another dog is heading toward us (even if the dog is off in the distance), Zoey stops, ignores the other dog, focuses on me, and looks for a treat.

At the dog park, while Corey chased tennis balls, I taught Zoey to "come." Since Corey chased balls incessantly, initially Zoey ran after her. Over time, I taught her to stop and "come." Now she only runs about ten feet away before she stops, turns, and the minute I say, "come" she runs back to me for treats.

After seven years together, while she's much calmer, un-

Casey

familiar surroundings still make Zoey uncomfortable and loud noises still scare her. She is friendly with people and dogs although she doesn't always play with the other dogs in my house. Unlike my other dogs, Zoey doesn't sleep with me. Instead, she's very content having her own space and sleeping in her own bed. If I'm sitting on the couch, she comes to me if she wants affection but doesn't hop up on the couch next to me. Essentially, Zoey lives life on her own terms and that's fine with me because she's happy, adorable, and I love her.

Compared to how Zoey was when I first got her, the change in her is extraordinary. She is extremely happy and gets excited anytime we go out for a walk, a ride in the car, or if someone comes over.

Equally extraordinary is the change in me since I got Zoey. As much as Zoey needed me, I needed her just as much. I was never very confident or had very high self-esteem, but by bonding with Zoey and helping her gain those attributes, I gained them as well. As she continued to calm down, my confidence increased. I always told people that I wasn't very patient. Now, because of Zoey, I am much more patient than I've ever been.

Zoey opened me up to the world of fostering and it's been incredibly rewarding. Last year, I fostered fifteen dogs. Because of my experience with (and all I learned from) Zoey, I search for dogs that might have a more difficult time getting adopted out: the fearful dogs or the older, senior dogs. I take in dogs that may need more time, space, and understanding, to get to the point where they're ready to be adopted. Depending on their needs, some are with me longer than others but every dog, and every experience, is incredibly rewarding.

While there's so much good you can do for a dog, there's also an equal amount—if not more—good a dog can do for you. I'm forever grateful to Casey and Zoey because, by bringing them into my life, they taught me so much about dogs, about life and love. And, especially, about myself.

# Chapter 22

# SARAH & ROCCO

## *I Started to Look at Everything Differently*

I LIVE ALONE AND HAD BEEN THINKING ABOUT GETTING A DOG. What I envisioned was rescuing a thirty-to-forty-pound dog who would be my walking, hiking, and traveling companion. I also wanted a black dog, because I knew typically they weren't adopted as quickly.

Since I was working in a corporate office in downtown Asheville and also going to college full-time, I decided the wisest thing to do was wait until the end of the semester to actively look for a dog.

Every day, Laurie, a friend who worked in the same building as me, went to the Aloft on her lunch hour to get the current Charlie's Angels Rescue dog from the hotel and take it for a walk. She always stopped by our building so everyone could meet the dog. Knowing I was eventually going to be in the market, she made sure I met every dog. Over time, I met a lot of dogs—puppies and adult dogs, big and small dogs—and while they were all cute and wonderful, none of them fit the bill.

One day, Laurie walked in with a little, scrawny, shaggy Yorkshire terrier-Chihuahua mix. I was on the phone when they walked over to my desk, so I quickly glanced down at him. The dog looked up at me and Laurie motioned for me to pick him up. I did, put him on my lap, and by the time I finished my phone conversation, he was sound asleep.

"Look how cute he is sleeping in your lap," Laurie said, smiling. "His name is Gremlin."

Before I could say a word, my phone rang again. I picked up Gremlin and handed him back to Laurie. "Ok, thanks. Here's your dog. I have to go."

The following Tuesday, Laurie came back with Gremlin. It was raining out and he was shivering, so I picked him up. The minute I did, he stopped shaking, and once again he settled into my lap and fell asleep.

At that time, dogs were flying out of the Aloft program and were being adopted after only a few hours or days. Yet, for some reason, Gremlin wasn't one of those dogs. After two weeks at the Aloft, no one had shown any interest in him. Knowing he was still waiting for his forever home, my heart began to soften.

One afternoon, shortly after Laurie and Gremlin left, a co-worker casually walked over, leaned on my desk, and said, "Gremlin is the ugliest dog I've ever seen."

I am sensitive and always stand up for the underdog, but even taking all of that into consideration, her comment really impacted me. For the rest of the day, I couldn't get Gremlin out of my mind and spent the next few days reading about him on the Charlie's Angels Facebook page. I learned he had been surrendered by a family who had seven dogs. When they were no longer able to afford their dogs, they surrendered all of them to a nearby shelter.

Time passed and with no one showing any interest in adopting Gremlin, the shelter placed him on the euthanasia list. That's when Charlie's Angels swooped in and brought him to their shelter. He was great with other dogs, but the shelter environment ultimately proved to be too stressful for him, so Charlie's Angels placed him in a foster home.

Something sparked in me. Once again, I began going through my checklist. He wasn't black but that wasn't a game changer. At eleven pounds, he certainly wasn't the thirty-to-forty-pound dog I envisioned. I wanted a dog who would be my hiking, walking, and traveling companion. From my experience with him thus far, Gremlin seemed to be more of a lap dog. On the other hand, as a student, having a dog hang out in my lap while I did my homework would be wonderful, too.

As I continued going through my checklist, I realized none of that mattered, because the truth was I wanted Gremlin. I filled out the application, and a few days later, Kim from Charlie's Angels called. "You've got a friend."

Having never had a dog before, I wasn't prepared and didn't have anything at my house for him. Before heading to the Aloft to pick him up, I drove to the store and bought everything he and I would need. As I carried him out, he shook. When I put him in my car, he shook. All the way home, he shook. I had read that it could take time for a dog and its human to get to know and get comfortable with one another, so I decided we would take it slow.

When we got to my house, I gathered him up in my arms and he continued to shake. As I carried him into my house, he shook. Once inside, I put him down, and he started to walk and sniff his way around. Within five minutes, he stopped shaking, jumped on my bed, laid down, and fell asleep. He was home and he knew it.

Originally thinking we would have a long adjustment period, I had bought a baby gate to keep him confined to one room while I was at work, but he never needed it. There was no adjustment or settling in period. He literally went from shaking and nervous to, "Oh, this is my life? Awesome!" in the snap of a finger.

I changed his name to Rocco, since I had just returned from a family trip to Italy and the name resonated with me. He liked it, too.

Next, I traded in my Volkswagen Beetle for a Honda CRV because I wanted something a little sturdier to protect Rocco. I added an elevated skybox car seat that allowed him to be comfortable while also sitting high enough to see out the window. As soon as school ended in May, we prepared for our first adventure.

I reconfigured the back seat so Rocco would not only be comfortable, he would also have multiple options for lounging. At certain times of the day when the sun came in the window, it bothered him so I wanted him to have the ability to move around and get out of the sun.

I packed the car very strategically. Since I made Rocco's food from scratch, I wanted easy access to everything I needed to fix his meals.

Once the car was packed, we drove west. Rocco was full of life and love and was always ready for fun. We regularly hiked at least five miles a day. As it turned out, I got my hiking dog after all! We were on the road a total of eight weeks and visited twenty-one states. In a single trip, Rocco had been to more states than most of my friends.

We're lucky to live in Asheville because it's such a dog-friendly town. Rocco was able to go with me to restaurants, breweries, and public places that have outdoor seating. Asheville's minor league baseball team, the Asheville Tourists, have a "Doggies On the Diamond" program every year where you can bring your dog to a game for free. Rocco and I went, and while he had absolutely no interest in the game, the snacks and food certainly held his interest.

Pixie (left) and Rocco

He had regular play dates and we went to the dog park. While I was at work, my neighbor kept Rocco and he spent the day at her house playing with her dogs in her big yard and loved it!

In November 2019, something unexpected and wonderful happened to me and Rocco.

While on our cross-country trip, Rocco and I visited a friend who lived in Michigan. Her Pomeranian/Chihuahua mix, Pixie, and Rocco instantly became best friends. It was tough leaving them because Rocco truly loved being with Pixie and she felt the same about him.

One weekend, I was on the phone with my friend when she told me they had decided to move to Florida. "I'm thinking of re-homing Pixie before we move."

The first words out of my mouth were, "I'll take her!"

Pixie moved in, and she and Rocco picked up right where they left off. They played, they snuggled, and just like true siblings, even got into a few arguments. Pixie moved in right before the pandemic and once I began working remotely, I had a chance to really connect with her, too.

Everything about my life changed because of Rocco. Even though I always loved animals, I never had one of my own. After Rocco came into my life, I wondered how I had gone so long without a dog. Because of him, I started to look at everything differently—and still do. I would much rather be home with Rocco and Pixie every night than out with my friends. In a sense, they are saving me money.

Every Christmas, I send Laurie a card to thank her for bringing Rocco into my life because she really was the ultimate matchmaker. Rocco didn't align with one thing on my original checklist for a dog, but Laurie saw past that and realized we were meant to be together. The truth is, in the end, nothing on that checklist really mattered.

I originally thought Rocco was going to be a lap dog. Unlike our first few times together in my office where he curled up in my lap, he turned out not to be much of a lap dog. However, when I'm not feeling well or sad, he always senses something is wrong, climbs into my lap, and stays close to me. He's sweet, loving, and very in tune with me. The bottom line is, Rocco is there for me when it matters the most.

Rocco and Pixie are my whole world. They are my heart. Rocco was the first to steal my heart and while I had always heard people say their dog was their best friend. I never realized this is what it felt like. It truly is magical.

# Chapter 23
## TENNESSEE

### *Over the Mountains*
### *to the Volunteer State*

IT WAS DIFFICULT PULLING OURSELVES AWAY FROM THE LUXURY and comfort of the Aloft on our final morning. Robb, Ava, and I had enjoyed cuddling together in the comfort of our plush king-size bed. Every morning, Ava loved having room service deliver bacon to our room for her.

Downtown Asheville had changed drastically since my days at Warren Wilson College. The Hot Shot Café, where I spent so many Sunday mornings eating scrambled eggs and buttery, cheesy grits, was long gone along with so many other businesses. In their place were a variety of eclectic and unique restaurants and shops. We loved walking and exploring and, with Asheville being such a pet-friendly town, Ava was able to explore alongside us. Every day, when we returned to the hotel, the first thing we did was stop and play with Daisy.

As much as we loved being there, the time had come for us to move on since I had an appointment in Knoxville, Tennessee. We checked out and grabbed an Uber back to the campground where we had parked our motorhome.

Since my appointment wasn't until the afternoon, we had time to forego the more direct and faster route via the Interstate and opted instead to take the more leisurely and scenic route along The Blue Ridge Parkway.

The Parkway connects two national parks, Shenandoah National Park in Virginia and the Great Smoky Mountains National Park in North Carolina. It's 469 miles of winding roads. With an average speed limit of 45 mph, it would take twelve to thirteen hours to drive it nonstop from end to end. Our drive from Asheville to Knoxville would only take approx-

Ava ordering bacon from the room service menu on our last morning at the Aloft

imately two or three hours, providing we didn't stop too often.

There's a reason the Blue Ridge Parkway has been dubbed "America's Favorite Drive" because, as you make your way through the picturesque, rural landscape of the Appalachian Highlands, you pass cascading roadside waterfalls, rolling hills, lush forests, and majestic mountain ranges off in the distance. Around every turn, there is another breathtaking view. In addition, for those who have the time, there are some fun stops along the way, including Gatlinburg, Pigeon Forge, and Cherokee.

As difficult as it was, we kept our scenic stops to a minimum and arrived at the Community Action Committee (CAC) building in Knoxville, a half hour before my scheduled appointment.

CAC is a local public agency that provides the community with a wide range of federal, state, and locally-funded programs. It was created in 1964 by Knox County and the City of Knoxville to uphold its commitment of: Helping People and Changing Lives.

The building itself sits on a rather unique, steeply-sloped, triangular site. The Fire and Police Departments occupy the lower level and the remainder of the building houses a variety of programs clustered along a wide, interior pedestrian "street" that leads to a large sunlit atrium.

I relaxed and waited in the atrium for my appointment with the Program Manager of Knox PAWS. Having witnessed firsthand the love and joy Brooke and Ava brought my parents as they entered their golden years, I was curious to learn more about Knox PAWS. All I knew was that it was a program geared toward senior humans and canines. That afternoon I learned the program, and its impact in the community, far exceeded anything I could have imagined.

# Chapter 24

# MONICA & KNOX PAWS

*Matching Senior Dogs*
*with Senior Citizens*

KNOX PAWS, PLACING ANIMALS WITH SENIORS, IS A SOCIAL SERV-
ice program that is part of the Knoxville/Knox County Community Action Committee Office on Aging. As part of the Office on Aging, we
knew seniors in the community were often lonely, anxious, and didn't
have much to do. The result was that many of them were spending their
days sleeping or sitting alone in their apartments.

Studies have shown the positive impact of placing animals with seniors—specifically in regard to getting them up, motivated, and into a
routine. Thinking it might benefit our seniors, we started brainstorm-
ing how to start such a program in Knoxville.

The Young William Animal Center, a local shelter, agreed to work
with us. After a local woman made a significant donation to start the
program, Knox PAWS was born. This was back in 2004. Initially, we only
covered the adoption fee for the animal but since then the program has
grown tremendously.

The majority of folks on this program have an average monthly income of $800 and 90% live in subsidized housing. There isn't a lot of
room in their limited budget, so we now cover adoption fees, pet deposit
fees, dog food and supplies, grooming fees, veterinary expenses, and
everything else responsible pet owners provide for their dog. We never
want money to be a barrier to a senior having a pet. Whatever their pet
needs, Knox PAWS takes care of it.

To qualify for the program, the client needs to be at least sixty years
old, live independently in Knoxville, and have an income at or below the

150th percentile of the national poverty level. Clients are also limited to having one pet at a time.

For a dog to qualify, it needs to be a senior pet (which we define as any dog six years or older). The average age of our pets is eight to ten years old but we have some old timers that are over fifteen years old.

Since most of the subsidized housing locations require that a pet weighs less than twenty-five pounds, the majority of our dogs are in, or well under, that weight range. If the housing management requires a pet deposit, Knox PAWS also pays that for our client.

Before a dog goes home with a client, we make sure they have everything they need: bowls, dog food, leashes, collars, harnesses, toys, dog beds, and blankets. When I first started working at Knox PAWS, I was surprised that one of the biggest requests was for doggie sweaters or jackets. It never dawned on me that, in the winter, people would be concerned about keeping their pets warm. I reached out to the community. As donations started arriving, we passed them on to our clients. They were thrilled. They love knowing their pet is warm, but also love seeing them in a new, clean sweater or jacket.

We have a wonderful groomer who bathes, brushes, and trims the dog, cleans their ears, cuts their nails, and also takes a picture of the dog after it's been groomed. If a holiday is approaching, she provides holiday-themed bows and bandanas. It's adorable to see the faces of our clients when we take their freshly-groomed dog back to them along with the photo. The photo immediately goes up on their refrigerator—as if it was their grandchild or other family member—and for many of them, it is. The majority of our clients don't have any family members living nearby so this dog truly is their family. It becomes their everything and what better place for a dog than with someone who is home all day to love and dote on them?

One of my clients always talks about how her dog got her into a daily routine of waking up, taking her medication, eating breakfast, and going outside. In addition to enjoying each other's company, the dog got her back into a daily routine of doing things and taking care of herself in a way she hadn't for quite some time.

Once a client qualifies for the program and is approved for a pet, we start talking about the kind of dog they prefer: a specific breed, color, male or female, long or short hair? Their answers are sometimes based on a pet they had in their past or a pet they've always wanted.

Knox PAWS maintains a great relationship with our nine shelter partners. We communicate every few days about pets that are available (or will soon be available) for adoption. Using the information the client provides allows me to begin honing in on adoptable dogs that might be a potential good match for them.

Pet Selection Day is an exciting day for the client. They're always eager to visit the shelters to look at available pets, even though they don't always find their perfect

Mr. G and Kyle

match the first time. Sometimes it can take a while but, regardless, we never give up. One client visited six different shelters before she found her perfect furry friend.

I had one client, Mr. G, who desperately wanted a dog. For quite some time, he'd been searching for one on his own but, time after time, he was turned down because he was in a wheelchair. At Knox PAWS we believe if you can love an animal, we will figure out a way for you and the animal to be together whether you walk with a cane, use a Rollator, or are in a wheelchair.

When I asked Mr. G what kind of dog he was looking for he said he didn't have a particular breed or even color in mind. "I'll know the right dog when I meet it."

Based on that limited information, we headed to the shelter and went up and down aisle after aisle. None of the dogs appeared to be the "right one" for Mr. G—until we passed a little Jack Russel/Parsons terrier mix, cowering in the back of his kennel. Mr. G stopped immediately and watched the dog.

"That's Kyle," the shelter worker told him. "He's eight. He was found as a stray and is very shy. He probably wouldn't work for you."

She continued to walk down the aisle but Mr. G didn't budge. He continued sitting in front of the kennel staring at Kyle. The shelter worker walked back and, again, tried to urge him on. "He's just going to sit in the back of his cage. Why don't we keep looking?"

And then Kyle saw Mr. G. He instantly ran to the front of his kennel and stood up so his paws and head were at a level where Mr. G could reach out and touch him—and Mr. G did.

We took Kyle out of the kennel and went into the visitation room. Kyle was amazing. He knew exactly what to do with Mr. G. He knew exactly how to walk around his wheelchair and knew exactly how much space and what kind of boundaries to give Mr. G.

We decided to do a foster-to-adopt with Kyle to make sure it would work. It did and the adoption was finalized.

We visit all our clients and their pets regularly, but we are also mandated to do reassessments twice a year to ensure everything is going well for both the person and the pet. At Mr. G and Kyle's one-year reassessment, I called to let him know I'd arrived.

As soon as his phone rang, Mr. G answered. Without even a hello, he said, "Meet me outside."

Thinking he was concerned because his home might not have been tidy, I assured him I didn't care if his house was a mess.

"That's not it. Just meet me outside. I'm already out here. Come over by the doggie side of the building."

I walked over. The minute I rounded the corner of the building, I saw Mr. G with a Rollator walking Kyle. His wheelchair was gone.

Six months later, I went back for another reassessment and, this time, the Rollator was gone. He and Kyle walked to the elevator, out the front door, and around the building. At the end of our meeting, they walked back together.

His primary care physician told us, "Walking his dog got him up and moving. Thanks to Kyle, he strengthened muscles he had lost. This is nothing short of a miracle and all because you placed this dog with him."

While Mr. G couldn't run marathons, he'd gone from a wheelchair to walking in eighteen months, because of Kyle.

And that's just one story. These are the kinds of things we see happen over and over.

Even when people think they know what kind of dog they want, many times they get to the shelter and the dog picks them. Once they do, it becomes an unbreakable bond.

If mobility ever becomes an issue for a dog, we provide a doggie stroller or whatever our client needs so they can continue going outside without fear or concern about trip or fall hazards. We do everything we can to make it safe and easy, and never a burden, for our client and their dog.

If a dog passes, we ask the client to wait at least ninety days to grieve the pet before getting another pet through the program.

If an owner passes, we take the pet back into our program and match them with another qualified applicant unless the shelter requires it be returned to them as part of their adoption contract.

In the event a client requires hospitalization or rehabilitation, we have a wonderful foster component within the Knox PAWS program where a foster will take the client's pet into their home and care for them until the person has recovered and returned home.

Our program is funded by donations along with any grants or funding I can obtain. I do a lot of speaking and community outreach and we're very lucky to have the support of so many in the Knoxville area. I've worked in animal welfare and rescue since I was fifteen years old and have also been able to use those connections to benefit our clients and their dogs.

Since 2004, we have matched over 170 clients and animals. We currently have seventy-four Knox PAWS clients. Even though I no longer have my own dog, I get to share in the love of over seventy clients and their pets.

# Chapter 25

 **MARY LEE & GRIFFIN**

*Not Perfect but Perfect for Me*

I ALWAYS HAD, AND LOVED, DOGS. BUT AFTER MY LAST DOG PASSED in 2018, I decided not to get another dog. Three years later, a friend told me about Knox PAWS. While it sounded like an interesting program, I still wasn't sure I was ready for, or wanted, another dog.

It took me forever to reach out to them, but I finally called and left a message for Monica. When she called me back, I was so happy because, by then, I'd changed my mind. I wanted a dog and companion.

Monica told me more about the program and it all sounded perfect. She also had a dog she wanted me to meet. We went to see it but it wasn't the right dog for me. Even though I always had little dogs, since I now use a walker, I was concerned.

"I'm sorry," I told her. "He's adorable but he's so little. I'm afraid he might trip me." I hesitated for a moment before telling her what else was on my mind. "The truth is, Monica, I don't want to leave here today without a dog."

Monica smiled and showed me a picture of another dog sitting on a couch. He was beautiful and, since he had short hair, I knew he would be low-maintenance. Thinking he might be a good fit, we went to the shelter to meet him.

The instant I saw Griffin, I loved him. Shocked that he was still at the shelter and hadn't been adopted, I finally asked the young man who worked there, "Why doesn't anyone want him?"

"He has an overbite," he said matter-of-factly.

"That's it?" I asked, flabbergasted.

"Yes, ma'am."

"Well, that doesn't bother me. Nobody's perfect."

I brought Griffin home to see how it would go. As soon as we walked into the house, I told him, "Griffin, it's just you and me here. There's no family and I don't get a lot of company so this is our home and the couch is all yours." I pointed to the couch, Griffin looked at me, walked over, jumped up, and took possession of it.

Griffin honestly settled into my life and my home without a problem. He was the most loving dog. Two days later, I told Monica I wanted him to stay. I had no idea how long Griffin had been at the shelter. However long it was, I was glad no one else had wanted him because now, he was mine. Like I told the young man at the shelter, "Nobody is perfect", but the truth was that Griffin was perfect for me.

I had his DNA done and he's a good mixture of just about everything: 12% Great Pyrenees; 43% American pit bull; 9.8% Labrador retriever; 8.9% Siberian husky; and 25.4% Super Mutt. The Super Mutt is basically a combination of every other type of dog you can think of—including Chihuahua. The only thing Chihuahua about him is maybe the curl in his tail.

When I got Griffin he was five years old; he's now six. It was obvious he already had some kind of training because, even when I first got him, if I asked him to "sit," he sat. He was housebroken which I definitely needed. He loves to be brushed and petted but, thanks to his short hair, he doesn't require a lot of grooming. And he's never had a problem with my walker.

The only problem we have right now is that he's a pretty big boy. After I got him, I fattened him up. I thought he looked good, but Monica and a few other people told me he needs to lose weight, so I put him on a diet. I cut down on his meals and cut out treats, but the problem is Griffin and I aren't very good at dieting. The other problem is anytime he looks at me with those big old brown eyes, I just can't say, "No."

I have a large fenced-in yard, but he doesn't like to exercise and, because of my walker, it's difficult for me to go out with him. Griffin's motto is: "Why walk when you can ride?" He absolutely loves going for a ride in the car.

Despite his size, Griffin thinks he's a lap dog. Anytime I'm sitting in my chair he comes over and crawls into my lap. He's too big. Half of him

Griffin

is in the chair and the other half is hanging off but I don't say anything. I'll just let him keep thinking he's a lap dog.

Shortly after he came to live with me, I had a piece of furniture I wanted to get rid of. For some reason, Griffin didn't want it gone and put up quite a fuss. I finally had to put him in the other room so I could get it out of here. Since then, I haven't gotten rid of anything. I tell people who come to my house, "This is Griffin's home; you're a guest, a visitor. You may consider him a dog, but he's my fur baby. He's my family."

I get Meals on Wheels and every one of the people who deliver meals to my house have fallen in love with Griffin. The man who delivers my medicine brings him treats and gets down on the floor and plays with him. My nephew came to visit last weekend. After spending time with us, he told me, "I'm so glad you have Griffin."

I am, too. I feel more secure having Griffin with me. I'm ninety-one and live alone and he's very protective of me. I don't think anyone would come in here if they saw him standing there barking at them.

He's truly the most loving and lovable dog and a wonderful companion. I honestly didn't realize how lonely I was until I got Griffin. He's been a God-send and now I'm so busy with him that I don't have time to get lonely.

He's also incredibly sweet, loyal, and caring. I recently had a coughing spasm and he came and sat next to me until it passed. No words can describe all the ways Griffin has helped me. I didn't realize what a huge difference he had made in my life until my friends started telling me, "You sound different now that you have Griffin." And it's true. I not only sound different, I feel different—and all because of Griffin.

Before I adopted Griffin, I asked Monica what would happen to Griffin if I had an emergency. Monica explained that Knox PAWS has people who would care for him until I was well enough to take care of him and myself again.

I was also concerned about what would happen to him if something happened to me. While I have a family member who loves him, in the event that didn't work out, Monica again assured me Knox PAWS would find him another home with another one of their clients. It was a huge relief for me to know that Griffin will always be taken care of regardless of what the future brings for the two of us.

When I adopted Griffin, Monica took him to a groomer and veterinarian. They also made sure Griffin and I had everything we needed. It's a wonderful organization and they are wonderful people to deal with. I honestly can't say enough good things about Knox PAWS and Monica. She is absolutely precious. The world needs more Monicas—and Griffins.

# Chapter 26
## VIRGINIA

*A Peaceful Day in the
Old Dominion*

LATE THAT AFTERNOON, WE LEFT KNOXVILLE TO DRIVE NORTH to our next destination, the Dixie Caverns campground in Salem, Virginia. I had hoped we would arrive in time to take a tour of the caverns, but they were already closed when we arrived, so Robb, Ava, and I went for a nice, long, leisurely walk and spent the night relaxing together.

The next morning, Christina from Deaf Dogs Rock was scheduled to pick me up at the campground and take me to their house for an interview. Instead, she called and asked if Robb and Ava would like to come along, too.

"Absolutely!" I told her, excited to have my traveling companions join me for this next adventure.

After giving me their address, we quickly finished our breakfast, cleaned, packed up, and began driving to their home outside of Salem. There are differing opinions on how the city of Salem got its name including one which says it was derived from the word "Shalom," meaning peace. Regardless of where the name came from, I can say with certainty that the feeling of peace was palpable as we drove through this magnificent area of the Shenandoah Valley, nestled between the Allegheny and Blue Ridge Mountains, past its pristine farms and wide-open fields where horses, cattle, and sheep leisurely grazed.

The moment we started up their driveway, we knew we were in a bit of a pickle. Their steep driveway and the semi-low clearance of our motorhome weren't a good combination. Christina's husband, Chris, came out to guide us in and, once parked, Robb, Ava, and I climbed out to meet and thank Chris. Out of the corner of my eye, I saw Christina walking toward us, a dog at her side. As I turned to greet her, I saw that she

Robb, Ava, and me visiting Deaf Dogs Rock

was communicating with the dog using sign language. I had never witnessed anything like it before and it was an amazing and remarkably tender moment.

After giving us a tour of their property, Chris and Christina invited us into their home to meet the rest of their pack. Their home, tastefully decorated in a white and turquoise color scheme reflected the personalities of its inhabitants: warm, welcoming, eclectic, and unique.

For Robb, Ava, and me, it was an incredibly peaceful and magical afternoon at Bluebird Farm.

# Chapter 27

# CHRISTINA & NITRO

*Deaf Dogs Hear With Their Hearts*

IN MIDDLE SCHOOL, I HAD A DEAF PEN PAL WHO LIVED AT THE Nebraska School for the Deaf. While I was familiar with deafness, I'd never given much thought to deaf animals or deaf dogs. All of that changed when I received a phone call from my friend, Rebecca, who worked at the City of Salem Animal Shelter.

"Do you have time to stop by today?" she asked. "There's a special puppy I want you to meet."

From time to time, I took photos of adoptable dogs and shared them on my social media pages to help them find a home. Assuming that was the reason Rebecca was calling, I agreed to stop by after work.

I arrived at the shelter shortly before they closed for the day and Rebecca met me at the front door. Together we headed back toward the isolation wing where new pups are kept until they are vaccinated. As we walked, Rebecca began to explain that one of their Animal Control officers had seen a puppy down by the Roanoke River so he pulled over, got out of his car, and walked over toward the puppy. He crouched down and the puppy ran toward him, unbridled joy written all over its face. It was a bitterly cold November day and the puppy, who was skin and bones, was extremely cold and shivering from head to toe.

As we reached the last kennel at the end of the hall, Rebecca stopped. I followed suit and, turning, looked into the eyes of a tiny, skinny white boxer puppy. He had one brown eye and the other was crystal blue and surrounded by a big round patch of brown fur. Even though he was emaciated, I knew as he grew and gained weight, he was going to be a striking dog, but what really got me was his blue eye. It was my kryptonite.

"He's a boxer," Rebecca explained. "We believe he was dumped by a local boxer breeder because he's deaf."

The puppy looked so vulnerable. Wanting to help get him into a good home, I began taking photos of him, as Rebecca continued talking. "I wanted you to take his photo, Christina," she said, pausing momentarily before continuing. "The other reason I wanted you to meet him is because . . ." She looked at me, and paused again. "I wanted to know if you and Chris might consider adopting him."

I stopped taking photos, lowered my camera, and looked at her, speechless. She wanted us to add a little deaf puppy to our family?

Rebecca had been to our farm and knew Chris and I had invested a lot of time, energy, and money into creating fenced dog areas so our three dogs would have places to run and remain safe. Rebecca knew our home would be the perfect place for a deaf puppy to grow up and be well cared for, but I was stunned.

"Let me check with Chris and see what he thinks," I told her.

I was confident there was no way Chris would want to adopt a fourth dog, especially a deaf puppy. As soon as he said, "No," I could go back to my original plan of sharing the puppy's photos and information on social media to find him a wonderful home.

I cuddled the puppy for about fifteen minutes, took a few more photos to share with Chris and my Facebook friends, then left the shelter and drove home for dinner.

I never mentioned the puppy until after dinner when Chris and I were relaxing. "Rebecca called today," I began, slowly. "She wanted to show me a deaf puppy." With that I showed him some of the photos I'd taken. "She wants to know if we want to add another dog to the family."

Chris sat silently looking at the photos. He got up from the table, started to walk out of the room then turned, looked at me, and said, "I think we should adopt him."

"You think we should adopt a deaf puppy?"

"Absolutely," he said with total conviction. "I agree with Rebecca. Our farm has all the separate fenced-in dog areas which would be perfect for a deaf puppy. He would be safe here. He would grow up with three other dogs who can hear. Our dogs love other dogs, and they all get along. What's one more puppy?"

I looked at him, still slightly dumbfounded. "Are you sure, Chris? We don't know anything about training or raising a deaf puppy."

Chris smiled. "How hard can it be?" Let's just go for it!"

My sweet husband Chris and I had been married for fourteen years. While he never ceased to amaze me, this was taking things to a whole new level!

The next morning, we called Rebecca to tell her we would adopt the little deaf boxer puppy. As soon as I told her, I knew she covered the receiver with her hand and told the shelter staff because the next thing I heard was a lot of whooping and hollering in the background. I started laughing, happy to know they were all truly celebrating our decision. I told Rebecca we needed to get puppy supplies and also get the house and yard ready for him so we would pick him up the next morning.

After hanging up the phone, Chris and I jumped in the car and ran down to our local pet store to get a crate, an exercise pen, a puppy harness, some puppy toys, and a puppy buckle collar. Since the shelter estimated the puppy was around eight to ten weeks old, we bought several different size collars and harnesses for him as he grew. We also wanted to get him an ID tag but he didn't yet have a name.

Years before, while driving to visit family in the Midwest, Chris and I passed through a town in West Virginia called Nitro. We agreed we would name our next puppy Nitro because it was such a cool name. Since the name seemed to fit our new deaf puppy, we purchased a new blue bone-shaped metal ID tag and had "Nitro" engraved on it along with our phone numbers and the words: DEAF DOG. Finally, since it was November and very chilly—and since Nitro was so skinny—we purchased a little blue sweater for him to wear when we picked him up from the shelter.

That night, Chris and I searched the internet for anything we could find on training, raising, or communicating with a deaf puppy. It was 2010 and there wasn't a lot of information available, but we were able to find a wonderful video on YouTube by American Sign Language (ASL) interpreter Alisha McGraw who had two deaf Boston terriers and a deaf boxer. In her video, Alisha showed all of the ASL sign cues she used with her three dogs. The video was a huge help. We watched it several times while taking notes and memorizing the ASL sign cues for things like "Eat", "Go for a walk", "Go potty", "Do you want water?", "Time for dinner", "Go for a ride", and so many more. Little did we realize at the time that Alisha and her video would one day become a very important part of helping us educate the world about raising and living with a deaf dog.

Chris and I stayed up until 1:00 a.m. gathering as much information as we could on living with and raising a deaf puppy. By the time we were done, we were so excited about adopting Nitro that we barely slept.

The following morning, we were the first people in the

Chris, Christina, and Nitro
Photo courtesy of Kenn Bell

parking lot waiting for the shelter to open. We couldn't wait to pick up Nitro but this would also be Chris' first time meeting him. The minute Chris took Nitro into his arms, it was love at first sight! The shelter staff was so elated for all of us and asked Chris and Nitro to pose for several photos for their adoption wall.

After getting Nitro settled in our car, Chris and I looked at each other, then at Nitro, and promised him we would protect him, love him, guide him, open up a new world of communication to him, and be his advocate for the rest of his life.

It had turned out to be an unseasonably warm November day, so we drove to our local coffee shop and sat outside. Nitro sat in Chris's lap. Over coffee (and a pup cup for Nitro), we discussed the best way to introduce Nitro to our three hearing dogs: Lexi, Tallulah, and Bailey. We knew they loved other dogs, and that the puppy would be fine with them. Since we wanted everyone to have an opportunity to get to know one another individually, we decided to do one-on-one meetings.

Back home, we began introductions. While a lot of side-to-side smelling and wiggle butts ensued, there were no issues or problems. Tallulah, our one-year-old Chug puppy, kept bringing her toys over and dropping them in front of Nitro, play bowing to try and get him to chase her.

Next, we spread a blanket on the ground and put all the dog toys on it. They had so much fun playing and chasing one another until they finally wore each other out. When we went back inside, Tallulah and Nitro cuddled up together on the couch and fell asleep.

We crate train all of our dogs, so we put a crate in our bedroom for Nitro to sleep in at night and another one in the main living room for naptime and mealtime. We placed his crate in the bedroom on an ottoman several feet from our bed so that when I was lying down, he would be eye level with me.

At night, if he whined or was restless, I did what I call "The Deaf Dog Lullaby" with my hand. Essentially, I took my right hand and, palm down and fingers facing him, made a wave motion over and over, similar to how a hula dancer moves their hands. Nitro found it extremely hypnotic and, within a few minutes, his eyes would grow heavy and he was sound asleep. The deaf dog lullaby worked like a charm and became part of our nightly routine.

For crate training in the living room, I randomly dropped a treat in Nitro's crate so he learned to go in and search for it. After a while, he started sitting in his crate waiting for a treat. Since he now associated treats with his crate, he learned to love it so much that if Chris and I decided to stay up past 10:00 p.m., Nitro went into the bedroom and cried until one of us went in and opened his crate for him. He liked routine and part of that routine was going to bed promptly at 10:00 p.m.

I began to notice that, other than when we were crate training, Nitro seemed detached and rarely looked at me. He seemed to be bonding with the other dogs but not his humans. One night, worried, I talked to Chris about it. "I'm afraid we may have bitten off more than we can chew."

"We'll be fine," Chris assured me. "But it might be a good idea to get some help."

I am lucky to be married to such a wonderful, pragmatic man who always has a solution to life's challenges because, once again, he was right. I was completely out of my comfort zone and needed help. The next day we found a training facility in our area and paid them a visit.

The training facility, Field of Dreams Training Center, was just up the road from us in Vinton. It was a really cool place and they offered a group positive reinforcement Puppy Class for Nitro. We learned that while they'd never had a deaf puppy in their training classes before, they didn't think it would be an issue since the classes are essentially geared toward training the handler how to train their own dog.

Positive reinforcement classes utilize clicker training wherein the sound of a clicker marks the exact second the dog makes the right choice. For example, with a hearing dog, the dog's handler gives the dog a verbal command or cue like "sit" and the second the dog sits down, the handler marks it with the sound of a clicker device followed by giving the dog a reward or high-value treat. This training method is repeated until the dog understands what the handler is asking them to do.

Since Nitro was deaf, we needed to modify his training which began with teaching him the cue for "watch me." Instead of the clicker to mark the exact second Nitro made the right choice, we used a thumbs-up sign.

The first night was spent doing "watch me" training. I pointed to my face and every time Nitro made direct eye contact with me, he got a thumbs-up sign, a smile, and a high-value treat like a piece of cooked hot dog. We repeated it over and over.

We then moved on to "sit" by giving him a visual command/cue and luring him into place with a high-value treat. As soon as Nitro sat down, we flashed him a thumbs-up sign, a smile, and gave him the treat.

We repeated it over and over. With every new sign or command Nitro learned, we could see a lightbulb go off in his head. As he began to understand what we were communicating with him, he got so excited. To see so much joy in his eyes with every new sign he learned melted our hearts.

Our trainer, Anne, constantly watched Nitro and marveled at how fast he was picking up all the sign cues. "He's such a good puppy," she repeatedly told us in her beautiful British accent and, in doing so, she was building my confidence. Nitro loved people, and while he truly adored Anne, when we were in class, he never took his eyes off me. The detachment I felt the first few weeks after bringing Nitro home vanished into thin air. Chris and I were beaming with pride over our absolutely adorable and extraordinarily smart Nitro.

Being deaf actually turned out to be an advantage for Nitro because he didn't hear, and wasn't distracted by, the other dogs. If a dog in the class was barking and having a fit, Nitro never once looked in their direction. Instead, he remained completely focused on his mom and dad—and, at times, Anne.

Every day we took Nitro somewhere—usually to the hardware store or to sit outside at the coffee shop—to make sure he would be well-socialized. We visited the local pet store weekly so Nitro could see other dogs, kids, and adults and practiced a lot of "sitting and waiting" to allow different people to come up and pet him.

We also employed the help of other people. After explaining that Nitro was deaf and still in training, we asked them to come toward him with the condition that they could only pet him if he was in, and stayed in, a sit. If he came out of the sit, they were to walk away immediately. Nitro figured out quickly that if he stayed seated with his bum on the floor, all these people would pet him. With children, he laid down so they wouldn't be scared. He loved sitting and soaking up all the love and attention.

At the end of his training sessions at the pet store, we allowed Nitro to walk down the toy aisle and pick out whatever he wanted. He loved stuffed animals and always took his time, carefully sniffing every toy. When he finally made up his mind, he would gently pick it up, put it in his mouth, and proudly prance to the front register making sure everyone who saw him knew he was a good boy and was getting a new toy.

Puppy training was going amazingly well, and Nitro loved learning all the new signs and cues. We also practiced grooming, touching paws, wiping paws, and massaging ears to get him used to being handled. Our veterinarian let us stop by so Nitro could hang out with their office cat. While using positive reinforcement training, he got used to stepping on the big scale to get weighed. Every day we made the most of every opportunity we had to teach Nitro how to navigate his silent world while also having fun and making it an adventure.

Shortly after Nitro turned five months old, we were in our backyard playing fetch. On one toss, I threw his ball but it rolled down an uneven part of the yard. Nitro was still in his gangly, uncoordinated phase. Since it had rained the day before, the ground was fairly soft. As Nitro ran to the bottom of the hill and approached our six-foot wooden fence, he tried to stop himself but his back legs folded under him. He gently got up, shook himself off, and began limping toward me holding his right foot up in the air, unable to put any weight on it. We rushed him to our veterinarian where an X-ray showed he had broken his toe. The vet put his leg in a splint and wrapped it so he could put some weight on it. They also gave us Tramadol for the pain, but the first night, he cried all night long. Realizing he was suffering more with the painkillers than without, we stopped them. Immediately, he did so much better and was able to get around and put some weight on his right leg.

Nitro continued to do well until four days later when he began acting completely different and refused to put any weight on his right leg. Knowing something else was wrong, we returned to our vet and found out the splint had turned and his toes were getting infected. The plan now was to soak his foot daily and rewrap his foot. It was important that we also monitor him and make sure he didn't hurt himself again. To do that meant attaching Nitro to either Chris or me until he was completely healed. Being tethered to a five-month-old, high-energy boxer puppy 24/7 was one of the longest and most challenging periods of our lives. Unbeknownst to us, it would also end up to be a huge blessing.

As Nitro began to heal, we went back to his Level One Manners class. He was excited to be back in class and see all his dog buddies and his favorite trainer, Anne. Chris and I also took him to the Gander Mountain store to walk around, practice his sit-and-wait, and meet new people.

With Nitro still tethered to us, we were all getting used to our new "normal." Next, we started doing directional training. If I was getting up from a chair, I gave him the sign for "up". If we were out in public and I was going to walk straight ahead, I pointed in that direction. If I was going to turn right, I pointed right.

After being tethered to us for eight weeks, Nitro knew and understood over forty American Sign Language cues. Chris and I now realized how much tether training helps deaf dogs like Nitro pick up on the smallest nuances of reading a person's body language. We decided, from that point on, to tether-train any deaf dogs we adopted because it was so incredibly valuable and helpful.

With Nitro excelling in his obedience and tricks classes, Jean Jadhon, a local reporter from WDBJ-7 News, reached out to do a story on him.

Excited and honored that our local news station wanted to put a spotlight on our very special puppy, we arranged to meet Jean (who is also a big dog lover) and her cameraman at the Field of Dreams Training Center for the interview. They filmed Nitro doing all kinds of sign cues and tricks. He was a joyful puppy learning sign language and, as a result, showed the world his superpowers.

The following day, Nitro's story hit the local news. Little did we know that a story about a deaf puppy learning sign language would be so popular that national networks would pick up Nitro's story. Friends and family members in other parts of the country started reaching out to Chris and me, telling us they saw Nitro's story on the news. We were shocked!

After the story hit the national news circuit, Chris and I started hearing from people all over the country. Some were looking for advice on how to train their new deaf puppy while others wanted to know if we knew of anyone looking to adopt a deaf puppy. We also started hearing from local shelters who had deaf dogs in their care.

In the back of our minds, every time we looked at Nitro we felt a pang of sadness because we knew other deaf dogs, like Nitro, were sitting in kill shelters across the country. Big dogs and little dogs who had no voice and, in most cases, had no chance of making it out of a shelter alive because, in 2011, deaf dogs were always the first dogs to be put on a shelter's euthanasia list.

My birthday was two weeks away and Chris kept asking me what I wanted. The more I thought about it, the more I realized what I truly wanted was to help deaf dogs and their families. For years, I had been writing a blog, "The World According to Lexi" about my dog Lexi, so I was familiar with the world of blogging and was also very connected to other pet bloggers. I approached Chris with the idea of working together to launch a special website to help deaf dogs all over the country.

Since it was summertime, and Chris was off from teaching, we spent the next two weeks working side-by-side on our computers surrounded by sweet Nitro and our other dogs. We learned WordPress and designed a beautiful website to support our mission of helping one deaf dog at a time. On August 1, 2011—my 52nd birthday—we launched our website, www.deafdogsrock.com, along with our social media platforms on Facebook, Instagram, and Twitter which we had simultaneously built. Once launched, we added photos and articles of Nitro in his training classes along with as much content as we could find—and I could humanly write. We also added "Happy Tails" stories and extraordinary deaf dog stories to help promote deaf dog adoption and change the perception that deaf dogs were hard to train or more aggressive.

As Nitro grew, we continued enrolling him in new training classes. Although he loved going to his classes, we noticed that around the thirty-minute mark, he would start to get bored with the repetition and begin verbalizing *very* loudly, almost as if he was saying, "Mom, I'm so bored!" Since he couldn't hear himself, he had no idea how loud he was. If that didn't work, he turned his body away from me thinking, I guess, that if he wasn't looking at me and couldn't see my sign or cues, he didn't have to participate.

I knew we needed to come up with something creative to keep him engaged in class. Knowing a deaf dog's sense of smell is remarkably strong (it's one of their superpowers), I tried a new approach. Anytime the trainer was working with other dogs and Nitro started to get bored or verbalize, I engaged him in scent games. After hiding a treat in each of my hands and putting them behind my back, I'd bring my closed hands back around in front of Nitro, bump both fists together, then separate them. This was Nitro's cue to pick one. He sniffed them both and then put his paw on the closed hand he thought held the treat. If he was right, I opened my hand and Nitro got the treat.

For another scent game we used three Solo cups. I put a treat under one cup, mixed them up, and then gave Nitro the ASL sign for "find." When Nitro was sure he'd found the cup that held the treat, he would put his paw on it and 99% of the time he was right. He absolutely loved doing scent games and we had so much fun!

We also played "Leave It", where I would put a treat down, give Nitro the sign for "leave it" and, if he went to eat the treat, I placed my hand over it. Eventually, he figured out that if he sat and stared at it long enough, then made direct eye contact with me, he would get a thumbs up and the treat! "Leave It" became one of his favorite games and we played it when we sat at outside cafes and coffee shops while also doing his eating-out training.

By the time Nitro was ten months old, he had passed all of his levels classes. Next, he took the AKC Canine Good Citizen Test. While they'd never had a deaf dog take the CGC test before, he passed it with flying colors. After earning his Canine Good Citizen certification, we enrolled him in a Tricks class and Agility just for fun.

In the meantime, our Deaf Dogs Rock website was keeping us incredibly busy. Every day, I was getting countless emails and messages about deaf dogs needing a new home, so Chris and I decided to add a form to the website where shelters and individuals could submit courtesy adoption listings to help deaf dogs find loving homes. I sent every person who listed a dog tips and tools they could use to screen interested individuals in order to try and keep their deaf dogs safe while searching for a new home.

An adorable eleven-month-old deaf boxer named Bud had been listed for adoption on our website for quite some time, so I finally reached out to the woman who listed Bud to see if we could help. She explained that she lived out in the country and wasn't having any luck getting him adopted. I reached out to friends at our local rescue, Angels of Assisi Rescue in Roanoke, to see if they would make room for Bud if Deaf Dogs Rock sponsored him into their rescue to pay for his neuter surgery. They agreed.

My friend Cherri and I met Teresa, Bud's owner, in West Virginia and picked him up. Poor Bud had been carsick the entire first half of his trip with Teresa so, by the time we got him, he was exhausted and went right to sleep in the crate I'd brought along for him.

We arrived at Angels of Assisi late in the day and all their kennels were full. Knowing I'd have to leave Bud in his crate alone in a strange place overnight made me feel sick to my stomach. Bud looked so much like Nitro. As an empath myself, I could feel what Bud was feeling, so I called Chris and told him what was going on. Hearing how distraught I was over the situation, Chris said we would go back first thing in the morning, get Bud, and foster him.

When we brought Bud home, he became fast friends with Nitro, Bailey, Lexi, and Tallulah. Nitro was in heaven to have another big goofy goober dog to romp and wrestle with. The following week, Bud was neutered. Concerned that Bud would run and play and break his stitches open, I tethered him to me. While he was tethered to my waist, I did the same training I'd done with Nitro. After one week, Bud was a total rock star. He followed my ASL sign directions perfectly, followed where I pointed, and his recall was 100%. I was so proud of him. Bud, of course, never left. He became a part of our family and we felt blessed to have him.

Over time, other deaf dogs joined our family: a little dark merle senior Chihuahua named Pepe who, until he came to us, had lived in a crate his entire life; and a Boston terrier puppy named Bowie who came to us from Austin, Texas, after his adoption fell through. Next was an eight-year-old senior deaf Australian cattle dog named Red whose human, Ricky, had recently passed from cancer. When we saw Red, it was love at first sight. Since we try to name our deaf dogs after rock stars, Chris changed Red's name to Cornell after Chris Cornell, lead singer and guitarist for the band Soundgarden.

All the deaf and hearing dogs in our home did so well. They played together, shared their big box of toys, chased one other, barked at each other, and settled down to nap together on the couch. It was a bit of organized chaos—and absolutely wonderful.

At mealtime, our hearing dog Tallulah took charge. She first ran to Bud and gently touched him to wake him up then proceeded to wake the other deaf dogs. I don't know how she knew they were deaf, but she did. It was so cute to watch her wake everyone up—and all of them would come over to me and remind me it was time to eat.

Many years later, Tallulah went completely deaf. At first, I didn't realize anything was different. One day we were out in the yard and she had her back to me. I kept calling her and she didn't respond. Next, I tested her while she was sleeping but, regardless of what noise I made, she didn't wake up. Since Tallulah was only eleven months old when we adopted Nitro, she knew all the signs and made the transition without any problem. Recently she's become slightly more vocal than she was when she could hear, but that's normal for a senior dog who is losing its hearing.

Over the next few years, our Deaf Dogs Rock community continued to grow in leaps and bounds. We were working with more shelters, individuals, breeders, and partner rescues across the country. Donations to sponsor deaf dogs out of kill shelters and into the safe arms of our rescue partners were flowing in. We sponsor approximately 250 deaf dogs into rescue every year and, to date, over 4,000 deaf dogs have been adopted from the 'Available Deaf Dogs' section on our website.

As word spread about our mission to save one deaf dog at a time, numerous media outlets reached out to us to share our information with the public. Deaf Dogs Rock has been featured in over thirty publications and books and featured on several prime-time television shows. Every year since 2015, we've celebrated annual National Deaf Dogs Rock Day on the fourth Saturday of September.

In 2014, Deaf Dogs Rock became an official 501(c)(3) non-profit, which allowed us to continue to sponsor and transport deaf dogs into rescue and also continue to travel and attend Pet Expos and Shelters to educate the public about deaf dogs. We have won four social media awards for Best Cause Blog and Best Micro-Blog from the Blog Paws Social Media community.

None of our accomplishments would have been possible if not for the inspiration and magic of our sweet deaf boxer Nitro.

Chris and I always say—and believe—our deaf dogs have superpowers. One of Nitro's magical superpowers is that he hears with his heart. We take his superpower very seriously, so much so that when we launched our website, our official logo became: Deaf Dogs Hear With Their Hearts.

Nitro was sent to us by a higher power to give us purpose, to teach us how to be in the moment and be intentional, and to inspire us to help deaf dogs in need. Although Nitro started his life abandoned, cold, and starving by the river, we believe God had bigger plans for him. He is a hero and living proof that the magic of one deaf dog, like our sweet Nitro, can change the lives of thousands of deaf dogs around the world.

# Chapter 28

# MARYLAND

## *Melting Down in the Free State*

WE LEFT CHRIS AND CHRISTINA'S HOUSE AND DROVE BACK TO the Dixie Caverns campground, once again, arriving too late to tour the caverns, but it didn't matter. Robb and I were content to sit outside with Ava and talk about our day and our trip thus far. It had been a remarkable and fun journey, but now it was rapidly coming to an end.

This would be our final night of camping because from here we were heading to Virginia where I had made reservations at a hotel. Not just any hotel but the hotel in Virginia where Robb and I first met and adopted Ava. I thought it would be a poignant stop on our trip; a full-circle moment to celebrate how far we had come together as a family.

Our last stop, before heading home, would be at House with a Heart Sanctuary in Maryland.

We pulled out of Dixie Caverns campground on the first of July. The morning was perfect: brilliant sunshine and azure blue skies without a cloud in sight. It was also hazy, hot, and humid, which didn't matter because we were comfortable thanks to the motorhome's air conditioning. On the three hour-drive, we continued talking about our trip, all we had seen and done, and the people and dogs we had met. We were laughing and having fun, but the fun really began when, one hour later, the air conditioning in the motorhome started having issues and finally gave out.

With every passing mile and minute, as the heat and humidity continued to rise, so too did the temperature inside the motorhome. I dipped bandanas in a bowl of cold water and ice and put them around Ava's (and our) necks to try and keep us cool. It didn't help a lot or for very long. The only thing I could think of was getting to our hotel, so we could get out of our pressure cooker of a motorhome and into the air conditioning.

We arrived late in the afternoon. After checking in, Robb went back out to fiddle with the air conditioning. Despite being incredibly handy and resourceful, nothing he tried worked.

Overheated and exhausted, the three of us piled onto the bed, ordered room service, and cranked up the air conditioning. It was sheer heaven.

We were scheduled to arrive at House With A Heart Sanctuary the next day between 11:00 a.m. and 2:00 p.m. when volunteers would be there to help with the dogs. It was a one-hour drive from our hotel. We stayed in the cool comfort of our room as long as possible, finally leaving at 10:00 a.m., hoping we would arrive before the heat of the day fully descended. By the time we pulled into the driveway of House With a Heart, the motorhome was already uncomfortably hot.

I texted Sher to let her know we were there. When she came out, I explained our situation, telling her we might have to cut my visit short since Robb and Ava would be waiting for me in the sweltering motorhome.

"I'll be right back," Sher said, disappearing into the house. Several minutes later, she came out carrying an extension cord and a portable air conditioner. Fully confident Robb and Ava had everything they needed to relax in air-conditioned comfort, Sher and I proceeded into her house.

I try, as much as possible, to go into every interview with very little (if any) information about the person or place I am scheduled to meet. That allows me to have a fresh perspective and an open mind, without any preconceived ideas. That day, walking into Sher's house all I knew was that House with a Heart was a senior pet sanctuary. In truth, what had originally drawn me to them was their two taglines: Love Lives Here and Kindness Counts.

Later that day, leaving Sher's home and the Sanctuary, I realized those tag lines perfectly encapsulated every being I met that day. On a grander scale, they were also the perfect summation of every person, organization, and dog we'd met while on the road.

# Chapter 29
# ✦ SHER & HOUSE ✦
# WITH A HEART

*Love Lives Here*

OUR MOTTO AT HOUSE WITH A HEART IS LOVE LIVES HERE AND, believe me when I tell you, that is a very different experience than the one I had growing up.

I was born in 1946 and my upbringing was riddled with alcoholism, physical abuse, and dysfunction. When I was seven years old, I accidentally broke a lamp. Knowing I was going to be in big trouble, I jumped out the first-floor window, landing in a pile of dirt and mud. My plan was to run away but there was a fence in my way and, as much as I tried, I couldn't get over that darn fence. Finally, I gave up and sat down in the mud and cried. Instantly, our family dog, Lucky, came over and licked my face. In that moment, for the first time in my life, I knew what love felt like. Everything else that had been going on in my life wasn't love. What happened with Lucky was love.

Our two dogs, Lucky and Terry, were both mutts, super sweet, and everything good in my world. They became the lights of my life. Every day, I came home from school, opened the gate, and ran into the backyard to see them and play

One afternoon, I came home and the gate was standing open. Terrified the dogs had gotten out, I started running around yelling for Lucky and Terry. My stepmother came out the front door with a smirk on her face, and said, "They're not here. Your dad took them to a farm today. They'll be better off." With that, she turned and walked back in the house.

Shortly after that, my father and stepmother broke up and I think taking the dogs to the "farm" that day was one of the first things they did to begin separating their lives.

To this day, I remember how I felt in that moment. I was so happy and excited to come home and see my beloved pups and when I saw the open gate, my heart fell. When my stepmother came out and told me the dogs were gone, I felt as though my heart had shattered.

When you're the victim of an uncaring person, you have two choices: you can choose to be the same as them, or you can choose to be the complete opposite. I chose to be (and do) the opposite. I wanted everything and everyone to be love and light, and for people to care about, and be kind, to one another.

I developed a passion and compassion for those I felt were most at risk: children, animals, and senior citizens. I got involved with pet rescue, worked with deaf children, and volunteered with seniors in hospice and at a nursing home. While I loved all of it, my true passion was working with animals.

My husband, Joe, and I had done animal rescue for years and people often reached out to us about dogs they wanted to surrender. We brought many dogs and cats home with us. In the process of finding them a forever home, we fell in love with each of them. We worried and agonized over whether we were placing them in the right home and with the right family but, in the end, we always did.

Over time, I started getting more and more calls from people who had an older dog they wanted to give away. I listened to story after story of a dog someone had raised from a puppy. They told me how much they loved the dog but now it needed a lot of medical attention and woke them up at night. The conversations typically ended with them telling me they couldn't put up with the loss of sleep, or the messes, any longer, and asking me to find their pet another home.

One day, while out to lunch with friends, we started talking about what we would do if money was no object. When it was my turn, I declared without hesitation and with absolute conviction and confidence, "I would save senior dogs. I'd keep them with me and never place them with anyone, so I would know, with certainty, that they'd be safe, happy, and loved for the rest of their lives."

I left lunch that day and drove home thinking about our conversation, amazed at the words that had come out of my mouth, but the more

I thought about it, the more certain I was that was exactly what I wanted to do.

I walked in our house and over to Joe, and said. "We need to talk." I told him what I wanted to do, ending with, "OK, here's the deal. You're either in it with me or you're not."

Joe smiled. "I'm in it with you, Sher. Let's get busy!"

The next day, I made an appointment with our vet. When I ran the idea past her, she told me I was out of my mind. Reminding me how upset I got when our dogs passed, she didn't think I could handle it emotionally.

While I heard her concerns, even more, I believed it was my mission and purpose in life. And that's how and when it all began.

I immediately filed for our 501(c)(3). In 2006, House with a Heart (HWAH) opened its doors and hearts to senior and special needs dogs. The deal Joe and I made at the start was that we would never have more than ten dogs in the house at any one time. When one dog passed, we would allow another one to come.

Joe passed in 2008. In the two years we ran HWAH together, we discovered an endless supply of people who wanted to give up their senior dogs. After Joe passed, I missed him so much, but caring for the HWAH dogs helped me through my grief.

It became increasingly difficult for me to turn dogs away. By 2009, I had thirty dogs at HWAH. I didn't have any volunteers, was doing it all by myself, and was beginning to feel overwhelmed.

A kind and caring lady heard about HWAH and called to volunteer. I am a very private person. Since she was only one person, I let her come. She became a close and trusted friend and constantly encouraged me to get other volunteers. I knew it made sense but the thought of constantly having other people in my home was very uncomfortable for me. Then, one night I was downstairs, exhausted, scrubbing and cleaning at 1:00 a.m., and realized she was right. I not only needed help, but also had to think of what was best for the dogs.

At the same time, we were featured on a local television station. As people began to reach out, our volunteer family began to grow. In addition to helping with the dogs, the volunteers created a web page. Step by step, things continued to grow and then I got a call from *The Today Show* asking if I would consider doing a segment.

Jill Rappaport came from New York City to visit and film a piece about our Sanctuary. After the segment aired, we were blessed with more volunteers and donations. We began doing short-term boarding for owners as a way to earn funds to pay for the never-ending medical care our dogs (I call them "our residents.") needed.

Today, we have almost fifty volunteers and need to space out the schedule to give every volunteer a shift. Over the years, we've developed procedures and ways of doing things that work for everyone – especially the dogs. I get up at 6:00 a.m. every morning to prepare breakfast for the dogs and administer whatever medications are needed. That gives me a few quiet hours alone with them before volunteers arrive. Volunteers are here from 11:00 a.m. to 2:00 p.m. every day. At 2:00 p.m., we close for a few hours of quiet. I'm on my own in the evenings and on Sundays, but gratefully our Resident Care Coordinator gives me a break and prepares the morning or evening meals several times a week.

If I'm ever sick (which thankfully has not been very often) volunteers are trained to step in and help. It's comforting to know there are wonderful people who have my—and the dogs'—back.

Over the years, a lot of dogs have found their way to HWAH and it's always fascinating when a dog picks their favorite person. Sometimes it's confusing to understand why they pick the person they do, but that's not for me to figure out—that's strictly between the dog and the person. Our dogs receive 24/7 care and are never left alone. The rule is if a volunteer can give a dog a better experience than they're getting here at HWAH, the dog is welcome to go home with them as a Forever Foster.

Monroe was one of those dogs. He was a special needs pup who came to the Sanctuary when he was only six months old. He was blind, had dementia, and walking on the bare floor made his feet bleed so we kept his feet covered with a special wrap the veterinarian gave us. Volunteers snuggled him in a blanket and he'd lie quietly in their arms and soak up all the love.

Feeding Monroe was a challenge. He wouldn't open his mouth yet constantly cried out from hunger. The neurologist determined at some point he'd been asphyxiated long enough to allow some of his brain cells to die. The result was that his brain no longer told his mouth to open so we began mashing up his food and feeding him with a syringe. We gave him water the same way. Since he was so young, there was a chance his brain cells would regenerate, and that became our prayer and hope.

For several weeks, we loved and cared for Monroe and continued giving him food and water with the syringe. One day, I told our vet, Dr. Neville, that I believed Monroe was getting better. She checked him and said I was wrong. Again, I told her I believed he was starting to see things and, again, she told me I was wrong. A week later, she admitted that maybe, just maybe, I was right. Monroe's brain had begun to create new pathways and he *was* getting better.

A few years ago, Monroe bonded with one of our volunteers, Karen. The love was mutual so Karen agreed to become Monroe's Forever Foster Mom. Monroe is now eight years old and living a wonderful life with Karen and Penelope, his doggie sister.

Piper is another heart dog who came to us, just like Monroe, as a special needs case when she was only six months old. The breeder told me she was only six pounds and not thriving. His veterinarian suggested she be euthanized, but he couldn't make that decision so he asked if we would take Piper for hospice care and let her go when she was no longer comfortable.

The day Piper arrived, she was so small and lethargic we didn't think we'd have her with us for very long. She had giardia-like symptoms and a specialist diagnosed a congenital liver problem. It was likely she would only live a few months. However, after extensive medical treatment, Piper began to improve.

As the weeks passed, Piper and Monroe bonded. Monroe would get a toy out of the toy box, bring it over to Piper, and they would play with it together. The first time Piper went to the toy box on her own and pulled out a toy, I cried.

One afternoon, Piper, Monroe, and one of our senior pups, Sally, were all playing together in the kitchen. For some reason, at one point Piper felt she was being left out and suddenly started beagle howling. We were all so excited that we started crying and sending out emails telling everyone that Piper was barking like a beagle. Woohoo! Her bark was music to our ears.

Piper, like Monroe, became another one of our Miracle Dogs. Those

Piper (left) and Monroe waiting for popcorn

two pups came here to die. Instead, they became best friends and blossomed together.

We've had so many special needs and seriously senior dogs over the years and so many remarkable stories that demonstrate the true healing properties and power of love and caring.

It is now 2023 and seventeen years have flown by. I am older and, as you get older, you start to think about taking care of the ones you will leave behind. I have everything taken care of in terms of life insurance, a Trust, and identifying people who will take care of each dog when I am no longer able.

I want to know that even when I'm gone our Mission of "Love Lives Here" and our passion for saving special needs and senior pets will continue. To ensure that happens, we have set up the House with a Heart K9 and Kitty Medical Miracle Fund which focuses on assisting other rescues and encouraging them to pull special needs and senior dogs and cats from shelters.

Since rescues generally don't want to take senior dogs because they are harder to adopt, we partner with approved rescues and offer them grants to help with medical bills. We also promote senior and special needs pets for adoption on our website and our Social Media volunteer promotes the pets on our social media platforms. With this program in place, I am confident the House with a Heart heartbeat will continue long after mine has stopped.

This truly has been *the best life ever*. All of the dogs who have come through HWAH have saved me, as much as I and the HWAH Team have saved them. They've shown me in unimaginable and unending ways that Love Lives Here and Kindness Counts!

# Chapter 30
## ✦ PENNSYLVANIA ✦
### Crossing the Border
### into the Keystone State

BY THE TIME WE PULLED OUT OF THE DRIVEWAY AT HOUSE WITH A Heart Sanctuary, the heat of the day had really set in. The two hand-crank windows on either side of the cab in the motorhome didn't allow for a lot of cross-ventilation. Whatever air movement did occur was mostly hot and humid. I sat in the passenger seat, promising myself I would remain calm and optimistic and focus on the fact that we were only three hours from home—until we pulled onto the Interstate and traffic came to a grinding halt. For five hours, we sat in the sweltering heat, in bumper-to-bumper July 4th weekend traffic.

Arriving home mentally and physically overheated, and drenched in sweat, was not the auspicious ending I had envisioned for our trip. I was overjoyed to see my sons, to take a shower, hang out in the air conditioning, and sleep in my own bed. It had been a wonderful and magical trip. But, for me, there's "no place like home."

Knowing the motorhome—as well as Robb, Ava, and I—needed and deserved a break from life on the road, I decided to focus the remainder of my interviews and visits in places that were an easy, short, drive from my home: Pennsylvania, New York, and New Jersey.

I began by heading across the border from New Jersey into Pennsylvania to talk with Edna. She had shared her story in *Magical Dogs 2: Connecting the Dots, Connecting the Dogs* but was now on a very different journey with a dog and I wanted to know more. Because of Edna, my path crossed with Sharon and Rebecca who each had their own incredible dogs and stories. But first, let's begin with Edna and Franklin.

# Chapter 31

# EDNA & FRANKLIN

*Good Morning, Franklin*

IT ALL STARTED IN 2017 WHEN I RECEIVED A TEXT MESSAGE AND pictures of an emaciated, defeated pit bull. My immediate response was: "Who is he and where is he?"

Through subsequent texts, I learned that while doing a sweep for stolen vehicles in Reading, Pennsylvania, the police ran the license plate on a vehicle parked in front of a row house. The vehicle came up as stolen. The officers walked up and knocked on the front door of the house, but no one answered. Next, they checked the property, but the only signs of life were the flies buzzing in the window.

Thinking someone might have died inside the home, they decided to do a welfare check and gained access. Entering, they called out, but, again, there was no answer. As they continued searching, they found the only occupants in the home: a female pit bull confined to the upstairs bathroom and a younger male pit bull in the basement.

The officers immediately contacted a shelter. Two shelter employees arrived and immediately determined both dogs were in critical, and possibly life-threatening, condition and needed to be transported to the nearby emergency veterinary hospital.

The female dog in the upstairs bathroom was leashed and slowly walked down the stairs but the male dog in the basement was skin and bones and too weak to walk so he was carried out.

Once at the emergency vet hospital, both dogs were immediately started on IV fluids. The vet tech, one of the first people to touch them other than the police or shelter employee, decided they needed names so the female was named Sally and the male Franklin (perhaps because he was found on Franklin Street).

Over the next few days, despite the extraordinary care and efforts of the staff at the emergency vet hospital, Sally's body continued to shut down and, several days later, she passed.

Franklin, on the other hand, had started a slow road to recovery. Four days later, he was released into the hands of the shelter, which is when the shelter manager sent me the text and photos. As soon as I asked for more information, she began to provide it.

"We scanned him for a microchip and he has one," she told me. "He's been adopted not once, but twice—the first time when he was a puppy. However, since the adopters' landlord didn't allow pets, they ended up bringing him to another shelter."

"Both dogs were then adopted by the same woman but at different times. Sally was adopted first and, we believe, was used for breeding. Franklin was adopted at a Clear the Shelter event, possibly to be re-sold, or for fighting. At the time, he was healthy and weighed sixty pounds. He's now twenty-two pounds, incredibly emaciated, and too weak to walk."

She ended her text by asking three words that would change my, and Franklin's, life: "Can you help?"

I typically take in senior dogs who are on hospice or aging. I've had dogs with kidney failure, cancer, geriatric issues, arthritis, and mobility limitations. I typically take in golden retrievers but I've also adopted pit bulls, including a pit bull puppy who had to have a leg amputated when he was only four months old.

I knew this dog was going to need time, a safe place, and a lot of love. I already had three goldens and two pit bulls at home. Did I have it in me? Did I have the time? Could I do it?

The person who sent me the text was someone I knew and respected. In turn, I knew she trusted me with the most fragile and needy so, looking down at my phone, I texted her back: "Yes, I can help."

I set up a crate with a new, clean bed in my kitchen and made sure all three gates in my house were secure. I brought out every extra gate I had and set them up, too. After researching the impact starvation and emaciation has on a dog, I made a list for the grocery store. I hung a sign over his crate that read, "Welcome, Franklin" and, before heading to the grocery store, prayed: "Please give me a strong heart and the ability to turn his life around."

The shelter was an hour drive from my home. On my way, I thought through every possible scenario and routine in my mind from playing, sleeping, feeding, pottying, to slow introductions between Franklin and the rest of my dogs.

I arrived at the shelter, parked my car, and grabbed a slip lead, a bag of treats, and my phone. After double checking to make sure the back of my car would be warm and comfortable, I took a deep breath and walked in. The Shelter Manager was walking down the hall toward me—and then I saw Franklin. My eyes instantly filled with tears as I knelt down on the floor. Franklin slowly walked over and put his head against my chest. He was so fragile that I was almost afraid to touch him—almost— but when I gently let my fingers touch his velvet-like fur, he trembled. I quietly whispered in his ear, "I promise to give you the best I have to give."

Together we walked out to my car and, knowing he was still too weak to climb in on his own, I picked him up and my heart broke. My vacuum cleaner and his crate back at my house weighed more than he did. However, I left that day with an advantage many rescuers don't have: knowledge about his past. Thanks to the Executive Director of the shelter, who was also a Humane Law Enforcement Officer, I had a documented past and knew a good deal of what Franklin had already been through.

Since a large part of that past included an ongoing investigation into a possible animal cruelty case, Franklin was considered evidence. I looked at him, relaxed and sleeping in my car, and decided I was going to post about him every day on Facebook. That would give people an opportunity to meet Franklin and follow his progress but would also help me keep track of everything in the event I ever had to testify in the court case. And so began the posts: "Good Morning, Franklin."

Back home, three Goldens and two pit bulls were waiting for us. I believe dogs heal each other and I have been honored to watch their incredible ability to do so on numerous occasions. Still, I always keep the 3-3-3 Rule in mind when bringing a new dog into my home. The rule, in short, says it generally takes three days for a dog to begin to decompress, three weeks for them to begin to settle in, and three months for them to build trust and begin to bond with you. While it is just a guideline, and every dog is different and unique, it's still a good rule to keep in mind. With Franklin, I knew it was probably going to take extra time and patience because he was so thin, frail, and had been through so much.

Franklin walked into my house and looked around with wide, curious eyes. My other dogs were at the gate, equally curious, but no one was barking. There were a lot of happy wagging tails. But, again, I wanted to take our time and do slow introductions. At the shelter, to allow him time and space to physically recover, Franklin had stayed in the Shelter Manager's office. While he appeared curious about the other animals and was never reactive in any way, I still didn't know how he would be around other dogs.

To ensure slow introductions, I gave Franklin the run of my kitchen since it was double-gated off from the rest of the house and my other dogs. The first night, as Franklin and I settled down on the kitchen floor to sleep next to one another, he looked at me and I reached out to hold him. As I held him, he sighed and relaxed, and I promised him we would give it our all and hope for the best. I took his picture for our first Facebook post: "Everybody roots for the underdog." Still holding him, we went to sleep.

As expected, everything with Franklin took extra time and extreme patience. He was more than forty pounds underweight, and while having him put on weight was important, I knew it needed to be done in a way his body could handle so I hand-fed him small meals multiple times throughout the day. I did that for a month before moving on to three meals a day.

Every night, I slept on the kitchen floor with him. While holding him, I always promised we would give it our all and hope for the best. And I continued to capture everything on Facebook.

As Franklin began to put on weight and gain back some strength, I decided to begin initial introductions starting with the most curious of my dogs: my two pit bulls, Summit and Woody. I put a chair next to the gate in the kitchen, sat down, and asked Summit and Woody to come and sit. They did and I rewarded them with treats. Franklin came over and I rewarded him, too. Any time they looked at Franklin (or Franklin looked at them), I gave everyone a treat. If they were calm, they got a treat. Next, I had them lay together on opposite sides of the gate so they could see and smell one another—and again I gave them treats. Everyone was getting treats at the same time.

I did that for about two weeks before deciding to introduce Franklin to one of my Golden Girls, Rosita. Knowing Rosita was sassy and always defended herself if needed, I started taking her and Franklin out together to go to the bathroom. They did fine.

Seeing how well he was doing with Rosita, and knowing he had put on even more weight, I closed the living room off with double gates and put Franklin and Rosita together. While they didn't try to play or snuggle, they calmly co-existed which was perfect.

Next, I started letting Franklin go out with all my Golden Girls: Magellan, Hope, and Rosita. I had him on a leash at first. Again, he was fine. We were now closing in on a month together and he was still sleeping in the kitchen at night and not really interacting with the other dogs.

Then one day all that changed.

I work nights and came home one morning absolutely exhausted. Without thinking, I let all the dogs out together. When I realized what I'd done I panicked for a brief moment then looked around. They were all fine. They were sniffing one another, but they were all calm. I laughed, shook my head, and thought, "Well, that worked out really well."

I still wasn't completely comfortable having them all together in a confined space inside the house but, a couple days later, I eased that restriction too. At last, they were all in the house together.

All in all, it took about thirty days. I may have been an overprotective and overly-cautious Mama Bear, but I wanted to make sure it went smoothly. I didn't need Franklin going through any additional stress or trauma in his life and I believe the prep work we did together up until that point made it seem normal when they were all together.

In the beginning it was always Franklin and Woody. I would hear a ruckus and go in and Franklin and Woody would be playing and Franklin would be sucking on Woody's ear. The two of them still play together the most, although the others get involved now, too. They all adore one another.

Franklin and Summit are the most accepting of other dogs I bring into our home. Woody, on the other hand, doesn't react, but his eyes get really big. If he could talk, I think he'd say, "What the heck! Another one? You brought *another* dog home?!"

After the local news station and newspaper did a story about Franklin, two little girls in the area were inspired to have a lemonade stand to benefit the shelter. Even though they didn't know Franklin, they wanted to help and ended up raising $537 in a single day.

I'd been taking pictures and posting each step of our journey on Facebook. Every morning we began our day with a "Good Morning, Franklin" post. Early posts were photos or videos showing Franklin's daily progress, weight gain, or his first time exploring, or doing zoomies, in my yard. Over time, you could see the physical changes taking place as he continued to gain weight and grow stronger—and you could see his confidence growing.

Social media has given us a virtual world where we can get to know people or animals without ever meeting them in person. And that's what started happening with our "Good Morning, Franklin" posts. After a few weeks, I started posting more colorful, funny photos and updates and people really responded. I continued doing that and people kept commenting about how much they looked forward to our posts and how much the posts helped if they were having a rough day or just needed a good laugh. If I was late posting in the morning, people messaged me to make sure everything was okay with Franklin.

Seeing people's reactions to our more creative and entertaining posts, I decided to continue doing them. On holidays, I decorated, and Franklin wore a variety of hats, bandanas, outfits, and sunglasses to celebrate. He dressed up as a soldier, a shark, a butterfly, and the Gorton fisherman (complete with rain hat and raincoat). In one post, he balanced a dollar bill on his forehead. He also talked a lot about one of his favorite people: the Chewy delivery person.

It also helped that Franklin has one outstanding physical feature: his left ear. It's large and stands up—even when he's sleeping. On occasion, he turns it like a radar dish. His ear became a prominent feature of many posts and, again, everybody loved them.

Not all of our posts are funny. From time to time, Franklin and I write posts to educate people about topics of concern relating to animals or dogs. A perfect example is when the woman who adopted Franklin, his abuser, claimed in court that the reason he was locked in her basement was because he was extremely aggressive. She said she threw food down to him using his "aggression" as an excuse to starve him. I posted a video of me hand-feeding Franklin who gently took food from my hand, and wrote, "Oh yeah, he's so vicious."

She had locked Franklin and Sally up in the house and abandoned the property—and them. Although they were able to locate her through Franklin's microchip and address records, honestly, had it not been for the police, both dogs would have starved to death.

The woman was ultimately found guilty of two counts of cruelty to an animal (one count for each dog), was fined $1,500 per dog, and sentenced to two years' probation.

Her sentencing was in July. A month later, in August, Pennsylvania passed Act 10 (also known as Libre's Law), a comprehensive and sterner law regarding animal abuse.

Libre was an eight-week-old Boston Terrier puppy that had been rescued from a breeder in Lancaster, Pennsylvania where he'd been left outside and was suffering from multiple medical issues. Fortunately, the person who found Libre nursed him back to health, but not before his story made headlines around the world in large part because the person responsible for Libre's neglect had only received a fine by the court.

Prior to Libre's Law, if a veterinarian saw an animal and suspected animal cruelty, they weren't required to contact the police. Social workers who did home visits and suspected possible animal abuse weren't permitted to report it. That all changed with Libre's Law, so there are now additional protections in place for animals.

Libre's Law also upgraded the charges that could be filed against an individual for animal neglect and cruelty. If Libre's Law had been in effect when Franklin's abuser went to court and was sentenced, the animal cruelty charges against her would have been upgraded from a misdemeanor to a felony and her sentence would have involved time in prison.

Abuse often starts with animals but oftentimes, if not addressed, will ultimately progress to abuse of humans and that is what happened with Franklin's abuser. She has since been involved in a domestic violence situation. She had four pages of various charges prior to what happened

with Franklin and she con-
tinues to be brought up on
different charges.

I am generally an intro-
vert. I don't socialize very
much and generally eat
90% of my meals at home
alone with my dogs. I'm
content living with my dogs
but, as anyone who does
hospice fostering knows,
you often end up carrying a
lot of grief. Even though
you know from the start
you're going to face loss,
sometimes the losses
mount up and become
overwhelming. When that
happens, it's necessary to

Good morning, Franklin

take a break for your own mental, emotional, and physical health. I don't
always take that break but I'm also no stranger to compassion fatigue. I
know the signs to watch for, so I try to be mindful if I think I've gone too
far.

With every dog, you learn a lesson. You grow deeper compassion,
deeper convictions, and you gain a better sense of purpose. With
Franklin, it's been a whole new level of lessons. Honestly, you can't go
through an experience with an innocent soul like Franklin without being
changed.

I think back to that day at the shelter, meeting him, touching him for
the first time, and feeling him tremble. Have you ever held something so
fragile that you can feel their trust? Every night as I laid next to him on
the floor and held him, I could feel that Franklin trusted me with his life.
Even today when I look at him lying on the couch sucking on his pillow,
I get a feeling that's hard to describe. It's trust, unbelievable love, and a
connection so strong that it defies words. I kiss him a lot and whisper,
"I'm not allowed to play favorites."

Every time I look into Franklin's eyes, all I see is love. I think he adores me as much as I adore him. If I'm confused, he brings my focus back. He calms me down when I'm angry. If I'm feeling lost, he helps me re-center myself. For me, Franklin is, in a word, magic.

# Chapter 32

# SHARON & BEARLY

*Healed by the Love of a Dog*

MY LIFE HAD BEEN PLAYING OUT LIKE A BAD COUNTRY WESTERN song for a number of years. As 2012 was slowly coming to an end, everything intensified.

My beloved husband of thirty-three years, Ray, passed away in early October after a heroic five-year battle with cancer. Three weeks before, my loyal and loving rescue dog, Big Buddy, had crossed the Rainbow Bridge. On top of that, I was having my own health issues.

I suffer from a genetic liver disease called hemochromatosis wherein the liver produces too much iron, which is then absorbed by the bone. The result of this absorption is that the bones become extremely fragile, thus creating another condition called spondylolisthesis.

While Ray was home on hospice care, I had to lift and turn him repeatedly and ended up with a severely broken cervical spine, three vertebrae fractures, and two dislocations. I was scheduled for major spinal surgery in early November 2012, followed by physical rehabilitation.

Alone and heartbroken, a deep sadness overcame me and I had one wish: to get healthy enough to adopt a dog. I desperately missed the love and companionship of a dog. My life felt incomplete and I wanted to share my home and heart once again with a special dog, perhaps a dog that needed me as much, or more, than I needed them.

By February, my surgery and rehabilitation behind me, I began searching online for a dog. I contacted Delaware Valley Golden Retriever Rescue (DVGRR) then sat back and anxiously waited.

DVGRR reached back out and said they had five potential matches for me. I couldn't believe my luck! On a brisk February morning, nervous and apprehensive, I drove to DVGRR to meet with Dennis, their Adoption Manager. I knew this meeting, and day, could change the course of my life and that, perhaps, my wish would come true.

When I arrived, Dennis and I sat down to discuss my options. We were in a room filled with dogs who had already been adopted and were just waiting to be picked up. As we talked, several dogs briefly approached me but didn't pay a lot of attention to me. Knowing they were already adopted, I tried not to pay too much attention to them either. However, one dog, a faintly white-faced golden retriever, kept pushing her way toward me. She kept staring at me, her tail constantly wagging. Again, I tried not to make eye contact or pay too much attention to her since I didn't want to get attached to a dog who already had a home. Then, she gently placed her head in my lap and looked up at me with the most incredible soulful brown eyes. I had no choice: I looked into her eyes and my heart melted. It felt as though I could see and feel her soul.

"Oh, Dennis," I quietly uttered, "I wish she was available."

Dennis grabbed her file and, after flipping through a few pages, said, "Actually, she *is* available, but I'm not sure she's exactly what you're looking for, Sharon. Her name is Bear and she's ten-and-a-half years old, a senior, and recently arrived from an SPCA in Oklahoma where she was relinquished by the only family she had ever known."

I looked down at Bear's head in my lap, looked up at Dennis, and said, without a moment's hesitation, "She's mine. I want her."

Within fifteen minutes we completed the paperwork. Later, as we walked together to my car, Bear looked up at me. My first thought was, "My wish just came true. I have another dog to love."

Bear jumped into the backseat, laid down, and slept the entire one-hour ride home. When we arrived, I brought Bear in and showed her around, then got busy putting her things away. Fifteen minutes later, realizing she had left my side and, not seeing her anywhere, I began to search the house. I finally found her curled up on a bed, sleeping peacefully, her paws wrapped around a stuffed golden retriever she had unearthed somewhere.

I was overcome with emotion because the bed Bear had chosen to fall asleep on was my husband Ray's bed. In that moment I knew, with absolute certainty, it was a sign from Ray that he had sent an angel named Bear to me.

I laid down next to her and began to gently stroke her soft golden fur. As she continued to sleep, I kissed her face, tears rolling down my cheeks onto her. I thanked Ray for sending Bear to me—and thanked Bear for finding and choosing me. Filled with a sense of peace I hadn't had for a very long time, I laid my head down next to Bear and fell asleep.

For the next few days, I gave Bear time and space to decompress from all she'd been through. She ate and explored our backyard a little, but for the most part she slept, thus earning her the nickname "Bearly"—as in, barely awake.

When family and friends stopped by to meet Bearly, for the most part, she never got up to meet or greet them. Instead, she preferred to continue sleeping in Ray's bed. She welcomed pets but even that happened in Ray's bedroom which had become her safe place. More than once, people asked, "Are you sure you did the right thing adopting such an old dog?"

My answer was always the same, "Absolutely!" because I knew she had chosen me and Ray had sent her to me.

However, over time, I, too, began to get concerned. Bearly continued to retreat into Ray's bedroom and seemed depressed at times. Finally, one afternoon, while she slept nearby, I pulled out the adoption book DVGRR had given me. It contained a lot of background information on her, including information DVGRR had obtained from the SPCA in Oklahoma where Bear originally came from. Opening it, I began to read.

Bear had come from a loving home with three children. Every night she slept with the thirteen-year-old son and, during the day, she was given the freedom to wander around their fenced-in yard while the family was at work and school. After ten years together, the family got a new puppy. After deciding they no longer wanted Bear because of her age, they surrendered her to the SPCA. When DVGRR agreed to take her, Bear was transported via a tag team rescue from Oklahoma to Pennsylvania, ultimately arriving at DVGRR on February 1, 2013.

Closing the book, I looked down at Bearly. My heart broke for this old girl who had been through so much both physically and emotionally. I was even more determined to make the rest of her life the best of her life.

On our first few walks together, Bearly struggled. She walked with a limp and stopped frequently. Her hind quarters seemed weak but a visit to my vet confirmed that, gratefully, there were no structural or muscular issues: she was simply overweight. I immediately changed her diet to pumpkin, green beans, weight management food, and baby carrots. She loved the food and slowly, the weight started to come off.

We awoke on our fourth day together to gently falling snow. Even though it was early morning and bitterly cold, we set out on our first adventure to the rural park near our home. Bearly was still overweight and unsure of herself, but together we explored and walked two miles—and she loved it! She rolled in the high grass, stalked a groundhog, and stopped to watch the birds. I gave her constant reassurance and called her by name and, by the end of our walk, I could see her body and soul start to relax.

From that day forward, regardless of the weather, our day began with a 6:30 a.m. walk. Along the way, we stopped to observe and absorb the natural beauty of the world around us, watched the sunrise together. Day-by-day, our bond grew stronger.

Several weeks later, Bearly and I woke up to a winter wonderland. The park was blanketed in snow, the white crystals glistening against the backdrop of sunshine and a deep blue sky. Bearly was so excited and kept pulling on the leash yearning to run free. I hesitantly unleashed her and off she scampered through the blanket of snow. Every 100 feet or so she ran back to me for assurance, then turned and ran ahead of me again. I was bursting with joy and smiling ear to ear, not only at the beauty of mother nature, but also seeing Bearly, my new best friend and constant companion, in her glory.

We were having so much fun that, despite the snow (and without realizing it), we spent two hours at the park. After returning home, we cuddled together in front of the fireplace. Bearly placed her head on my lap, just like she had done the day we met at DVGRR. But this was the first time she had done it since I brought her home. For the first time in a long time, my entire being—mind, body, and soul—relaxed. Tears of contentment and love streamed down my cheeks. Thanks to Bearly, happiness had quietly crept back into my heart and life.

That night, for the first time since she came home with me, instead of retreating to Ray's room, Bearly followed me into my bedroom and stood wagging her tail and pawing at the side of my bed. I patted the bed and Bearly placed her front paws up on the side of the mattress. I gently lifted her onto my bed. Together, we slipped under the covers, our heads resting together. I stroked her soft fur and kissed her precious face as we both drifted off to sleep. Neither of us moved an inch all night. It was probably the best night's sleep either of us had in a long time.

Bearly

As winter turned to spring, Bearly and I continued our daily walks and adventures at the park while watching the grass turn a vibrant green, stunning wildflowers bloom, and the wildlife become more active and abundant. As I stopped to pick flowers, Bearly used her God-given retriever instincts to stalk the birds which had come to life and were merrily singing all around us. With spring also came the rain and many mornings we returned home wet and muddy, but happy and grateful for our time together.

In late spring, Bearly and I began to see groups of pre-school children at the park. Although they were at a distance, they still called out to Bearly. As soon as she heard them, her tail started wagging. I knew she wanted to meet them so several days later we walked toward them. After getting permission from their teacher, I invited the children to meet her. Bearly sat calmly as the children lovingly began to pet her. I could tell from her expression and demeanor that she was delighted to be with them. I couldn't help but wonder if she missed the children she had lived with for over ten years and if, in some way, these children were helping to fill that void. Now, along with our daily walks, spending time with the preschoolers became a part of our daily ritual.

One morning, while watching her with the children, a light went off in my head. Everywhere we went, people loved Bearly and she, in turn, loved them. Realizing how special Bearly truly was, I decided it was time we had a talk. "Bearly," I began. "You have a gift and I think we need to share that gift with others. What do you think?"

She looked up at me, happy, her tail wagging.

Now that I had her approval, as soon as we arrived home, I reached out to Bright & Beautiful Therapy Dogs. Three weeks later, Bearly passed the tests for her Canine Good Citizen and Therapy Dog certification. She could now spread her love and magic to others.

We began going to the nearby school, visiting the children we had crossed paths with on our daily walks. We read books to them and Bearly often dressed up as one of the characters. She also dressed up for holidays.

From the school, we spread our wings and began reading to children every week at our local public library. Bearly became a local celebrity among the parents, but even more with the children.

Since Bearly was a senior we didn't want to ignore the elderly human population, so we began visiting a local assisted living facility. She easily and effortlessly navigated her way around walkers and wheelchairs and made bedside visits. We took photos of Bearly with the residents and, after having them framed, gave them to the residents along with Bearly's pawprint.

Bearly became an ambassador at DVGRR-sponsored events to advocate for other dogs and assist in getting them adopted. Regardless of how much we did, Bearly could never get enough. She was social; she was loving; she was special. Bearly, who was once a shut-down, depressed old dog was coming to—and enjoying—life.

Between our long daily walks and all the social interaction and stimulation, Bearly was thriving. It was glorious to see my girl living the life she deserved. In turn, my life was complete and my heart was overflowing with joy.

By the time summer arrived, Bearly's weight was down nearly fifteen pounds. No longer limping or struggling on our walks, we visited new parks and set out on new adventures. One morning, I walked Bearly down to the creek and she stood there, looking up at me, unsure what to do. I took a step into the water, "It's okay, Bearly," I assured her. "Let's go."

She immediately followed me into the creek and began prancing in the cool running stream, biting at the water, and pawing at the fish. She loved it so much, and since the creek ran parallel to the footpath, we continued walking in it for over two miles. It was a refreshing, fun treat for both of us.

Our summer adventures got even more exciting with the introduction of early morning rides on my brother Joe's pontoon boat. It was incredible to see Bearly standing majestically at the bow, nose sniffing, and tail wagging on high alert for turtles, herons, fish, or even an occasional eagle soaring overhead.

Afterwards, we went for a swim. Bearly retrieved sticks and swam out to my raft. I don't recall ever feeling more at peace, loved, and content as I did in those moments when we were together in the cool water, the sun glistening off Bearly's golden coat. This extraordinary girl had not only changed my life, but my entire being.

My days and life were now centered around Bearly's enjoyment and contentment. Her happiness was my happiness. Every morning after our walk, we sat on the couch, her head in my lap, and I asked her "What are we going to do today, Bearly?"

Her ears would perk up, her tail would start wagging, and her dazzling brown eyes lovingly gazed into mine. In those moments, I knew she was telling me she didn't care what we did as long as we did it together—and it was the same for me.

Bearly was my heart, my soul, and my life. I had always heard people talk about their heart dog . . . their soul dog . . . but I had never experienced it until Bearly came into my life. From Bearly I learned that no matter what is going on in your life, no matter how sad or heartbroken you are, the love and companionship of a soul dog can heal everything.

# Chapter 33

# REBECCA & SUMMER

*Bringing Comfort to Those in Need*

IN THE SUMMER OF 2005, I WAS IN A REALLY GOOD PLACE. MY first job after graduation was in my chosen career and I had just bought my first house. It was beautiful and it was mine. Only one thing was missing: a dog.

My entire life, other than when I was in college, there had been a dog by my side. Now, for the first time, I would be living alone without family, roommates, or a dog so, after moving into my home, I began my search for a canine roommate.

Although I had grown up with Labrador retrievers, I always loved golden retrievers. I kept going back and forth, undecided between the two, until the answer came to me in a most unexpected way.

My sister treated me to a massage for my birthday. At the end of the massage, the therapist asked if I was familiar with Reiki. At the time, I didn't know anything about it. She explained it was an energy healing technique and that sometimes, while doing it, she got information or messages.

"During your massage I kept sensing something and would love your permission to do some Reiki and see if any messages come forward."

Things like that intrigue me, so I agreed and she began. Almost immediately, she said, "I keep getting an image of an older person, a woman, with a blonde dog. Does that mean anything?"

At the time my grandmother was living with my parents, so I knew she was the older person. As for the blonde dog, I knew what that meant as well. I knew it was a sign. On the car ride home, I looked at my sister and announced, "I'm getting a golden retriever."

On a rainy, hot, humid July morning, several weeks after moving into my home, a friend and I got in my car and drove to a local farm. Since I live in Lancaster County, the East Coast capital of puppy mills, I told my friend to be mindful and look for any signs that the farm was a puppy mill. Gratefully, it wasn't.

As we got out of the car and began walking toward the barn, the farmer let the puppies out and they came running toward us. One puppy ran directly to me, sat down in front of my feet, and looked up with the most incredible soulful eyes. I knew immediately she was my dog. I brought her home, gave her a bath, and from that moment on it was the two of us starting life together—but first she needed a name.

Since I'm not a fan of human names for a dog and prefer something different, something unique, for weeks I struggled with choosing a name for her. Her father's name was Goldie, her mother was Sunny, and she had been born on June 3 but none of that struck a chord with me. Then one night, while watching *The OC* on television, there was a character named Summer. I liked the name so, from that moment on, she was known as Summer Gold Sunrise—Summer, for short.

Years before getting Summer, in the weeks following the 9/11 attacks, I felt both hopeless and helpless. Beyond donating blood and money, I didn't know what else I could do to help. When I saw people working with their dogs at the World Trade Center, I immediately thought: "When I get my next dog, I want to do something with my dog to help people."

Even though Summer was only a few months old, those memories were still fresh in my mind so I started taking her to work with me. I had a Master's Degree in clinical psychology and was working as a therapist at a day treatment for at-risk youth. While I'm not sure I had a clue what I was doing, Summer knew exactly what to do. Very early on, Summer showed me she was extremely instinctual and had an amazing ability to read people and know exactly what they needed. And the kids loved her.

After completing obedience classes, we moved on to therapy dog training. Summer loved going to class every week. She loved working, training, going to work with me, and connecting with people. She never

Summer

wanted to miss out on anything and, even though we were constantly on the go, she loved it.

Shortly after turning one, Summer passed her therapy dog certification and we immediately began going to nursing homes, reading programs, and schools. She loved it all—and everyone loved her.

We visited various nursing homes and, once a month, we visited a nursing home where a dear sweet couple lived. Both the husband and wife loved Summer, but the husband had a special attachment to her. Summer knew where their room was and would sit quietly at their door and wait for the husband to let us in.

Since there were two of them living in the apartment, they had a larger room with a separate sitting room. For years, that's where we sat and visited. When the husband's health started to decline and he was no longer able to get out of bed, we began spending time with him in his bedroom.

After the husband passed, the wife moved into a smaller, single room. The first time we visited after she moved, Summer went to their old room and sat outside waiting patiently for him to let her in. It ripped my soul. When I finally got her to move away from their door and took her to the wife's new room, Summer immediately connected with the wife, knowing instinctively that the wife was now her responsibility.

We usually visited nursing homes as a group. One day, while waiting for the rest of our group, a woman walked over to Summer and me. As I began to introduce Summer to her, she smiled, interrupted me, saying, "Oh, I know all about Summer! My father talks about her all the time."

In that moment, I realized how many times in life we may think we aren't doing much for someone when, in reality, what we're doing means everything to them. And it wasn't me; it was Summer. I was the lucky person to be on the other end of the leash who got to watch it all happen.

For years, we had been doing therapy work with my friend, Chris, and her dog, Beamer. In 2010, Chris approached me. "I found this organization," she began, "and we're doing crisis work with them now. It's different than therapy work but I think you and Summer would be really good at it."

I smiled. "I really don't need one more thing to do, but tell me about it anyway."

"With therapy work," Chris explained, "you know where you're going, you know the population, what you're going to see, and how long you'll be there. Your job is essentially to make people feel better for an hour, and leave. Crisis work is very different. With crisis work, you walk into a man-made or natural disaster. You're dealing with a high-stress situation and environment, and a lot of emotion. There's no way to determine in advance exactly what you'll be walking into or how long you'll be there."

Immediately, my mind went back to 9/11. I remembered watching the people working with their dogs at the World Trade Center and telling myself that when I got my next dog, I wanted to help people with my dog. I looked at Chris. "Where do we sign up?"

At the time, certification involved an initial evaluation and, assuming you passed that, moved on to a four-day training that was held hours away from our home. We passed the screening evaluation and, two months later, proceeded to training. During training, Summer and I were placed in a variety of situations and scenarios to see how she handled the environment and stress. They also evaluated how I, as her handler, supported her and the individuals we were serving, while simultaneously dealing with everything going on around us.

The training took place at the U.S. Coast Guard Station in Erie, Pennsylvania and, for those four days, we were put through a lot. They watched how Summer handled different surfaces she had to work on including the spiked surface of the docks. We went out on a boat with the Coast Guard. Actors created different scenarios to see how Summer and I would physically, psychologically, and emotionally handle unknown and unexpected situations. We sat through hours of training, stayed in a hotel, and practiced etiquette skills.

Summer handled every situation with ease and confidence. She had a quiet presence about her which everyone noticed. They commented on her eyes and the soulful way she took everything in. The same eyes that had captured me the first day we met were now becoming her trademark. It wasn't just people who watched, and were impacted, by Summer. Her presence also drew in other dogs. Many times, they looked to her for support when they felt stressed. A touch from her reassured other dogs, just as it did people.

*USA Today* was working on a feature about the dogs who were training that weekend and they took a picture of Summer alongside one of the actors. The photo ultimately made the banner of the national newspaper.

After passing the training, one of the first major things Summer and I were asked to respond to was the ten-year anniversary of 9/11. It was an all-day event being held in New York City that involved ceremonies to support survivors as well as family members of survivors and non-survivors. For me, it was a full-circle moment. 9/11 had been the reason I originally wanted to get a dog and do this kind of work and now here we were—Summer and me—doing what had once only been a dream.

With crisis work, every situation is different and many times requires travel to other states. During her years of service, we went to Alaska, twice, including once to support the FBI with an active shooter drill. The purpose of the drill was to see what, if any, impact canines had on people waiting to be interviewed after an event. The drill ultimately determined that the dogs made a difference. Having a person interact with a dog prior to being interviewed, versus standing around talking with other people, allowed people to be calmer and provide more accurate details.

Back home in Lancaster County, Pennsylvania, early one January morning in 2011, four students from the local high school were tragically killed in an auto accident. Since it was a small town and a tight-knit community, there were obvious concerns about the impact the accident would have on the other students. Mental health teams were brought in to talk to the students and allow them to sit and process the death of their friends. Our job was to support the mental health professionals, but what happened that day was something very different.

Chris and I brought Summer and Beamer. The students sat and talked with their friends but refused to talk to any of the mental health professionals unless Summer or Beamer were nearby. If either of them was near, once a student started petting them, they slowly started to talk. We ended up spending the entire day at the school until the last student left.

We did similar work in North Carolina, after the youth group leader of a local church committed suicide.

At every location, Summer instinctively knew not only who needed her but what they needed. Even in a crowded room, she always gravitated toward the person who needed her the most—and I knew to trust her. I knew if we were walking and she stopped next to someone there was a reason, a purpose, and it was important for me to standby quietly and wait. She had a quiet presence with people, and any time Summer looked at someone with her incredible eyes, it was as if she was reading their soul.

Every April, the American College of Veterinary Ophthalmologists (ACVO) offers free eye exams to service, therapy, and working dogs as their way of giving back to the dogs who give to others. The first year after Summer received her therapy dog certification, we went to the event. I wasn't concerned but it was a free eye exam. The test came back that Summer had Golden Retriever Pigmentary Uveitis (GRPU), a common, inherited ocular condition in golden retrievers which can threaten their vision.

I had never heard of GRPU but the ophthalmologist explained that, since we were catching it early, we would start treating her with eye drops and continue checking her to stay ahead of it. I was grateful because, if not for ACVO and their generosity in offering the free annual eye exams, I never would have taken Summer to have her eyes examined. For years, her vision remained stable.

One day, something unexpected happened but, as is typical with Summer, even those things can turn into something amazing.

In October 2014, I noticed a tiny bump on Summer's chest. It was so little that I wasn't overly concerned but decided to show it to our veterinarian anyway. The vet tapped it, and immediately said, "We're taking this off on Monday." By the look in her eyes, I knew before I knew.

The tiny bump turned out to be apocrine carcinoma: skin duct cancer. The same day I got that call, I got another call telling me my grandmother died. I thought back to the day so many years before when the massage therapist told me she saw, "An older person, a woman, with a blonde dog." As I began making some of the most difficult decisions of my life, I was filled with a sense of peace knowing my grandmother was watching over Summer.

Summer underwent surgery to remove the growth. The day she had her sutures removed we learned the margins hadn't been enough to get all the cancer so she went back for a second surgery, which was followed by six months of chemotherapy. People questioned why I would make Summer go through all of that because she was a perfectly happy dog. "She doesn't know she's sick," they would tell me—but I knew. Many disagreed with my decision to explore all my options since she was ten years old. But, for me, age is not a disease and, after conversations with her oncologist, and serious soul searching, I knew we had to try everything. After all Summer had done for others, I owed her a chance to fight and see if we could get past this. I knew I had to do whatever I could for her so we did, and she beat it.

The downside was that the therapy organization considered her immunosuppressed since she'd been undergoing chemotherapy and, even after she was cleared by the oncologist, wouldn't allow her to do any crisis work.

Summer had already been restricted from working until her incision was fully healed, but this was a dog who had been working for nine years. She didn't know how *not* to work and, now that she wasn't working, I watched her get more and more depressed. I knew if she could no longer do therapy or crisis work, she would shut down and I would lose everything so we switched organizations. Summer passed all her tests, and we started working again beginning with flights to Kentucky to train new crisis canine teams.

While Summer was officially cancer free and our battle with cancer was behind us, a new fight surfaced. In September 2016, her battle with GRPU really ramped up and then she was diagnosed with glaucoma in one eye and was scheduled for eye removal surgery.

The diagnosis came one week after Summer received the Wodan Animal Hero Award, the Pennsylvania Veterinary Medical Association's annual award which recognizes "the courageous and heroic acts of Pennsylvania animals in the preservation and protection of animal or human life." Summer was chosen for the award "in recognition and appreciation of her longtime generosity of spirit and healing in service as a therapy and crisis response dog both in Pennsylvania and beyond and bringing comfort to those in need."

Several weeks after the surgery to remove her eye, Summer went completely blind in her other eye.

When people told me, "OK, it's time to retire her" my response was always the same: "Summer will tell me if she wants to stop. She'll tell me when it's time."

The thing people didn't understand was that Summer did what she wanted. She wasn't doing any of this for me. She truly lived to do the work we were doing; she lived for people. She was the most social dog I ever met and I believed in my heart, if I took her work away, she would die, so we continued working.

Before she went blind, Summer could walk into a room and know who needed her the most. Maybe she smelled something in their body or sensed their stress level. She visited with everyone but, if somebody really needed her, she wouldn't budge from their side. That was her "tell sign" for me.

It happened all the time and not always when she was working. It happened at the grocery store or at a park. A person looked perfectly normal, and most times didn't realize they needed her, but as soon as they started petting her, they began talking and whatever struggle or concern they had came out.

Even though she was now completely blind, she was still Summer and still incredibly intuitive and fiercely independent. She somehow made eye contact even without being able to see. People watched her and she inspired them in new ways. After the cancer and her eye issues, Summer began to reach people in a way she never had before.

Our first major assignment after she was officially blind was to support Red Cross shelters in Texas following Hurricane Harvey. Most of the people at the first shelter we visited had been homeless before the hurricane and survived the hurricane by hunkering down under overpasses and bridges. They lost what few meager possessions they had and now they had nowhere to go.

One gentleman, prior to coming to the shelter, had been living behind a bank drive-thru. When Summer and I arrived at the shelter, he came right over to us and started petting her. A while later, the Red Cross public relations people asked him to tell his story and he started talking about how nice people had been and how the shelter had helped him. The entire time he continued petting Summer. Pausing, he looked down at her, and said, "You see this dog? She came all the way here to help me and she's blind. If she can do it, I can get back up and start over, too."

That was the connection Summer made with people. She'd always had an impact on people but her impact now was different. Her story and her ability to overcome all odds inspired others and showed people that they, too, could overcome any obstacle placed in their path.

We worked at another shelter in Texas where FEMA was giving out checks to people so they could relocate and start over. At the end of one of our days, Summer and I were waiting for the other team members when an older gentleman looked at her and smiled.

"You can pet her," I told him.

It was obvious he'd seen her missing eye. As he began petting her, I shared her story with him. Summer didn't move or turn her head or body. She stayed firmly planted in her spot which was her sign for me that she was going to stay by him. She knew, on some level, that he needed her.

Finally, he stopped petting her. "Go ahead. You can go see other people. They probably need you more than me." Again, Summer wouldn't move.

"Actually, she's content where she is," I told the gentleman.

"I'm fine. I don't need her," he replied. I knew he was a proud, and tough, gentleman, but Summer wasn't moving.

"For some reason, Summer feels you need her more than you realize so we're going to stay here with you," I told him.

He continued petting Summer and, as he did, he started to get emotional.

"You can hug her if you want," I told him.

And he did. He leaned down, hugged her, and started to cry. Ashamed and embarrassed that he was crying, he immediately apologized.

"The last time I checked crying was a human emotion," I quietly said. "And you're human, so it's fine."

This man had already lost everything in Hurricane Katrina and now, twelve years later, he lost everything again in Hurricane Harvey. While FEMA had given him money to relocate, it meant driving states away where he knew no one.

As he began walking toward his car, we walked alongside him. "Thank you," he said over and over. Then, looking down at Summer, he said, "If she can do it, I can do it too. I can start over."

Before he got into his car, I asked him if he wanted me to take a picture of him and Summer on his phone. "That way, when you get to where you're going you can look at it and maybe it will give you the strength and inspiration to keep going."

"I would love that."

I took a picture of him and Summer and we watched him get in his car and drive away. You never know who you're going to meet, the situations you'll face, or the impact you're going to have but, time and time again, I witnessed Summer change people's lives.

One of my earliest memories of working with Summer was during our monthly visit to the local hospital. At the end of every visit, we went through the emergency room. Since it's a secure area, we had to wait and get permission from the check-in desk before entering.

On this particular day, three dogs and three handlers were waiting when a man walked out, saw us, stopped, and stared. He never said a word but you could see he was uncomfortable. My first thought was that he was afraid of dogs. Finally, he turned to the woman at the desk and asked, "Why are dogs here?"

After we explained, he got extremely tense. "My son was brought in today because our neighbor's dog bit him."

We asked which room his son was in. He pointed to a room in the back corner, and we promised him repeatedly we would avoid that area. We kept our promise and didn't go anywhere near the back corner.

Later, I saw the father walking toward us. "My son knows the dogs are here and wants to see them."

From working with kids dealing with trauma, I know sometimes they are more resilient than we give them credit for and that was the case with his son.

The other dogs with us that day, a Shih Tzu and basset hound, were low to the ground and the boy couldn't see them so the ladies who had them picked them up for the boy to see. I had trained Summer to do "paws up" where she put her front paws on the side of the bed so a person could see her. The minute Summer put her paws on the edge of his bed you could see his eyes light up. Their connection was immediate. The other dogs went over and stayed next to the boy's mother but Summer continued to stand at the boy's bedside. She stood there the entire time they stitched him up. While I know standing that long couldn't have been comfortable for Summer, she stayed because she knew the boy needed her.

In 2016, Summer and I were part of Camp Susquehanna, a free sleepaway summer camp sponsored by the Burn Prevention Network for children ages seven to seventeen who had suffered burn injuries. Many of the counselors were either nurses in a burn unit or burn survivors themselves. Summer attended the camp for three years and while the kids all loved her, the connection she had with them changed over the years.

The first year we attended, Summer didn't have any medical issues; the second year, she was post-cancer; and the third year, she was blind and had undergone surgery to remove her left eye.

After her eye removal surgery, the kids related to her differently. She now had scars, her face was disfigured, and she was blind. During one of the activities, the kids were supposed to share their burn stories, but they were resistant to talk. I told them if they were worried about sharing, Summer would be happy to listen to their story.

One of the kids immediately piped up and asked what had happened to Summer so I shared her story. I told them how, after her surgery, I was afraid people would be scared of and avoid Summer because of her scars and how she looked. When I finished, one by one the children came up, put a hand on Summer, and shared their stories. In doing so, they were able to share their story with the group. Summer connected to all the burn survivors through her scars and she empowered them to not be ashamed or scared. She gave kids the courage to participate in discussion groups and share the story of their injuries or about new and scary activities or situations they had overcome.

And that's the power of the work Summer—and all these dogs—do and the connection they make. Sometimes what appears to be something small or uneventful turns out to have the biggest impact and can change everything for someone. Summer taught me that love is blind and how important it is to enable the ability, not the disability.

Helen Keller once wrote, "Although the world is full of suffering, it is full also of the overcoming of it." Summer lived and modeled that truth. Despite her own battles, she never stopped guiding people through their own healing process and sharing her love with them.

# Chapter 34

# NEW YORK

## *Busting Loose in the Empire State*

AS A VOLUNTEER FOR ANIMAL ALLIANCE OF NEW JERSEY, I HELPED at adoption events. Every time I saw on their Facebook page that a dog who had been at an event had found their forever home, I celebrated. Because of Kimber and Animal Alliance, I knew how much those moments and connections changed life for the dog as well as the humans who had opened their hearts, arms, and home to the dog.

Photos of one dog, an adorable, scrappy-looking little pup named Buster, occasionally popped up on their page. He was an alumna of Animal Alliance. From the little bit they shared, his start in life hadn't been that great but it appeared all of that was behind him. He was now living a big life in The Big Apple.

Curious to learn more about Buster and his journey, I reached out to his mom, Jacqueline, to see if she would be willing to share their story.

It was no big surprise when I heard back from Jacqueline. Just like her dog, she was a spunky, bundle of energy. "I'd be thrilled to share Buster's story!" she said.

Buster, like so many other dogs, didn't just overcome, but defied the odds that had been placed against him early in his life. He let go of his past, moved on, embraced his inner champion, and was now living an amazing life.

# Chapter 35

# JACQUELINE & BUSTER

*From Street Dog to Champion*

MY FAVORITE WORD IS SERENDIPITY AND I BELIEVE MY STORY with Buster embodies the true meaning of that word: that events develop or occur by chance and the results are happy or beneficial. While at first, it seemed that Buster and I were two beings who would never meet, we did, and the result has absolutely been serendipitous.

From the time I was two years old, my most vivid memories all revolve around wanting a dog. Every year, my Christmas list for Santa had one thing on it: a real live dog. Any holiday or occasion that involved a gift, I asked for just one thing: a real live dog. Every time I opened a box, whether it was the size of a ring box or the size of a television, I always said, "I hope it's a real live dog." My family tried to appease me with stuffed dogs, plastic dogs, and literally anything but a real live dog.

My grandparents and parents always had dogs, so I didn't understand why I couldn't have a dog of my own. Of course, I was too young to understand that dogs were a lot of work and, since both my parents worked, they didn't have the time to supervise, train, or care for a dog.

My grandparents, who lived across the street, always had purebred poodles. When my grandmother's dog, Pepper, passed she reached out to the breeder and asked if they had any black poodles. The breeder had a litter with one black poodle, so my grandparents got him.

The weekend the puppy was delivered to them, my grandparents were scheduled to go out of town for a business trip. Unable to bring the puppy with them, they brought him over for us to watch. Since the puppy didn't yet have a name, I decided to name him. He was black with a white stripe and the only black and white dogs I'd ever seen were Dalmatians.

Being too young to differentiate between breeds, and knowing Dalmatians were firehouse dogs, I named him Sparky. From that day on, Sparky and I were inseparable. When my grandparents returned from their business trip, I never gave Sparky back. He was now my dog.

Our family spent every summer at our beach house. I wasn't supposed to leave the house. But I was strong-willed. Every day I put on my bathing suit and went to the beach with a leash-less Sparky tagging along beside me. We spent the afternoon running in and out of the waves and playing on the beach until it was time to go home.

The ice cream truck passed us every day. One day the driver stopped and gave me a free mint chocolate chip cone. The first thing I did was bite the bottom off the cone. As the ice cream melted, it dripped out the bottom of the cone onto Sparky. When my family found us, they took a picture of me standing eating my ice cream cone with Sparky next to me, smiling, drops of green melted ice cream all over his beautiful black fur.

Sparky became my protector, best friend, and also got me through one of the hardest times of my young life when my parents divorced. After Sparky passed, my mom got a cream-colored poodle who was fiercely independent and very smart (both typical characteristics of the breed). We named him Spunky and then my mom decided to add another dog to our family, a cream-colored cockapoo named Buster the First.

One day, while he was in a gated area of the house, I watched Spunky maneuver the gate with his nose just enough so he could slip through. Buster the First was right behind him. It was clear that Buster the First was silly and fun, but Spunky was definitely the brains of the outfit.

In April 2012, I found myself in-between apartments and also in-between in my life. I had signed a lease on a new apartment but it didn't begin until July. In the interim, I decided to move back home with my mother for a few months.

Both Spunky and Buster the First had passed, and my mother kept saying, "I have to get a dog. I don't have anything to walk. I just want another dog."

Our family had always gotten purebred dogs, mainly poodles, from breeders and we didn't really know much about rescue. Knowing she wanted a dog to love, I suggested, "Why don't we adopt a rescue dog?"

Mom agreed—as long as it was a cream-colored poodle. I told my friend, Maureen, and together she and I started looking. A few weeks later, Maureen called. "I have a dog for your mom. It's a cream-colored poodle I found online at a place called Animal Alliance in New Jersey." We live in New York. At the time, I didn't really use GPS and thought it would be a quick trip over the bridge into New Jersey. It wasn't. Two and a half hours later we pulled into the parking lot at Animal Alliance to meet Ashton, an older poodle whose owner had passed. He was exactly what my mom wanted, but the feeling wasn't mutual. Ashton wanted absolutely nothing to do with us. He loved Annie, the woman who ran the rescue, and refused to come near us. My mother was devastated, and me being the one who had pushed the idea of rescuing a dog, felt responsible.

"We have a back-up," Annie told us. "We just pulled him from euthanasia. His name is Tito and he was just neutered so he may still be a bit groggy but he sort of meets your requirements for a cream-colored poodle."

We agreed to meet Tito and, before long, Annie walked in with what looked like a cream-colored drowned rat. But the drowned rat came right over to us and sat on my feet. I kept trying to egg him over to my mom and as soon as he rolled over on his back for us to rub his belly, my mom said, "I'll take him!" Honestly, mom wanted a dog so badly that I think if Annie had brought her a cream-colored half dog-half squirrel my mom would have taken it!

Tito, we learned, had been found as a stray on the streets of Philadelphia and taken to Animal Care and Control. The hair by his mouth was so severely matted he couldn't open it to eat. Likewise, the hair on his back end was so matted he couldn't go to the bathroom. In short, he was a mess and the decision was made to euthanize him.

When the young girl who worked at Animal Control was instructed to take him into the back to be euthanized, she saw his pink paw pads. Realizing he was a puppy, she thought, "I can't do this to a puppy," walked out with Tito in her arms, and drove straight to Animal Alliance of New Jersey, a no-kill shelter near where she lived. It was estimated that Tito was between six to eight months old and had probably been on the streets for at least five of those months.

It became obvious very quickly after we brought Tito home that, based on his start in life, he had no idea how to be someone's dog. He drank out of puddles and didn't know how to walk up stairs. He had trust issues and wasn't used to being given food so instead he stole food off the table. Just like Spunky and the original Buster, he was an escape artist and searched for any small slat or space to slither through and sneak out. From the outset, we knew we wanted to honor my mother's beloved Buster the First so we changed his name to Buster the Second.

As a teacher, I had summers off. Since I couldn't move into my new apartment until July, my mother and I took Buster to our beach house. He loved every minute there. Since our house opens onto the beach, Buster spent his days walking across the sand to the water, taking a dip, then coming back to relax on a lounge chair on our deck.

In July, I moved into my apartment but continued going back and forth to the beach to spend time with my mother and Buster. In September, I returned to work. A few weeks later, my mother called. "I think Buster is depressed."

"What do you mean?"

"He doesn't want to do anything. He seems sad. He won't come upstairs to sleep and sits in front of the window all day staring outside."

As we continued talking, I learned she and Buster hadn't been getting along. It wasn't anyone's fault. My mother realized it had probably been too soon for her to get another dog to try and replace her beloved Buster the First.

In addition, the new Buster's personality was eons apart from her first Buster. My mother wanted a dog to sit in her lap and that certainly wasn't Buster the Second! DNA tests confirmed he was a terrier mix and he had the typical terrier disposition: fearless, stubborn, independent, and smart. He was also full of energy and barked all the time.

Feeling guilty that I'd inadvertently gotten my mother into this situation, I enrolled Buster in an agility class. I thought it would be a fun thing for us to do together while also giving him an outlet for all his energy. I knew Buster was a dog who needed a job and maybe agility would fulfill that need.

Agility helped in so many ways. It not only gave us something to do together but Buster loved it and emerged as the star of the class! Then, one night in class, everything changed.

After taking a jump, Buster stopped, and rolled over on his back. "C'mon, Buster," I said, "Get up. Let's go. You have to run." No matter what I said or how much I encouraged him, Buster refused to move.

I looked at Kim, our trainer. She was smiling. "He's pissed at you."

I was shocked. "Why? I didn't do anything."

"Because you bring him here and do all this fun stuff with him and then you take him back to a place he doesn't want to be."

I knew what Kim meant. He didn't want to go back to my mother's house—he wanted to be with me. Two things stood in my way: the first was my life.

I was living a life that wasn't beneficial (or necessarily even healthy) for me but making changes was difficult. I was focused and driven, which often made me unapproachable. I had no time for people or friends or anything other than what was already on my daily schedule. At that point in my life, if you weren't in a time slot, you simply didn't exist. The agility class was Buster's time slot. I didn't have another time slot or any extra room for him in my life.

The other thing standing in my way was my new apartment. When I signed the lease, I didn't have a dog so the fact that the apartment building didn't allow dogs wasn't a concern. I explained all of that to Kim. "Order a sherpa bag and bring it to the next class."

I ordered the bag and brought it to class. "Now what?" I asked.

She patterned the command "Hide" with Buster and taught him how to jump in the bag and lay down. Every time he did it, he earned a treat.

"OK, now what?" I asked.

"Sneak him into the building," she said, as though it was the obvious choice.

"Are you crazy? Buster is a barker. How am I going to sneak him into my building?"

"Just do it," she said.

And I did. I was a nervous wreck, but I did it. When we got home, we took the stairs to my second-floor apartment so as not to run the risk of seeing someone (or someone seeing him) on the elevator. Despite being a go-go-go, barky dog who liked to be in charge, somehow Buster understood from the moment we entered the building and my apartment that he had to be quiet. Whenever he had to go potty, I put him in the bag, went down the stairs, got in my car, and drove him a few blocks away.

For five years, Buster and I lived that way. For five years, I snuck him in and out of the building and we continued doing agility.

Dogs competing in agility are placed in a class based on their height with many of them being purebred dogs who have come from a long line of agility champs. Since Buster was a mixed breed, he was registered as an All American.

Agility is a timed competition where the dog is tested on their ability to complete a course in an exact order following the commands of their handler. Courses typically have between fourteen and twenty obstacles made up of tunnels, A-frames, tire jumps, weaves, and a variety of other obstacles. The dog and handler don't know the layout of the course beforehand although the handler is given eight minutes to walk the course without their dog. Points are awarded based on time and proper completion of the course (minus any errors the dog may have made on the course).

Agility requires confidence because both you and the dog must perform in front of an audience. You need to know your dog inside and out, how they turn, and what spots will be tough for them. It requires incredible focus on the part of the dog because they need to block out everything and everyone around them and listen only to you. It also requires athleticism and the ability to follow their handler's commands to maneuver around an obstacle course.

At our very first agility class the trainer gave me one simple rule to follow: "You should be the most fun thing to your dog."

That is the best piece of advice I ever got. By following that one rule Buster always stays incredibly focused on my cues and directions. He continued to excel and qualify in almost every run—and the two of us connected in an indescribable way.

We went to weekend trials throughout the northeast. In his first competition in May 2014, Buster took first place. As his ribbons started to rack up so did his ability and notoriety.

In 2017, after acquiring sufficient points in AKC sanctioned events, Buster qualified to compete at The Westminster Masters Agility Championship, which is the crème de la crème of agility competitions. You need the highest title level to get into Westminster and Buster had it. He earned it and deserved to go so off we went to Westminster!

We were so nervous or, at least, I was. Out of 900 dogs at the event, they picked Buster to be the focus of a *New York Post* article based on the bio I had written about him. It was a wonderful article—and, the following week, I got a letter from my apartment building telling me Buster and I had to move out. I knew the day would come, but I never thought it would come via an article in *The New York Post*!

In our new building, I always let Buster run from our apartment door to the front door of the building. One day, shortly after we moved in, as Buster ran toward the front door, I saw the door man standing there, watching. "Don't worry," I assured him. "He's super well-trained and would never leave without me."

The doorman looked at me, smiled, and said, "Oh, I know."

"Really? How do you know?"

Pointing at Buster, he said, "I know Little Simba." He explained that he called him that because the way Buster's hair had grown out made him look like Simba, the lion in the movie, *The Lion King*. When I told him his name was Buster, he continued, "Well, then, Buster likes to run around during the day up and down the halls."

"Oh, no. I'm not around during the day and certainly don't let him run around. You must be thinking of another dog."

"Come with me for a second," the doorman said. We walked over to the security cameras and he pulled up footage from the prior day and there on the screen was Buster running up and down the hall! I was completely baffled.

A few days later, I came in and the doorman showed me more footage of Buster running up and down the hall, and the doorman taking selfies with him.

"What's going on?" I said.

What was even more confusing is that it didn't happen every day but, eventually, I figured it out. In our old apartment, whenever I closed the front door behind me it automatically locked. I assumed it was the same with the door in my new apartment, but it wasn't. I needed to turn the lock on my new door before closing it behind me. The new door also had a rubber strip at the bottom which sometimes slid back and forth.

If I was in a rush and the strip slid to one side when I closed the door, it left a small crack. On those days, Buster finagled his nose into the crack and eventually worked the door open. Once the door was open, he was a free man! He ran up and down the halls or headed down to hang out with the superintendent or socialize with the doorman. After a while, the doorman or super put him back in my apartment and locked the door. Buster legitimately had another life I knew nothing about!

Now everyone knows him. All the firemen at the firehouse across the street know him. The EMS workers let him sit in their truck. This seventeen-pound mostly Shih Tzu and Silky terrier mix has captured the heart of everyone he's met.

And me? I'm the lucky girl who once dreamed of having her own dog and hit the lottery. He's my reason for living, breathing, and grinding my teeth.

Buster has competed at Westminster every year since 2017. In 2021, he was chosen to do the Westminster Press Preview, which aired on Fox 5 News. In it, Buster showed what the sport of agility is all about. He made the finals, but was injured so my vet immediately began to work on him. That night he came back, gave it his all, and ended up placing seventh.

In October 2021, Buster tore his left rear ligament. I thought it would retire him from agility, but within three months he was healed and went on to win another title. It seemed like nothing was going to stop him!

I'd been warned that when a dog tears a ligament in one leg, there's a good chance they will go on to tear the ligament in the other leg. In March 2022, that's exactly what happened. Buster was on the course and on a run when suddenly he stopped, held his leg up, and couldn't move. I carried him off the course and found he had torn the right rear ligament worse than he'd torn the left.

From March to August, we did everything: acupuncture, chiropractic, laser, rehab, everything. At that point, I was uncertain if Buster would ever be able to compete again and was devastated—not so much for me, but for Buster. He'd been a working dog for ten years and now he wasn't doing anything and was getting really depressed. It was difficult for me to see him so sad, so I enrolled him in scent work in May. He loved it and became a scent work star, too.

The number twenty-five has always been significant to Buster and me because he was adopted on April 25 and got his first championship title on August 25. Even though we were doing scent work, I was getting depressed, too, so I went to a sacred grotto which was said to have healing waters flowing from it. I said a prayer, put some of the water in a bottle, and went back to my car. I made one stop on my way home. As I got out of my car, I looked down and lying on the ground next to my car was a silver-plated medallion. I picked it up and looked at it. There was one thing engraved in the metal: the number twenty-five. In that moment, I knew Buster would heal and be fine.

I took the medallion to have it made into a necklace and when they asked if I wanted the scratches buffed out, I told them, "Absolutely not!" Our flaws and imperfections, just like the scratches on the medallion, were what made us—and our journey—special. I wanted them to stay.

We got vet clearance in June 2022 to go back to agility and I wore that medallion our first time back in the ring and haven't taken it off since. Two months later, Buster was back and stronger than ever. In three months, he earned his Preferred Championship title which can sometimes take a dog years to achieve.

With Buster fully healed, I decided to submit his profile to a dog talent company because everyone was always telling me how smart, expressive, and personable he is. At his first audition, straight out of the gate, he landed his first job.

The job was for Buster to be part of a public service announcement a company was doing for pets and people. It consisted of five different segments—the majority were still shots with the exception of one, which was a commercial. Buster was hired for the commercial.

The subject of the PSA was geared toward anyone who had a pet and may have fallen on hard times. It directed them to organizations that would help them feed or care for their pet.

The film company took over a home in Philadelphia and completely transformed it for the commercial. Actresses were hired to play the mother and daughter. In the storyline for the commercial, the daughter had a dog named Walter and everything in her life focused on him and, especially, around feeding him. Now, she and her mom had fallen on hard times, and they were struggling to feed Walter.

On the day they began shooting the commercial, things didn't quite go according to plan. First, the little girl playing the daughter kept calling the dog Buster so, by the end of the day, they changed the script. Now, rather than a dog named Walter, she had a dog named Buster.

When Buster refused to cooperate with the car scene as it was written, once again, the script was changed to allow Buster to run down the block like he wanted to do all along.

Buster somehow finagles every situation and ultimately gets his way every time.

While I stood watching that day, I suddenly had the realization that this was Buster's first time back in Philadelphia since the day he was picked up as a stray. This was the same place where he was supposed to be euthanized. All that love, all that potential, could have been extinguished, but thanks to the kindness and compassion of that young woman and Animal Alliance of New Jersey, Buster and I are both living our best life.

Through everything, Buster never gave up—not once. My mother calls him "The little dog who could" and I think it fits him perfectly! He has taught me so much about resilience, perseverance, and tenacity. He is well-adjusted and filled with a fierce determination. No matter what happens, Buster simply shakes it off, kicks some grass over it, rolls with it, and keeps on going. He's been in so many situations where even the strongest human would have given up and thrown in the towel, but not Buster. He goes out and performs no matter the conditions or what he's been through and always comes back stronger than before. In the process, he's gained the support of even the biggest skeptic.

Before Buster, my life was somewhat toxic but now, because of him, my entire life has been transformed.

I got engaged at a very young age but not because it's what I wanted. The truth is, while I always saw myself with a dog, I never saw myself married or with children. Regardless, I thought it was the logical trajectory for my life: you go to college, you get married, and you have kids. But at the last minute I couldn't go through with it and cancelled the wedding. Everybody was upset with me and, being so young and lacking confidence, I questioned my decision.

From that point, I questioned everything I did and most times felt I was making wrong decision after wrong decision. It didn't help that I was also a perfectionist and couldn't accept failure. If something wasn't perfect, I simply didn't move forward. In short, my life wasn't going anywhere at all, but I kept living that life because I could control it. People wanted to be part of my life but, because I couldn't control them, I turned them away.

I was a Pro-am competitive ballroom dancer. Although I was ranked very high in the country in my division, I was stressed. I barely slept or ate. My life revolved around work, dance, and more work. When Buster came into my life, I let go of the compulsive need to constantly work and stay busy because now I had to get home for Buster. I was accountable and had to be somewhere for another being. Thanks to Buster, I now had a positive, rather than a toxic, focus in my life. My life had meaning.

For over ten years, my dance partner didn't understand and told me, "It's just a dog. You do too much for him."

Even though he and I had parted ways, we kept in touch. Recently, he found himself in a difficult situation. In the midst of it, he connected with a street dog in Bulgaria whom he named Bobsom. When we talked about it, he said, "I was always jealous of you and Buster and what you had. Now that I have Bobsom, I understand. She's given me a new purpose in life."

My childhood wasn't easy, but it was made easier because of Sparky. There were times I wondered if Buster was Sparky reincarnated.

My mother used to watch Buster for me while I worked. One day, I picked him up but we had to get home quickly. After Buster and I were settled in the car, I called my mother from my car's speakerphone so she could tell me about their day. "He's probably going to need to rest when you get home," she said, "because he barked all day long. He wants what he wants. The only other dog that was more persistent than him was Sparky."

Buster sat quietly in the passenger seat next to me. When I stopped for a red light, I turned to him, and said, "Are you Sparky?"

Buster looked at me. When I turned back, I noticed the license plate on the car in front of me. It said: SPARKY. I still have the photo of that license plate on my phone.

One year, at the start of school, the teachers were asked to write about

Buster
Photo Courtesy of
Venture Photography-Greenwich

someone who had characteristics we wish we had—someone we respected and emulated. This is what I wrote:

*Mine isn't a person. It's my dog, Buster. Everything I strive to be is what Buster is or has shown me.*

*I have learned to give others the benefit of the doubt and to let things go. I was always the one that could not let things go; I had to prove my way was the right way. At times it led to a verbal fight or confrontation. Buster taught me to let it go because honestly who even cares about this nonsense? Instead of engaging in a fight like I would have years ago, I simply shake my head, say, 'Great. Sounds good', and walk away.*

*I always felt I knew better than anyone but it turned out I learned the most by listening to a being that could not speak.*

*Buster has taught me that the most important things in life are to love and to trust. He also showed me how to stop, slow down, and smell the flowers.*

*He has taught me how to laugh at myself and that it is okay not to be perfect. Buster has always done things his own way and has royally screwed up on a course and then stood and barked at me. I learned I had two choices: I could get upset or roll with it.*

*Realizing there was nothing I could do, I laughed it off just like all the others were doing—and, time and time again, I heard people say, "I love watching that dog!" Buster's mistakes are what make him lovable. He would be running his own course and the entire audience would be laughing and cheering for him. From Buster I learned that it was okay to make mistakes because it made you more relatable and approachable to people.*

*For years, I had not been open to other ways of doing things but Buster has shown me there are a lot of ways to get something done. As a result, I have become a nicer person and, I believe, a nicer teacher.*

*Others probably thought this seventeen-pound matted, disheveled dog would always be the underdog but he has shown everyone—he has shown the world—that it does not matter what your pedigree is. What matters is your heart.*

Sometimes I think back to the time Buster and I went to our first Nationals together. We hopped on the redeye to Reno, Nevada, and arrived at 2:00 a.m., completely lost, and not knowing where to go or what to do. After a sleepless night, I held Buster the next day as we walked into the arena. Looking around, my first thought was: How did we get here?

This dog has taken me on the journey of a lifetime and helped me create a life I never imagined for myself. I have learned more from my seventeen-pound street dog than any human has ever taught me.

The truth is, Buster isn't perfect—none of us are—but we are perfect for each other.

# Chapter 36
 **NEW JERSEY**
*Back Home
in the Garden State*

AND LAST, BUT CERTAINLY NOT LEAST, IS MY HOME STATE OF NEW
Jersey. It's often a misunderstood state. Many people's perception of New
Jersey is what they see flying in and out of Newark International Air-
port: oil tanks and industrial parks with New York City as a backdrop.
To them, the fact that New Jersey is known as The Garden State is a mis-
nomer.

That, however, is not my New Jersey. My New Jersey has rolling hills,
sprawling farmlands, quaint towns and villages all conveniently located
a short one hour drive from New York City, Philadelphia, the Jersey
shore, and the Pocono Mountains. Despite the reality of high taxes and
the threat of overpopulation, I still choose to make it my home. Therefore, I decided to make the final chapter of this book be a tribute to dogs
and people that hail from the place I call home.

Since I know a lot of people and dogs here in New Jersey, it was a bit
overwhelming initially to decide whom to include. I decided, just as I
do with my acts of kindness, to sit, wait, pray, and trust my intuition.
Once again, the people and dogs found me.

Joseph Frazz is a world-class photographer with an incredibly keen
eye and instinct for capturing the right shot at the right angle at the right
time. His photographs of animals and humans have a unique perspective
and astonishing depth. In addition, he is a wonderfully kind human
being and very active in the world of animal rescue.

I met Joe while working on *Magical Dogs 2: Connecting the Dots, Connecting the Dogs* and was fortunate to have his photo of a dog named
Dot on the cover of that book. Now, hoping we could work together for
the cover of this book. I reached out to him. While texting back and

forth, I had a gut feeling I needed to ask him if he knew anyone I might want to interview for this book. He responded with one name: Robin Hall. Just like with his photos, Joe's instincts were spot on.

The names of two other possibilities had been running through my mind for months. They were people and places I had briefly mentioned in Kimber's story: Hound Hunters of New Jersey and Animal Alliance of New Jersey.

Kristy, who inspired me to write *Magical Dogs 2: Connecting the Dots, Connecting the Dogs,* had since joined forces with another person to form Hound Hunters of New Jersey. Over and over, I saw that the work they were doing was extremely impactful and wanted to know more. I reached out to Kristy who immediately put me in touch with her partner, Jeanette, who shared her (and their) remarkable story and journey.

That left Animal Alliance of New Jersey: the place and the people who had changed my, and Kimber's, life. Knowing the world of rescue isn't an easy one, especially for those on the frontlines, I reached out to Annie, the person and force behind the rescue. Knowing how much she already had on her plate, I was incredibly honored and excited when she agreed to tell her story.

I believe these three stories capture the heart of my New Jersey: strength, resilience, and most of all, kindness.

# Chapter 37
# ✦ ROBIN, HAPPY ✦
# & PETUNIA
## *It's All About Happiness*

I'D JUST STARTED VOLUNTEERING WITH ELEVENTH HOUR RESCUE and, in an attempt to find my niche, was trying different things. I helped at events, did a chili cook-off, helped with adoption applications, went on several transports, and was thinking of fostering.

One night, while helping with a transport, I saw a dog come off the transport vehicle, immediately walk over to someone who was sitting on the ground, and sat down in their lap. I couldn't believe how sweet and loving he was. My first thought was, Oh my God! Who is that dog?

Even though the dog went home with a foster that night, I kept thinking about him. The next day, Eleventh Hour sent out an email saying they were looking for a new foster for him because his current foster's dogs wouldn't accept him and were bullying him.

I immediately knew I wanted to foster him, so after work I stopped at the rescue and picked him up. He hopped in my car, rested his head on the console, and looked at me. I turned my head, looked at him, and thought, "What in the world did I just do? I don't know anything about you and I've never fostered before." In addition, my daughter had just had a baby and was living with us.

The entire trip home, all I kept thinking was, "What in the world am I doing?" He just kept looking at me and, every time I looked over at him, my fears and concerns began to dissipate. There was something about him. I also knew, since we were fostering him, I had an "out" because he wouldn't be with us forever.

His name was Happy. From the get-go, he was the easiest dog ever. He was great with our other dogs and my grandson, and was truly perfect.

The day after I brought him home, I received word that a woman had filled out an application and wanted to meet Happy. I contacted her and we talked about Happy. During the course of our conversation, I heard myself tell her, "The dog just came here and I really love him. I'm thinking of keeping him."

I hadn't planned to say that and hadn't yet said those words out loud to myself or the rescue. They literally just tumbled out. The woman was wonderful and extremely understanding. "If it's meant to be and you want to keep the dog, then keep him."

And that's how we ended up keeping Happy.

Happy had been at a shelter in Georgia. He had a large scar in the shape of an "X" on his forehead and, even though it was an older scar, the hair had not grown over it. The shelter said the "X" meant he'd probably been branded for dog fighting, but considering how docile he is, and how much he loves other dogs, it probably didn't take them long to realize he wasn't a good fit for fighting. Luckily, he ended up at the shelter.

Many shelters in the South, due to overcrowding, only keep dogs a few months. But, several months later Happy was still in the shelter, probably because he was such an easy, loving dog. Eventually, Happy was pulled by a rescue and placed in a foster home before ultimately being pulled by Eleventh Hour Rescue who brought him to New Jersey.

He was housetrained, crate trained, loving, affectionate, gentle, got along with everybody—and deaf. I'd never been around a deaf dog before, but Happy made it effortless. He knew several hand signals and his deafness was never an issue.

Before Happy came into my life, what I knew about pit bulls was based on the stereotypes I'd heard or what I'd read in the media. I was fortunate to have Happy teach me the truth about pit bulls because, as a result, I now have five. I don't think I would have any of them if not for Happy.

Happy truly was the best advocate for adult shelter pit bulls. When I first adopted him, I wanted to change his name but everywhere we went, people said, "He's such a happy dog! What's his name?" When I told them his name was Happy, they smiled, laughed, and said, "Perfect!" and I realized he really *did* have the perfect name.

Happy and I went everywhere together. I have a picture of him at my

Robin and Happy
Photo courtesy of
Joseph Frazz Photography

daughter's baby shower relaxing in the middle of thirty women. You could have a house full of people and Happy never cared.

They say a deaf dog's other senses are heightened and it's true. With Happy, it was something else: he and I were incredibly in-tune with one another. Even if he was sound asleep, and I quietly tip-toed into another room, he immediately woke up and followed me. He always had one eye—or a sixth sense—focused on me.

One day, a friend who also volunteered with Eleventh Hour, told me she'd begun volunteering at a shelter in Newark. "Robin, those dogs really need our help. They're overcrowded and completely inundated with pit bulls."

Before Happy, I wouldn't have considered going with her. Now I had more experience and a different perspective.

The first time we went to the Newark shelter, I was completely overwhelmed. The shelter itself isn't in a great area but walking into the shelter was very intimidating. They had at least 200 dogs and, as we walked down the aisles together, it was impossible to talk or hear one another. The level of noise and reactivity were like nothing I had ever seen or heard before. As a result, most of the dogs were extremely stressed and didn't show well.

I left, went home, and thought about my next step. While it was overwhelming, I also knew those dogs needed help, so I started doing events. A few months later, I took time off from my job, got more involved, and eventually started doing evaluations.

The majority of the dogs were adult dogs and the stress level in most of them was very high. In many cases, you had to go up to a dog several times, sometimes for weeks, before you could even begin to try to take them out. When you did, you always had to have a pouch with high-end treats. Sometimes they came off their bed and approached you for a treat.

Sometimes they came to you. As soon as you tried putting a slip lead on them, they went to the back of their run. Sometimes they just barked and growled. We knew it was all mostly fueled by fear but we always let the dog's reaction and our intuition guide us before we would try and take them out.

I always walked the kennel with two other girls, Sherri and Jenn, to decide who we were going to take out to evaluate. There was a white and brindle spotted bully with a big head. Since she slightly resembled a pig, I named her Petunia after Porky Pig's girlfriend from the Looney Tunes cartoon. For some reason, Petunia didn't like Sherri or Jenn but she was always wiggly and friendly with me. One day, I put the slip lead on her and took her outside to get comfortable before going into a room for evaluation. She was great with me.

In the evaluation room, you see how a dog responds to being petted and handled. You give them a toy and then take it away. You put a bowl of food down, all the while taking notes and writing their reaction. Again, Petunia did great.

After that, every time I went to the shelter and Petunia saw me, she went crazy and started jumping up on her fence, barking, and wiggling her tail as if to say, "Take me out!"

The shelter is located in an industrial area with no grass. It's not great for the dogs, but some of them have a lot of energy and want to walk regardless. Other dogs enjoyed hanging out in my "dog car", an old Jeep I have just for dogs. I keep a bed and toys in the back along with bowls and treats and the dogs love it. After a while, the dogs got to know my dog car and got excited anytime they saw it when we went out. Some jumped in the hatchback, played with the toys, and hung out with me, while other dogs jumped in and slept. They simply wanted some peace and quiet.

Every time I went to the shelter, I took Petunia out. She loved to either hang out on the sidewalk outside the shelter, or in my Jeep. We sat on the sidewalk on a blanket with a toy and, other times, we sat in my Jeep as she watched the world go by. She never slept. She was content playing with toys and hanging out with me.

Over time, we got closer and closer. As she slowly gained more trust in people, I started taking her to events with me. The thing about Petunia is you never had to wonder if she liked you or not because she always let you know. She was fine with women but was leery and more fearful of men. She clearly didn't like one particular older gentleman who volunteered at the shelter. Whenever I had Petunia, I remained extremely mindful of who was around us. One day, when another volunteer had Petunia, she bit the gentleman's pant leg. Another time, a man came in dressed up in a Michelin man costume and Petunia grabbed at him. She didn't break the skin, but many times if a dog bites someone, regardless of the extent, the dog pays the price.

Petunia had been in the shelter for eleven months when a lady came to meet her. I was concerned because you never know if a dog will like someone, but Petunia liked this woman and the woman wanted to adopt her.

I sat down and wrote the woman a two-page letter telling her everything I knew about Petunia. I stressed to her the same things I stress to everyone: "You have to be mindful; you have to be careful with strangers."

She read the letter and said she understood. She had a fenced-in backyard for Petunia and we exchanged phone numbers in the event she ever had any questions or concerns.

Everything was going fine, and then Covid hit and the woman's twenty-year-old son moved in. Straight out of the gate, Petunia didn't like him. I had explained in my letter the need to acclimate Petunia to strangers and make sure introductions were done the right way. Unfortunately, that didn't happen and Petunia bit her son. The lady messaged me and said her son was afraid to come out of his bedroom. I told her to keep working with her.

Since Petunia was muzzle trained, I also encouraged the woman to use the muzzle when she walked Petunia in her neighborhood, but she didn't. One day, while walking around the neighborhood, a male neighbor approached them. Petunia was fine and the man was able to pet her. A few days later, they met the same man again and this time when he went to pet her, Petunia bit his finger.

The next text I got from the lady simply said, "I'm done. She's going back to the shelter."

I knew surrendering Petunia back to the shelter meant she would be labeled forever. I knew the shelter didn't care what happened or what part the person played in the circumstances. Petunia would pay the price.

Petunia came back to the shelter and the shelter manager immediately said, "We're not adopting this dog out."

I tried explaining to him what I knew about Petunia, but he didn't want to listen.

"What if a rescue wants to pull her?" I asked him.

"No. She's a liability." His mind was made up.

Three times a week, when I was at the shelter, I took Petunia out. I knew they weren't going to let her live in the shelter forever. The clock was ticking.

Petunia

I was crying all the time and constantly asked my husband, "What am I going to do? I'm not going to let her die, Mike. This lady failed her. Petunia is fearful of certain things but she always shows you when she's fearful. What happened wasn't her fault."

My husband looked at me and said, "If you want to bring her home, bring her home."

Petunia is good with other dogs, particularly male dogs, but I knew she wouldn't get along with one of our females, so living in our house wasn't an option. Now what?

My husband is a contractor and together we came up with a plan. It was a huge commitment for both of us, but we knew it was the right thing to do for everyone, especially Petunia.

We have nine acres of land and a couple of outbuildings. We took one of the outbuildings that was a little distance from our house and started renovating it for Petunia. My husband and his crew installed electricity, heat, and air conditioning. They put up sheetrock and poured the floors. They installed a guillotine-type door so she could go in and out of a huge fenced-in play area.

Petunia's Hut has a living room complete with a leather couch, pillows, blankets, chairs, a rug, a dresser with a television, a basket of toys, and a basket of bones. Stairs lead up to a landing which has a bed and is fenced off for her safety. It's nicer than many people's apartments.

Almost everything in Petunia's Hut was donated by friends. In addition, so many people knew about Petunia and what we were trying to do, they donated to help offset the expense of everything. Everybody was happy and excited to help us bring Petunia home.

Shortly after she arrived, packages started showing up on our doorstep. Chewy boxes filled with toys and bones were delivered. A woman made a needlework pillow with her name on it which we put on her couch. Another woman painted a portrait of her and we hung it in her house. To this day, I decorate inside and outside her hut on every holiday. Even though the place is always immaculate, I want it to stay that way. On Sunday mornings I sweep, clean the carpet, and wash everything down. Petunia knows our schedule and watches for me on Sunday morning.

Every morning, after taking care of my other dogs, I go out to see Petunia before heading to work. After work, I let Petunia out first. We have four fenced-in acres so she roams and explores and, when she's done, I put her back in and feed her before going to take care of my other dogs. We have the same routine every day and she knows it well.

I help review adoption applications for Eleventh Hour and typically take the applications out to Petunia's house. She lays down on the floor next to me while I go over them.

If my daughter is away, Petunia and I go to her house and swim in her pool. Petunia loves to go out in the car and I take her to parks. Regardless of where we are, I'm always very cautious and mindful of other people and dogs and keep spray on me because I know it's my responsibility to protect her. Petunia is very predictable and I know her triggers, so I'm mindful of those triggers.

At times, from a human perspective, I want more for Petunia and question whether this is truly the life for her. Then I look at her and see that she's happy. It may not work for another dog, but for Petunia it's perfect. Anytime we're together she lays on the floor next to me and chews a bone. She's relaxed, confident, and happy.

She's lucky but I'm lucky as well because, in my life, I've been blessed with Happy and Petunia, two of the happiest dogs ever.

# Chapter 38

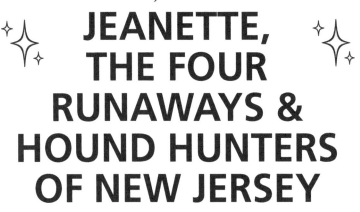

# JEANETTE, THE FOUR RUNAWAYS & HOUND HUNTERS OF NEW JERSEY

## *We Are That Someone*

IF YOU ASKED ME FORTY YEARS AGO WHAT I WOULD BE WHEN I grew up, even though I always loved animals, I never would have guessed this would be my future.

Growing up, my best friend had horses. Her mother was a groomer, so we spent a lot of time hanging out in the barn where her mom worked. Since the facility also offered dog training, we played with all types of dogs—big dogs, small dogs, old dogs, puppy dogs, and even deaf dogs. Without realizing it at the time, we were learning a lot about dog behavior and training.

When I was five years old, my father walked into the house after work one day and shouted, "Surprise!"

We turned to look. In his arms, was an adorable little black and white Labrador/hound puppy. On his way home from work, my father crossed paths with someone giving away puppies and he decided to get one for our family. My mother was busy raising four children under the age of five and was more apprehensive, and not quite as excited, about the puppy as my father and the rest of us.

We named the puppy Fred and he turned out to be a great dog and much-loved family member. Fred went camping with us, grew up with us, and we did everything together. Fred was afraid of thunder and several times during a thunderstorm he got out of our backyard but my mother knew how to lure him back. She grabbed a few of her homemade Italian meatballs and headed out to search for Fred and, without fail, he always followed her and her meatballs back home.

Fred was the first of many pets to come along throughout my childhood because somehow it seemed lost dogs, puppies, cats, and kittens always "found" me. We were able to reunite lost animals with their owners. Over the years, I also learned how to properly care for and love a pet.

After getting married and giving birth to my son, I got an amazing yellow Labrador retriever named Boomer. I was still young and unaware of the dog overpopulation problem decided to breed Boomer. In the litter, one of the puppies was born with crushed ribs and wasn't breathing. We nursed him back to health and decided to keep him. The puppy, Jake, grew up to be a healthy dog and lived a good long life.

Using what I had learned during my childhood about dog training, I helped a friend train and show her Neapolitan Mastiff. Together, we managed to win several dog shows before I moved out of that chapter of my life and straight into the next chapter: the world of animal rescue.

In 2010, I was divorced and raising my son, Justin when I decided to continue following my passion for animals by fostering puppies for Eleventh Hour Rescue. Justin gave so much love to every puppy that came into our home and it was wonderful to see the puppies thrive and help them find their perfect forever home.

We had been fostering dogs for two years when, one day, we received a call about a dog named Josie. A young Kelpie mix, Josie had been adopted by a family in Fredon but had managed to get away and was on the run. We lived close to Fredon and offered to help.

The rescue had a humane trap which we set up to try and catch Josie. But, when she refused to come near the trap, we devised another plan. We opened the front door of the house, trailed food in, and sat and waited.

Thankfully, we didn't have to wait very long. Josie took the bait and, as she walked into the house, we shut the door behind her. Once inside, we put a leash on her to secure her from running again, but her adoptive family decided she was too frightened to stay with them and surrendered her back to the rescue.

Seeing how incredibly scared and skittish Josie was, Justin and I didn't want her going back into a kennel environment. We also knew she needed to learn how to live in a home, so we decided to foster Josie. After being with us for nine months, she was adopted into a wonderful home in Rockaway. The next morning, she was spooked by something, escaped out the front door, and took off into the woods.

Since we had been able to get her back once, I knew we needed to try again. We headed to Rockaway with the humane trap. After finding out where she had been staying in the woods, we set it up. Once again, we waited. The next morning, we checked the trap and found a mother possum and six little newborn babies inside. We relocated the possum family to a safe place and went in search of sweet Josie.

About a mile away, I saw Josie standing up on the mountain ridge. She watched me approach and, as I got closer, she ran. I knew not to chase her. Hoping she'd come back to me, I sat down on the rock where she'd been standing and waited.

Several minutes later, Josie slowly approached me. Avoiding eye contact, I slowly held my hand out toward her. Once again, she ran. I continued to sit and quietly talk to her, telling her all the wonderful treats I was going to get for her. Very cautiously, she approached me and began to smell me. After resting her head on my back for a while, she finally laid down on a rock near me just out of my reach. I sat with her for about fifteen minutes offering her food, but she wouldn't budge or get any closer. As soon as I began to slowly reach out toward her, she ran off, only this time, she left the area.

Those few minutes with Josie were some of the most tender, sweetest moments I'd ever had. Heartbroken, I sat on the rock crying.

I know something now that I didn't know back then: Josie was in Survival Mode. When a pet is lost, going into survival mode is what, quite literally, helps them survive while they're on their own in the wild. It's part of who they are. Their natural born instincts create a fear wherein they don't trust anyone or anything. That fear ultimately helps keep them safe and also helps them find food and water to survive.

On Josie's second day out on her own, I knew I had to step up my game if I was going to beat her at her survival game. I brought Jake with me because Josie loved Jake with a passion. After putting Jake on a thirty-foot lead, we headed into the woods and I talked loudly mentioning my son Justin and my dogs Jake and Boomer. I asked Jake if he wanted to go for a walk or wanted to eat. I used all the key phrases I could think of that the dogs under my care, including Josie, heard repeatedly.

Before long, Josie came running down from the same rock ledge where I saw her the day before. I quickly sat down on the ground as Josie ran like a freight train straight for us. Excited to see Jake, she started jumping for joy. Jake was happy to see Josie, too. As they began playing, I slowly stood up, happily cheered them on, and began walking down the hill. They both followed me. Ahead of us was a fenced-in area with an open gate and, as the three of us entered it, I closed the gate. I had preemptively placed people around the exterior of the fence in various locations in case Josie went into the enclosure and tried to escape and that is exactly what she tried to do. As soon as she realized what had just happened, she was terrified and tried to jump the fence but, everywhere she turned, someone was standing outside it. She finally stopped and looked at me with total fear in her eyes. I slowly walked toward her, saying, just as if we were home, "Josie . . . sit," followed by "Josie . . . wait" and Josie obeyed. She sat and waited for me to put a leash on her.

We brought Josie back to the family and talked to them about all the steps they could take to safeguard her including what type of collar and leash to use and how to keep her safe in the home.

Josie was my second experience searching for a lost dog and there was something about it I loved. Maybe it was the soft gentle moment I shared with her in the woods or seeing how much she trusted me to keep her safe. Maybe it was being able to outsmart her while she was in survival mode—or maybe it was a little of everything. Whatever it was, I was hooked.

Eleven months later, I received a similar call. "Jeanette, a dog went missing in Stillwater. He's very frightened and they can't find him. Can you please help?"

Justin and I immediately met with the foster family and learned that the dog, a Corgi/Chihuahua mix named Brett, had recently come to New

Jersey. His foster family decided to take Brett on a field trip to a nearby river. After attaching Brett to a picnic table to keep him safe, they were relaxing when something scared him. He broke the leash and ran. They tried running after him, but he was too fast. The family was devastated.

We put up posters and spread the news about Brett on social media, and quickly received calls from several people who had seen him. I had purchased a few trail cameras. Now that we had a starting point, we placed them at feeding stations in the vicinity where Brett had been seen. Once we identified the path he was taking, we set up a humane trap, but Brett didn't want any part of it. A baby bear cub, however, found it intriguing and wandered in, but the cub's mother wasn't very happy and ended up destroying it. Unfortunately, it was the only trap we had.

That was back in the early days when I didn't have a lot of equipment. Without a trap, we built a makeshift enclosure in the backyard of an abandoned house along the path Brett was travelling. We filled the back of the enclosure with rotisserie chicken, bacon, burgers, and a big pork neck bone. It smelled delicious. Then we tied a rope to the door of the enclosure and the foster parents and I hid inside a shed on the property.

In the dark and silence of the night, we heard the familiar jingle of Brett's collar coming up the hill. We peeked out as Brett reached the door of the enclosure. He hesitated then, very slowly and cautiously, walked a little further in. We were sweating and anxious. When he finally reached the back of the enclosure, knowing this was our shot, we pulled the rope tied to the door and jumped out of the shed. One person went into the enclosure and grabbed Brett, another grabbed the door and held it shut, while the third person waited outside the enclosure in case Brett tried to jump over the four-foot-high barrier. After being loose for over a month, we finally got him!

Although Brett's foster parents loved him and had worked incredibly hard to help get him back to safety, they ultimately decided it was in Brett's best interest to go to a different foster home where, after months of rehabilitation, Brett was adopted by a great family.

Seven months later, in early February 2015, a scruffy little Shih Tzu mix named Marley got out of the play yard at the Eleventh Hour Rescue Kennel Facility in Randolph. Kristy, another volunteer at Eleventh Hour, reached out to me. "Jeanette," she said, "I'll buy rotisserie chicken or whatever you need. Just tell me and I'll get it and I'll also come out and help you." And she kept her word.

It was February and getting colder with every passing day. A lot of people were concerned for Marley and showed up to help. The fire department loaned us a thermal imaging gun to see if we could find any evidence that Marley was hunkered down in the woods surrounding the kennel property. People put up posters, spread the word, and contacted psychics. We finally got word that Marley was possibly hanging around on a back street about a mile from the rescue and that was where we began our search.

The owners of the property where Marley had been spotted gave us permission to search but warned us to be very careful. They explained that even though their property was fenced off, it was a very large parcel of land and they didn't know if other possible dangers or hazards were lurking anywhere. Kristy headed in one direction and I headed in another searching for paw prints in the snow. Although I was being careful, the snow made it hard to see what I was walking on when, without warning, SPLASH! I fell waist deep into a septic hole.

I crawled out and when Kristy and I decided the search was futile, we headed back toward her car to try another location. I never said a word to Kristy about what happened, but as soon as we got in the car and shut the doors, Kristy began to gag. "What is that smell? It's awful!"

I looked at her, smiled sheepishly, and said, "I kind of fell into a septic hole." With that, Kristy grabbed a can of awful-smelling melon-scented air freshener and began to cover me in it. I could barely breathe from the spray, but we were also laughing hysterically. I'd never met Kristy before that day and this was our first experience together. Earlier, I'd asked her to hold a piece of frozen dog poop in her pocket for evidence. She never questioned why. She just did it. By the end of the day, Kristy and I had bonded and a friendship was born.

After receiving a new sighting of Marley, we set a humane trap. That night, as snow fell and the wind whipped around us, Kristy and I sat huddled under blankets waiting, hoping to hear the sound of the trap door closing. During the night, the temperature dropped to ten degrees below zero. We were beyond cold, but at least we had one another and blankets. Marley was out, alone, in the cold and falling snow.

"Dear God," I said to Kristy, "we can't let that little dog freeze."

But all we could do was sit, wait, and listen—and then my cell phone rang.

On the other end was Linda from Eleventh Hour Rescue. "We have Marley," she said. She explained that a couple had been looking out their back door at the falling snow and saw something on their porch. When they went out to investigate, Marley was huddled under their barbecue grill cold, tired, and trying desperately to stay warm.

Linda had hurried over to their house and found Marley, freezing and near death, so she rushed him to the animal hospital. After a brief stay, Marley was released, recovered completely, and went on to live a very happy life.

Moments like that change you. Shared experiences like that change relationships. Sitting together on that cold, winter night, huddled under blankets, hoping to hear the sound of the trap door closing, solidified the friendship Kristy and I had begun only a few days earlier.

After Marley, Kristy and I decided to continue working together. We started out by helping find the lost pets of our rescue's adopters, but it soon expanded to helping anyone in need. At times it was heart-wrenching and difficult, but it was also incredibly rewarding and exhilarating. In the process, our friendship kept getting stronger.

Kristy gives everything she has to these animals who have no voice. We share a common love for helping and rescuing animals, but we bring different strengths to the table which, I believe, is what makes us a great team.

We love helping to reunite families with their dogs and with every dog and family we helped, we wanted to help even more. It was difficult because we were searching in our spare time and paying for everything out of our own pockets. We only had regular trail cameras, which took still pictures, no video, so every day we had to go into the woods with our laptops, take the chip out of the camera and put it in our laptop to check for pictures to see if the dog had been there. It was extremely time consuming and it also breached the area we were trying to keep quiet and undisturbed so the dog would come back.

We also only had one trap which meant we could only help one family at a time. We wanted to expand our knowledge as well as our resources and talked about getting some new equipment. Since that wasn't realistic, we learned little tricks. One of the tricks was to put reflective tape on the door of the trap. With so many animals in the woods, traipsing in and out all night long, checking a trap wasn't the best idea. The tape allowed us to see at night from a distance using a flashlight whether the door was open or closed. Admittedly, it wasn't the best system, but it was better than nothing.

In 2016, we began talking more seriously about starting a non-profit so we could help reunite more families with their lost pets. We began to expand our equipment by purchasing cameras that recorded video with sound. With the new cameras, whenever motion was detected, images were sent directly to our cell phones allowing us to respond more quickly. We built our first enclosure and acquired an additional trap. Those improvements helped us to be more effective in helping families— like the families of Limmony, Lola, Apollo, Oak, Benny, Maizie, and Carter (just to name a few).

I personally have four runaways living with me: Hannah, January, Chrissy, and Sheba. They were all very skittish dogs that never had a home or family, didn't know when or where their next meal was coming from, and never felt loved or secure. Kristy and I captured each one and they all have their own story and are extremely special to us.

My first runaway, Hannah, arrived in New Jersey in June 2016. She was a black Lab mix and extremely scared, but she found her forever home quickly (or so we thought). A couple of hours after being adopted, she pulled the leash out of her owner's hand and thus began her five-month journey.

Shortly after she went missing, we received the first sightings of Hannah when people saw her running across the golf course at the Metuchen Country Club. Our team of volunteers drove almost two hours to hang posters and speak to people in the community. Cameras and feeding stations were put into place along the edge of the golf course and it wasn't long before we had Hannah on camera eating the food. The trap was set. Now we needed to wait for Hannah to make her move.

Night after night we watched as Hannah came looking for food but always refused to enter the trap. After befriending a fox and a skunk, all three of them started showing up together. Before long, Hannah decided to move on.

Every day, she traveled miles along major roadways, dodging cars, and escaping injury time after time. She visited Roosevelt Park and the South Plainfield Country Club. Wherever she was spotted, she ran from everyone and everything.

Since Hannah always seemed to gravitate back to the Metuchen Country Club, we enlisted the help of the golf course maintenance crew. They often saw Hannah early in the morning out on the course enjoying the quiet and serenity before the golfers arrived. Although she was becoming more comfortable with the maintenance crew, she still wouldn't allow anyone to get near her.

While we were working hard setting up enclosures and traps, Hannah was running around stealing golf balls off the course and taking them into the woods. She stole hats, shirts, shoes, and literally anything the maintenance crew mistakenly left out. Residents saw her running happily along the beautiful greens, barking as she chased golf carts and mowers. The golf course had become her playground. The ponds on the course were providing her with plenty of water and the maintenance crew had begun to feed her breakfast, lunch, and dinner. Hannah seemed to love her life.

In turn, the maintenance crew loved Hannah. Even though they tried every day, it didn't matter to them that they could never touch or get close to her. They wanted her to stay forever, but we knew living on a golf course wasn't the best home for her. What would happen when winter arrived and it got cold?

With all our failed attempts at trapping her, we knew the only way to get her was to have the maintenance crew begin feeding Hannah inside the maintenance building. Every day, she came a little farther into the building until she was finally eating in the center of the garage. One day, like every other day, Hannah arrived promptly at 9:00 a.m. for breakfast. Thinking nothing of going into the garage, she walked in and began to devour the food as the garage door was quickly closed. When Hannah realized what happened, she panicked and began to run around in circles to escape. Everyone waited for her to calm down. When she did, we were able to approach her, get a leash on her, and secure her in a crate.

Hannah was transported to my home to decompress and begin rehabilitation. While she was slow to trust, with the help of my other dogs, she became more comfortable. She's still fearful of thunder, gunshots, loud noises, and is leery of crossing thresholds between rooms or when going outside. Even after being here all this time, if she gets scared, she still runs under the porch and hides for hours without making a sound. Sadly, I don't think Hannah will ever overcome those things. But as far as being a member of my household, she's as perfect as they come. Despite her fears, she's extremely happy and has bonded deeply with another one of my runaways, January.

January was an adorable little ten-month-old beagle mix puppy who had spent the early months of her life in Georgia alone, scared, confused, and constantly on the run. She was ultimately given a golden ticket to the possibility of a new life and home in New Jersey and arrived in January 2017 (thus her name: January). Immediately, she was adopted into what everyone thought would be her forever home.

Less than twenty-four hours later, January escaped and was back on her own in completely new and unfamiliar territory. Six weeks later, a bad thunderstorm forced her to take refuge in someone's open garage and the people were able to get her and return her to her adoptive family.

The following day, the family decided to take a leisurely car ride with January. After pulling over on the side of the highway in a neighboring town to look at something, they opened the car door to get out, and instantly January was off and running again.

For the next two winters, January proved to be methodical, mindful, and invincible. She survived a score of bad snowstorms and scaled four-foot fences in a single bound to get away from us. Several times a day, she crossed a busy highway, always stopping to look both ways before crossing. The one time she forgot to look both ways she was hit by a car and dragged several hundred feet, but when the car came to a stop, January jumped up and ran off into the woods.

We used regular box traps and enclosures. We made a fancy catapult trap that would catch her in a net and even a trap that was buried underground. We tried using several different fenced-in backyards and considered digging a hole and placing sticks over to camouflage it so she would fall into it when she went for the bait. Regardless of the type of trap we put out for her, nothing worked. It felt like we were trapped in a bad episode of Wile E. Coyote trying to catch the Roadrunner with January laughing at all of our attempts, and saying, "Try again, people!"

After eighteen months on the run, once again a thunderstorm drove January into someone's open garage for refuge. Out of the blue, we received a call.

"I think I have your dog," a woman said.

"A little beagle?"

"Yes."

"Great! Please don't let her out! We're on our way."

The woman was silent for a moment. "I just fed her and let her out to go potty," she said. Our hearts sank. We expected to hear that she had run off again. Instead, the woman said, "She came right back in and is sleeping on my pillow."

Relieved, we exhaled and arrived at the woman's home in record time. After thanking the woman profusely for her kindness, we took January directly to the vet. In addition to being extremely afraid, January was positive for heartworm, Lyme's Disease, and anaplasmosis. She also had evidence of burns on her body probably from the exhaust on the car the day she was hit. I brought her home with me to allow her to decompress and treat her illnesses.

That was five years ago and January is still here. She is extremely happy and comfortable with my pack and our routine. The other truth is that I become attached to them. They mean so much to you and it's hard to let them go into what could be another potentially dangerous situation. She's an amazing, loving dog, and welcome to stay here forever.

The story of Chrissy, my third runaway, began in September 2017 and is one Kristy and I reflect on often. Chrissy and her sister, Janet, were collie-sheltie mixes who, on the day they were adopted, arrived at their new home. Within hours, Chrissy escaped and was on the run.

We immediately set up cameras in several locations throughout nearby Echo Hill Park in Clinton Township. We tried several traps but the cameras clearly showed she was not food motivated and wouldn't go near the traps. She was scared and mistrustful.

She constantly eluded hunters and coyotes, ran the trails, and hid in the brambles. Several coyotes started coming to the location and ultimately between the coyotes, people out looking for her, and the start of hunting season, Chrissy left the area.

It was mid-December. The weather was getting cold and we were getting tired. Trapping a dog is a huge undertaking and commitment. You can't just start and stop when things don't work out, the weather changes, or you get tired. You can't get attached or emotional and must be committed to seeing things through while also balancing your work and family life and taking care of your own pets. Through it all, posters need to be put up in surrounding towns and the search must go on!

After receiving reports that Chrissy had been spotted four miles away on River Road in Flemington, we went to the new location and set up several traps, including a big bear trap, as well as a net suspended in the air that would fall on her if she walked through the area. Nothing worked. Chrissy was too smart for anything and everything we tried, so we decided to bring her sister, Janet, to the location. We walked Janet around to try and entice Chrissy to come out of hiding. After hours of walking, Janet was tired and we had to call it a day.

Next, our cameras started capturing pictures of Chrissy and a coyote she had apparently befriended on her journeys. We had endless footage of the two of them prancing together and eating the food we were putting out. While one ate, the other would stand watch. Then the other would stand watch, while the other one ate. It was amazing to see the relationship that had developed between a domestic dog and a wild coyote. This went on for weeks while we tried to figure out new ways to capture her.

The last time Chrissy was spotted on camera was August 28, 2018. We continued to put food out for her for weeks—and then months—but she didn't return. We were devastated and felt like we had failed her, but we never gave up. We constantly drove through the area looking. It was as if Chrissy had simply vanished.

On May 15, 2020, in the middle of a worldwide pandemic, a woman posted on Facebook that she saw a dog, possibly a collie, cross Bartles Corner Road outside Flemington. Could it be? Was it even possible that eighteen months and two winters later, it was Chrissy?

We immediately headed back to her old familiar stomping grounds, set up cameras, a feeding station, and waited. That evening around 9:00 p.m., the cameras started to ping our phones. It was Chrissy. She was alive! We were in shock. After all this time, she was back.

We wasted no time setting up a twenty-five-foot-long enclosure and filling it with cheeseburgers, rotisserie chicken, liverwurst, bacon—you name it, we put it in there and the stinkier the better.

That night, around midnight, Chrissy showed up and walked around the enclosure several times. She began to walk into it, but after only a few steps, she turned and decided she didn't like or trust the arrangement, and quickly left.

The next morning, at daybreak, our cameras caught Chrissy wandering back and looking into the enclosure. She knew there was food. Now it was a matter of being brave enough to go in after it. Ultimately, her nose and stomach won the battle and she started walking down the twenty-five-foot corridor. We held our breath. Finally, we heard the glorious sound of metal on metal as the door slammed shut and locked. Chrissy immediately swirled around in a panic as we ran and surrounded the enclosure.

The flood of emotions we felt in that moment was overwhelming. Almost three years of our lives and countless blood, sweat, and tears were over! We cheered and hugged. As the sun began to peek over the horizon, we cried tears of happiness and success that Chrissy was finally safe.

We took her to the vet and aside from being covered in ticks she was in surprisingly good shape. The man who initially adopted Chrissy and her sister Janet almost three years earlier had decided he no longer wanted either of them. He had returned Janet to the rescue the day after Chrissy ran away so, after getting Chrissy cleaned up and on medication for several tickborne illnesses, she went back to the rescue, too, since they were now her rightful owners.

When the rescue told us they were going to keep her as a member of their family rather than adopting her out, we were thrilled and relieved. It seemed like everything had finally come together for her. For the next year, they sent us videos of Chrissy running in their yard and relaxing on the deck. She looked healthy and happy and the people seemed to really love her. We were ecstatic until the following year when things went sideways.

I don't know exactly what happened. But, at some point during the second year Chrissy was with them, the rescue turned into a hoarding situation. The police came and took the owners of the rescue to jail, while Animal Control came and brought the dogs to several different shelters. News of the situation spread like wildfire and when it reached us, we were crushed. Chrissy had meant so much to us and we had fought so hard for her. It was heartwrenching to finally get her back after almost three years on the run to have her end up in a hoarding situation.

We reached out to the owners of the rescue and asked them, over and over, "Where is she? Where's Chrissy? How dare you! We want her back!"

The owners of the rescue were in jail and had no idea where Chrissy had been taken, but a colleague from NJSH Pet Rescue, a local rescue, reached out to us. They had contacts at some of the shelters in Brick Township and had found Chrissy at one of the shelters. She was in good condition and being taken care of medically. The shelter released Chrissy to NJSH Pet Rescue and I'm now fostering her.

She's doing great and is learning how to live in a home. More importantly, she's learning to be a dog. Out in public she has trouble on a leash and is very scared and shy, but, at home, she loves playing with the other dogs. What happens in the future for Chrissy depends on whether she's able to be rehabilitated to the point where she can go into a home.

Based on all she went through, in some ways Chrissy is like a feral dog. If she ever went missing again, she would instantly go into survival mode. Knowing that, it would have to be the right home and the right situation, so I would know she would always be safe. While it would be nice to find her that home, she's certainly welcome to stay here with me.

And my final runaway is Sheba, a beautiful golden retriever who spent the first five years of her life as a breeding dog. When the breeder no longer needed or wanted her, he gave her to an older gentleman whom he knew who wasn't in the best of health. Sheba hadn't been off the farm very often, so when the man took her home it was a whole new and extremely scary world for her. When he took her out on a leash (something else she had probably never done) she pulled, knocked him over, and took off running.

She was on the loose for about a month when my phone rang and someone said, "Can you help with Sheba?"

"I would love to but there's one problem," I said. "I had a tumor on my pituitary gland and had brain surgery yesterday. I'm still in the hospital, but tell me more."

After pausing to process what I had just shared, the person continued. "We know approximately where she is because we hear her barking in the woods, but we can't get her."

I hung up the phone and called my sister, Tina. "Can you go to my house and get my cameras and traps?" I gave her the location and she set everything up.

Sheba refused to go into the trap, so I knew we needed to switch things up. The day I got out of the hospital, since I wasn't allowed to drive or do anything strenuous, I asked my son to help me. We set up an enclosure and put out fresh food and cameras then came home to see if we would have any better luck. Every day, until I was allowed to drive, my son drove me over to freshen the bait. For the next month, we tried different methods and foods to get Sheba to enter the enclosure, camouflaging it with fresh branches and leaves every day, until finally, she was comfortable enough to go in.

My heart broke for Sheba because she was completely shut down. She'd never been exposed to life outside of the breeding kennel and didn't know how to be a dog. She also had nowhere to go. With the blessing of her former owner and the kennel where she originally lived, I put her in my car and brought her to my house. Every day, Sheba and I reach milestones—big and small—together. It's incredible to be a part of (and witness) her slow transformation. I'm certain Sheba is very happy where she is and will never leave here. This will be her forever home.

In 2021, after working together for six years, Kristy and I finally formed an official 501(c)(3) non-profit: Hound Hunters of New Jersey, Inc.

People always ask us why we do what we do. The answer is simple: we're needed. After working in rescue for so long, Kristy and I had seen so many dogs that had never lived in a home and were living on the street, or had been severely neglected or abused. We consider searching for lost dogs to be a different layer to animal rescue.

The Four Runaways (from left to right):
Chrissy, Hanna, Sheba, and January

The other factor is the families. When dogs are lost, people are un-derstandably frantic. It is emotional, scary, and stressful. People in that frame of mind can easily be taken advantage of because they are vul-nerable and not thinking clearly. We want to help people who aren't in a position to help themselves during a crisis.

People typically reach us through our Facebook page. We've been all over the state of New Jersey although some areas are more difficult than others to get to because I have a full-time job, still foster for the rescue, and have my own dogs. If we can't physically help someone immediately, we offer advice and try to guide them in the right direction. Our advice varies since every dog is different and you need to take into considera-tion things like the dog's personality, where they came from, as well as a person's history with the dog.

People don't realize how resilient and wise dogs are. Think back to Chrissy. Here was a dog that had been out for almost three years, yet when she was found, she was in surprisingly good shape. Dogs instinc-tively look for food and water. When they go into survival mode, every-body and everything is the enemy. Even though they keep running, it also helps keep them safe.

Having your dog go missing is the worst feeling in the world. I know because I had two of my own dogs go missing. When it happens, you go into a different state of mind. You're so upset that you can't think straight. In a situation like that, it's nice to have someone be the level-headed calm person you can use as a crutch to get through it. It helps to have someone humanize the process and guide you step-by-step on what needs to be done and also provide you with the resources to make those steps a reality.

Hound Hunters of New Jersey is that someone.

# Chapter 39

## ANNIE, DOLLIE & ANIMAL ALLIANCE OF NEW JERSEY

### *A Love Like No Other*

IT'S REMARKABLE THAT THIS IS WHAT I'M DOING WITH MY LIFE because I never had a pet dog growing up and was always fearful of them.

After my husband, David, and I moved to rural New Jersey from New York City, he got me a sweet little Maltese to help me get over my fear of dogs. I named her Dollie after my beloved grandmother who had been my best friend and biggest fan my entire life. His plan worked. I loved Dollie beyond measure and, as I always say, Dollie kicked open the door to my heart. Soon after Dollie came into our lives, we started talking about getting another dog.

One day, while Dollie and I were out for a walk, we crossed paths with one of my neighbors.

"Your dog is so beautiful," she said.

"Thank you," I said, smiling at Dollie. "My husband and I are planning on getting a second one."

"I hope you're going to rescue your second dog."

Looking at her, puzzled, I said, "Rescue? A purebred Maltese? I don't think so."

"Believe me, it's possible. Just check out Petfinder online."

It was the late '90s and the internet was just getting going. Determined to prove her wrong, I went online and checked out Petfinder. Sure enough, just as my neighbor had said, there was an array of perfect, gorgeous, small, purebred dogs at shelters all over New Jersey and Pennsylvania waiting to be adopted—including a nine-month-old purebred Maltese named Little Mighty. He'd been the victim of domestic violence and, as a result, had a broken leg. The leg had been operated on and he had pins to help stabilize it and help it heal properly.

I drove to the shelter. When I arrived and started walking around, I couldn't believe what I was seeing. "Look at all these beautiful dogs!," I said to the shelter manager. "I thought shelters only had big, unruly dogs. Do people know dogs like this are just waiting to be adopted?"

"Ha!," she said, "I wish. We need more people like you to spread the word."

Little did she know that, with those words, she had planted a seed in my mind. I adopted Mighty on the spot. He was smart, intuitively knew Dollie was the boss, and quietly followed behind her. From the very first day, they got along beautifully!

At the time, I was working in transfusion medicine for Abbott Laboratories. Every day I went to work in New York City dressed in typical corporate attire: a suit. Day after day, I sat in meetings thinking about what I'd seen at the shelter, what the shelter manager had told me, and about the perfect little dog we'd just adopted. I loved Dollie and Mighty so much and knew more animals, just like them were sitting and waiting in the shelter. In 1997, knowing I had to spread the word and help those animals, I started volunteering with a local animal rescue, Animal Allies, and helping at The Trenton Animal Shelter.

I loved helping. But, even after my husband remodeled a section of our house so I could start fostering dogs, it still didn't seem like enough. Day after day, I sat through meetings at my job thinking about what else I could do to help animals. Finally, in 2001, after volunteering for a number of years, I took a one-year leave of absence to see how I could grow my involvement in animal rescue.

Eight months into that year, I had a ruptured ectopic pregnancy. It wasn't just a medical emergency, I was dying. I collapsed at home and was raced to the hospital by ambulance. Upon arrival, my blood pressure was 56/23 and I needed immediate blood transfusions. As I lay in the emergency room watching the nurses squeeze the bags of blood to try to get them into me quicker, I heard the doctors tell my husband I needed emergency surgery. I knew full well I was dying. Yet I was entirely at peace. I had no fear at all. The only thing I kept thinking was, "Thank God I did work I love these last few years!"

All I could think about were the animals I had helped and the animal-loving people I had met. I was so grateful to God that I'd stepped off the corporate track, did work that I truly loved, and made a difference in the world. I promised myself that if by some miracle I pulled through I was never going to do anything else.

I went into surgery and flat-lined three times. One and a half liters of blood from the burst Fallopian tube was removed from my abdomen and there had been enough internal bleeding to kill me. When the surgery was over, the doctors told my husband I was amazingly lucky to have survived.

I woke up in the ICU, looked at my husband, and said, "I'm never going back to work. No more suits for me."

David smiled. "You're on morphine, Annie."

"I'm serious. I want a big property and I want to build a kennel and help as many animals as I can. That's what I want to do."

My husband, being a good sport, simply said, "Sure, honey. Go back to sleep."

Later David told me that my eyes were so clear and focused that he knew, on some level, I was very serious about the words that had come out of my mouth.

And I was. I moved out of ICU the next day. Three days later, I left the hospital and David and I immediately began searching for property. Nine months later, we found a nice house on an eleven-acre parcel of land. It had a 3000-square foot outbuilding where the prior owners had housed antique cars. It was perfect, so we bought it and moved in. David immediately began researching what we needed to do to make the outbuilding a fully-compliant New Jersey-licensed animal shelter. It took six months to renovate. We put in an epoxy floor, fiber-reinforced plastic walls, and acquired stainless steel enclosures in order to comply with New Jersey state guidelines for animal shelter construction.

Honestly, not many men I know would move their entire life to build a shelter in their backyard because their wife had a crazy dream. But that's exactly what David did. He's always been my biggest supporter and I'm immensely grateful he believed in me then and now.

I settled on the name "Animal Alliance" hoping that an "alliance" of people would someday join me in this work. Knowing my first members of the alliance would have to be a veterinary team, I reached out to my dogs' veterinarian, Belle Mead Animal Hospital, to see if they would sign on to be Animal Alliance's veterinarian and do all necessary medical work, including spay/neuter for all the animals that would be rescued, and if they would offer me a discount.

Looking back, I realize how preposterous that must have sounded to Dr. Joe Martins who, as a thirty-year-old veterinarian, had just bought the practice. But after listening to my vision, he agreed to climb on board for the adventure with me. He also allowed Animal Alliance to hold adoption days in their lobby on Saturdays and Sundays. From the start, there were such long lines of people waiting to see the animals every weekend that the Fire Marshall finally sent a notice regarding the number of people allowed in the lobby at one time. Seeing the line of people wrapped around the building on our first adoption day, meant one thing to me: the time was right to start a new animal rescue!

With a veterinarian lined up, in mid-to-late 2002, I formed a rescue partnership with Philadelphia Animal Care and Control. At the time, that one inner city shelter was taking in 35,000 animals annually and was in desperate need of rescues to assist them. Every week, I went and took ten to fifteen dogs and drove them straight to Belle Mead Animal Hospital for medical care and attention. We saw so many egregious cases of cruelty and neglect. Dr. Martins adopted one of our first dogs, Lola, a sweet dog that had been deliberately set on fire and was suffering from excruciating burns.

My husband David donated money to help Animal Alliance get started. Even though we built the kennel on our property to accommodate between fifty and sixty dogs, it was quickly filling up. At first, I took care of the dogs myself. Before long, I hired staff to assist me. The dogs all got time in a fenced-in play area. But, as the rescue grew, we welcomed volunteer dog walkers to our property to also take dogs for long walks.

People interested in adopting a dog filled out an application online and I met with them personally at either Belle Mead Animal Hospital or Dogs and Cats Rule (a nearby pet supply store) since, understandably, David drew the line at having strangers come to our home to see the dogs. Diane Hutton, who had volunteered with me in the past, became the co-founder and Adoption Coordinator at Animal Alliance. She processed the applications that came through Petfinder and coordinated every adoption. Our first year, we adopted over 500 dogs.

Everything was going great until 2006 when I was diagnosed with breast cancer. It had already spread to my lymph nodes so I knew I had a battle ahead of me. It felt eerily reminiscent of, years before, laying in the emergency room with the ectopic pregnancy. Once again, my first thought was, "Here I am again at death's door." But the feelings that followed that thought were very different this time. This time, I felt so incredibly blessed. In the five years since my last medical emergency, I'd been doing work I loved so much and found so rewarding. I was immensely grateful I hadn't spent those years slogging it out in the corporate world, but was doing meaningful work on behalf of animals in need.

I immediately had a double mastectomy followed by thirty rounds of chemotherapy. Twice a month for fifteen months, I spent hours getting IV treatments to fight the cancer. It was a hard-fought battle, but no matter how sick I was, the dogs in the kennel on my property gave me the strength and the will to live. My oncologist cautioned me that, since I was immunocompromised, a dog bite could cause a serious infection and suggested I limit my contact with dogs. I listened to her, but every night I limped out to my kennel to visit the dogs in residence on our property.

One week, while getting treatment, I overheard two oncology nurses talking. Each one had a cat who recently had kittens. "We're trying to find homes for the kittens but it's difficult," one of the nurses explained.

"Unfortunately, the cost of spay and neuter is so expensive," the other nurse said. "There's no place to go for people on a budget to get their pet fixed."

I knew they were right. We can't adopt our way out of the pet overpopulation problem. It's futile. Spay and neuter was a critical component and I knew Animal Alliance needed to address the problem. Sitting there, bald and sick from chemotherapy, tethered to my IV pole, I sent a message to my Board: "We need to open a low-cost spay and neuter clinic." And we did.

Two years after my cancer diagnosis, Animal Alliance opened Planned Pethood in Lambertville, New Jersey, a clinic which offers low-cost spay and neuter surgery for dogs and cats. Located in a strip mall on a highway, the clinic spays and neuters approximately 2,500 animals a year.

A few years after opening Planned Pethood, the motorcycle show-room that had occupied a giant space adjacent to it became available. I knew the universe was telling me it was time to open a shelter and move the dogs from the kennels on our property to the space next to the clinic—so we did.

When we had our grand opening in 2012, we subsequently started a cat adoption program in the shelter which quickly became a runaway success.

The original shelter on my property is still there, but I use it now for dogs with special needs or who are having a problem living in a shelter environment. It's a very small group of animals but I'm glad we have an alternative for them.

We've done 30,000 spay and neuter surgeries since we opened Planned Pethood. Every year, we adopt out between 600 and 1,000 dogs and cats. After ten years of rescuing dogs (primarily from Philadelphia Animal Control and Trenton Animal Shelter), we formed a partnership with a shelter in Byron, Georgia, where the pet overpopulation is in-credibly severe. Each month, we take approximately thirty dogs from this rural, underserved, impoverished area and pay to have the dogs transported to us by a USDA-registered transport company.

Our cat adoption program has grown by leaps and bounds. In addi-tion to a space allocated for them at the shelter, we now also have a cat adoption center where cats live full-time at a Petsmart in Flemington, New Jersey. The cats primarily come from cat rescuers in Newark who are frequent customers of our clinic.

Today, most of our adoptions are still driven by Petfinder and people still apply online to meet specific animals. They also meet our dogs at

Mighty (on left) and Dollie
with Annie

adoption days held at various locations in and around Hunterdon County.

I think back to the day Dollie and I were out for a walk and my neighbor suggested I rescue my next dog. Back then I didn't believe it was possible to adopt a purebred Maltese but now I know that twenty-five percent of the dogs in shelters are purebreds.

While one person and one conversation changed the trajectory of my life, the truth is, at the end of the day, everything happened because of my intense love for a little dog named Dollie. In a most transformative and enduring way, Dollie showed me that the love of a dog is like no other. I'm doing this work in memory and honor of Dollie, and every dog I have loved since.

# Epilogue

# THE MAGIC OF A DOG

YEARS AGO, AS A YOUNG GIRL TERRIFIED OF DOGS, I NEVER IN MY wildest dreams thought these books, or any of this, would or could happen. Even, years later, when I wrote my Life List and added "#7: Own a dog" and "#21: Write a book", I never imagined those two dreams would blend and mesh the way they did. I never envisioned a dog named Brooke would find her way into my life, open the floodgates to my heart, and completely change me and the trajectory of my life.

Before bringing this book and journey to a conclusion, there's a story I have not yet shared with you—a story that began the day Brooke crossed over the Rainbow Bridge.

The week before she passed, Brooke had her one and only seizure. Veterinarians and specialists gave us various opinions and degrees of hope. Brooke vacillated between being our vibrant, energetic, happy little girl to being withdrawn, sullen, and oddly aloof. Robb and I promised her, and one another, that we would honor, respect, and care for her, take it day-by-day, and figure it out together.

One week later, Robb, Brooke, and I were at my house packing some things up to head to his house. Robb had built a bridge over a small stream in his backyard which we named The Brooke-Lynn Bridge. She loved hanging out there with us and since the weather was relatively mild, we decided to spend time together on her bridge.

Before leaving my house, Robb went upstairs. After a few minutes, he came back down with a curious expression on his face. "What's with the butterfly in your bathroom?"

"Butterfly?"

"Go look. There's a butterfly flying around the bathroom upstairs."

Thinking it was a joke or prank, I decided to play along and walked upstairs to find a yellow swallowtail butterfly. It made no sense. It was March, in New Jersey. It was cold and definitely not butterfly season.

Confused, I walked downstairs, looked at Robb, and shrugged my shoulders. "Honey, I have no idea where that butterfly came from."

With no flowers inside or outside my house to sustain the butterfly, I googled "what to feed a butterfly." An article said to slice up an orange and cut across the grain at regular intervals so the butterfly could easily reach the juice. I did what they suggested, put the orange on a plate, carried it upstairs, placed it on my bathroom counter, and walked out.

Over the next hour, I went up several times to check and the butterfly was still fluttering around. Convinced it would be fine, Robb and I finished packing up. Before leaving for Robb's house, I walked upstairs one last time to check on it. As I neared the top of the steps, I saw the butterfly lying on the threshold of my bedroom, lifeless.

The moment I saw it I knew. The butterfly had been a messenger that Brooke would be making her transition.

Several hours later, after spending time on the Brooke-Lynn Bridge with Brooke, we went into Robb's house. As he and I held her, we thanked her, and told her how much we loved her. Gently, she transitioned from this world to the next.

I googled the spiritual meaning behind seeing a yellow butterfly. One said it was a sign of hope and new beginnings; another that it was a sign of upcoming change or a new direction in life. Either, and both, made sense and were accurate depictions of what happened on that day with Brooke as well as what would happen in the months and years that followed.

That spring and summer, my yard and gardens were filled with swallowtail butterflies. Every time I went outside, a swallowtail followed me wherever I went.

One day, a piece of art popped up on my computer which had a dog (who ironically looked exactly like Brooke) and a butterfly, and said: "When you believe beyond what your eyes can see . . . signs from Heaven show up to remind you that Love never dies." It was precisely how I felt about all that had been happening since the day Brooke passed. I bought it.

As a writer, I vacillate between periods of confidence in my work and serious self-doubt. On the day I sent the first draft of this book off to my editor, I asked Brooke for a sign to let me know she still believed in me, the Magical Dogs, and this book.

Robb, Ava, Kimber, and I headed to the cabin to relax. At some point in our first few days there, Robb was working outside when he spotted something lying in the driveway. Our driveway is a fairly large, wide open area. For days, we'd been driving cars, trucks, and ATVs across it. Kimber and Ava had been running and playing on it constantly. We walked over it repeatedly while working or when heading out for walks. Yet there, in clear sight in the middle of the driveway, in the path we had been using over and over, Robb found a swallowtail butterfly. It was lifeless but still beautiful and perfectly intact. He picked it up, carried it inside, and placed it on the window ledge which held pictures of Brooke along with her ashes. He never said a word to me.

Several days later, I was sitting at the table in front of that window working on the Acknowledgement section of this book, when I glanced up briefly and saw the butterfly. Gasping, I put my hand over my mouth and walked out onto the porch. "Robb, where did that butterfly come from?"

When he told me the story—I knew. It was New York State, still cold, and definitely not butterfly season. Yet, just like the butterfly we'd found in my house all those years ago, there it was. Again, I knew. Brooke had sent me a sign, another butterfly, to let me know she was still with me and was still cheering for me, the Magical Dogs, and this book.

Whether you believe or align with any of this (or you think I've completely lost my marbles), isn't important. What *is* important, and what I hope you take away from this, is the bigger picture: that dogs don't randomly appear in the world or our lives nor are they here by accident or coincidence. Rather, they come into the world, and our lives, for a reason, purpose, or lesson (and sometimes all three). And when they leave this world, signs show up to remind us that "Love never dies." That is a dog's superpower, their magic.

What I wrote on my Life List all those years ago about wanting to own a dog isn't accurate. No one *owns* a dog. Rather, you are *blessed* with a dog.

I have now spent years of my life writing about dogs. Through them and their stories, I've felt and experienced every conceivable human emotion: joy, love, laughter, sadness, grief, despair, triumph, admiration, and pride. It's impossible to devote that amount of time and emotional energy to something and not be changed. And every dog, every story, has changed me—in all the best ways.

At this moment in time, I have no idea if this will be my last dog book. As always, I'll let the dogs guide me. If they say there's another book that needs to be written, I'll follow their lead because, from them, I've also learned to always stay open to possibility.

Regardless of what happens down the road, I hope you've enjoyed the magical dogs you've met. And, through them and their stories, you've been changed—in all the best ways.

For that, my dear reader, is the true magic of a dog.

# Acknowledgements

THIS BOOK HAPPENED BECAUSE OF A VILLAGE OF KIND, LOVING, magical beings—human and canine—beginning with the incredible people who willingly, honestly, and courageously shared their stories. Without them, this book wouldn't exist. They are (in alphabetical order by last name): Brianne Land Altice; Monica Brown (Knox PAWS); Jeanette Campbell (Hound Hunters of New Jersey, Inc.); Ron Danta (Danny & Ron's Rescue), Claire Desilets (Nuzzles & Co. Purple Paw Program); Rebecca Diamondstone; Edna Gorby; Robin Hall; Cameron Hollingshead; Corinne Humphrey; Cathy King (Canines With a Cause); Emma Kaye Ledbetter; Chris and Christina Lee (Deaf Dogs Rock); David McCartney; Liz McCauley (Cape Coral Animal Shelter); Jennifer Montgomery; Sherry Lynn Polvinale (House with a Heart Sanctuary); Danny Robertshaw (Danny & Ron's Rescue); Sarah Rosario; Sharon Schultz; Bill and Mary Ann Serridge; Laurie J. Smith; Jacqueline Soccodato; Anke and Ralf Sturm; Annie Trinkle (Animal Alliance of New Jersey); and Mary Lee Trott. You are my heroes.

To my editor, Joy Stocke, you are the bees knees, darling. The relationship we have built is both unique and sacred and involves massive amounts of trust and respect on both our parts. You always believed in me and this book. You dusted me off and kept me writing and focused when I was weary and you did it all with a sprinkling of your classic light-hearted humor. I love you and love working with you. Thank you for everything. Every. Little. Thing.

Immense gratitude to my exceptionally talented Creative Dream Team who have made this and every one of my books all they could be: my graphic designer, James Lebbad of Lebbad Designs; photographer extraordinaire, Joseph Frazz of Joseph Frazz Photography; and my layout designer/artist Susie Kenyon of Sans Serif Book Designs.

I am extraordinarily blessed with a family who has always believed in me and my dreams and have, individually and collectively, given me the time and space to pursue them: Robb, Sean, Mel, Cameron, Jackson, Mike, Kerri, Charlotte, Henry, and Joe. Thank you all. I love you—always have, always will.

To my friends and neighbors who, for far too long, never complained when my reply to any of your requests has been: "I can't. I'm working on the book." Thank you for your patience and understanding. Guess what, kids? The book is done. I'm done. Let's have some fun!

A special thank you to: Ken Bell, Venture Photography-Greenwich, Dave Norton, and Joseph Frazz Photography for granting me permission to use your photographs; Ben and Ellie Beans for allowing me to borrow your vintage luggage for the cover photo; and Scott and Robyn Mikaelian for letting us converge on your driveway for the cover photo shoot.

To the village of dogs who inspired this book (and the other *Magical Dogs* books), you have changed me—in all the best ways. I am honored to have been the one to share your stories with the world.

And last, but most certainly not least, to my very own magical dogs: Brooke, Ava, and Kimber. Thank you for choosing me. I love you.